Planning Models in India

S. P. Gupta
foreword by
Harry G. Johnson

The Praeger Special Studies program—
utilizing the most modern and efficient book
production techniques and a selective
worldwide distribution network—makes
available to the academic, government, and
business communities significant, timely
research in U.S. and international economic, social, and political development.

Planning Models in India
With Projections to 1975

Praeger Publishers   New York   Washington   London

PRAEGER SPECIAL STUDIES IN INTERNATIONAL ECONOMICS AND DEVELOPMENT

PRAEGER PUBLISHERS
111 Fourth Avenue, New York, N.Y. 10003, U.S.A.
5, Cromwell Place, London S.W.7, England

Published in the United States of America in 1971
by Praeger Publishers, Inc.

Library of Congress Catalog Card Number: 75-155214

Printed in the United States of America

To my Parents

The examination of Ph.D. theses is a mixed pleasure, if a pleasure at all. Many are both inadequately
written and excessively narrow in the conception of
their problem. This book, though originally presented
as a Ph.D. thesis at London University, is something
altogether different. Dr. Gupta has set himself,
and completed, the ambitious task of using dynamic
linear programming, with nonlinear variations, to
check the consistency and feasibility of Indian development planning. The results are of great general
interest. Dr. Gupta finds that the existing planning
models lack (a) integration among the technical,
behavioral, and fiscal aspects of the plan, (b) integration among the macro, sectoral and micro aspects
of the plan, and (c) explicit intertemporal phasing
of the plan variables. He emphasizes the importance
of the fiscal implications of the plan in the assessment of its feasibility, and finds that proper phasing
of the plans would reduce India's aid requirements
by 20 percent. The Final Fourth Plan is found to be
easily feasible, with no additional tax efforts and
half the expected foreign aid. This last finding
suggests that Indian planning has gone through a
typical cycle, from excessively ambitious and highly
inefficient planning to overly-cautious and probably
still inefficient planning.

This is a book for those who take planning seri-
ously and are concerned about the difference between
ideal planning and planning in practice.

Arising from my experience both as a practical
planner with the Indian Planning Commission and as
an academic economist, I have felt the need to bridge
the gap between practice and theory in economic planning. On the one hand, the formulation of practical
plans tends to evolve from meetings, conferences,
technical reports, and memoranda based mainly on the
experiences of different official and unofficial
agencies, the results of which are often regarded by
academics as being completely devoid of any rational
theoretical considerations. While one would wish to
qualify this criticism insofar as the theory used is
often implicit in the plans, it must be admitted
that the presentation of policy objectives at a very
general level in the official plan documents gives
no clear insight into the theory and techniques used.
On the other hand, I have frequently noticed the
suspicion of planners regarding the practical usefulness of the theoretical planning models formulated
by academic economists. To dispel this notion, I
have tried to demonstrate their usefulness by developing a theoretical planning model and working out
its empirics within the terms of reference set by
the practical planners.

In Part I of this book, an attempt is made to
bring out the explicit and implicit features of the
Indian plans prepared to date. Part II constitutes
the development of a multisectoral, intertemporal
programming model for India, containing both dynamic
and recursive elements. In it, I have discussed not
only technical and behavioral constraints, but also
those derived from the type of public policy adopted.
The presentation of the model attempts to map, sector
by sector, the movements of the major economic variables over time, in optimizing conditions; and to
study the sensitivity of plan allocations to alternative government policies and alternative values of
the major relevant parameters. Part III is devoted

to estimating the technical and behavioral parameters
for the above model. Part IV discusses the computational stages and the economic implications of the
model.

In the Appendix, an attempt has been made to
render the present model operational by demonstrating
especially how it can be made amenable to quick revision from time to time. As an illustration, the up-
to-date information on the Indian Fourth Plan has
been incorporated into the model frame, and its basic
consistency and feasibility have been tested.

The writing of this book was made possible because of the great help I received from many of my colleagues in the University of Manchester and the Indian Planning Commission. My special debt is to Professor J. Johnston of Manchester University for many helpful comments; and to Professor Harry G. Johnson, of the University of Chicago and the London School of Economics, and Professor J. A. C. Brown of the University of Oxford, for their valuable suggestions as examiners of the Ph.D. thesis on which this book is largely based.

For computation, my sincere thanks go to Mr. S. Moore of the Econometrics Department of Manchester University, and for general comments to Mr. C. H. Kirkpatrick and Mr. J. Bradley of the Economics Department.

For secretarial help and general forbearance I am indebted to my wife.

CONTENTS

LIST OF TABLES

LIST OF CHARTS

LIST OF ABBREVIATIONS

ASI	Annual Survey of Industries
CSO	Central Statistical Organisation
CMI	Census of Manufacturing Industries
ECE	Economic Commission for Europe
GDP	Gross Domestic Product
GNP	Gross National Product
IAMR	Institute of Applied Manpower Research
ISG	Inter-industry Study Group of the Indian Planning Commission
ISI	Indian Statistical Institute
NCAER	National Council of Applied Economic Research
NSS	National Sample Survey
PPD	Perspective Planning Division
Rs.	Indian rupees
SSMI	Sample Survey of Manufacturing Industries
VNR	Van Neumann Ratio

Planning Models in India

The discussions of planning problems in this
book have been confined to the stage of plan formulation. Even this limited task was found difficult
since, in official plan documents, the majority of
the assumptions and methods underlying the plan were
not specified in an explicit manner. This difficulty
was partly overcome by an examination of unpublished
technical papers and working sheets written by different government and nongovernment agencies in
connection with the formulation of the Indian plans.
Many of these were found to contain an explicit
specification of the assumptions and methods being
used. The disadvantages of drawing on this host of
background papers and studies is the lack of uniformity
in methodology and sources of information, coupled
with the difficult task of trying to assess the
exact role of the different bodies in the final plan
formulation. This is attempted in the first part of
the book.

In Part II, a suggestion is made for an alternative planning model for the Indian Fourth Plan,
broadly dividing it into two stages: a steady-state
formulation and a transient-state formulation. The
model is confined to the period 1964/5 to 1975/6,
and is presented in an optimizing framework, making
the basic assumptions as realistic as possible in
the light of information available up to 1964. The
period between 1969 and 1975 is taken to cover
approximately the fourth Five-Year-Plan period (postponed by official decision from the original plan
period spreading from 1965/6 to 1970/1). In addition,
the sensitivities of any given scheme of plan allocation, as against alternative aid possibilities,
different likely export performances and various
alternative rates of time discounting, are also explored. Further, it is emphasized that the feasibility
of a planning model is to be judged mainly in terms
of the feasibility of its fiscal implications.
Accordingly, an attempt has been made to develop and

analyze these fiscal implications in depth.

In Part III, an attempt is made to analyze and describe the structure of the Indian economy in great detail. This is done for four main reasons : In the first place, any choice of planning technique could not be made in isolation, independently of the existing structure of the economy; second, familiarity with the past is essential for the successful assessment of the likely future changes in a perspective plan; third, the efficacy and merits of existing planning techniques could only be judged in the light of the economic structure prevailing at the time and its subsequent changes; fourth, any realistic planning model of India must be based on detailed technical coefficients derived from the actual economic structure. By elaborating the structure of the Indian economy in this way and by following through the changes in it, the author has presented the picture mainly in a conventional inter-industry form, in order to cater to the needs of the inter-industry model which is developed subsequently.

The formulation of a modified plan brings out distinctive features of the Indian economy that have an important bearing on planning. They are the growing interdependance of her activity sectors, the absence of any "block structure" of the economy, and the presence of a number of very simplified stable functional relationships between many of her major economic variables (like outputs, inputs, capital stocks, inventories) and the price structure, which are seen to hold over time. The first feature suggests that a planning model in India short of a comprehensive plan frame will fail to give unbiased estimates of the plan targets; the second feature gives one confidence in the use of simple linearized relationships in building some such comprehensive planning model.

In Part IV, the empirics of the proposed computable model are explored. In this attempt, the following limitations on the present model become noticeable:

First, limitations of computer facilities and the varying degree of information in the different sectors of the economy place restrictions on the possible level of disaggregation that can be adopted in the model.

But the danger of this leading to significant aggregation bias has been avoided by breaking up the model into several suitable submodels and working with each of these submodels at different convenient levels of disaggregation, before finally integrating them into the comprehensive structure. The steady-state model, the export submodel, and the income consumption submodel are examples of this approach.

A second limitation of this model is a comparatively simple lag structure of one-and-a-half to two years for investments in a few specific sectors. Contemporary literature includes a number of attempts to use more complicated lag structures; unfortunately, all of these are highly conjectural and unrepresentative.

Third, the model's behavioral relations are highly aggregative. But considering the macro nature of the tools used for implementing the Indian plans, this is hardly a serious limitation.

Fourth, the present model, like most of the other members of the family, has no separate treatment for pricing problems or financial institutions. All the relevant variables run in terms of constant prices. This approach assumes away any exogenous change in the price structure and fails to spell out the activities of the financial institutions of the society, e.g., in terms of "the quantity of money to be created," or "the rate of interest to be instituted." However, the above limitations may not be very serious, because if a bottleneck has no occasion to appear in a well-planned economy, and if all price changes are well anticipated beforehand (i.e., endogenous) then the quantity layouts in the plan are likely to be price neutral. Also, if the financial sector of the market is under the strict control of the planning authority, then neglect of

this sector may reduce the coverage of the plan but
need not disturb the basic structure of the model.

A final limitation of this model is that some
of the assumptions and the values of the exogenous
variables used are in places slightly backdated. This
is inevitable in the case of a model of the present
size, which would unfortunately almost always take
more than two to three years to build, whereas the
information in most sectors would flow in with a
time lag of one to two years. But in the Appendix
it is demonstrated how these models could be made
timely and operational at a slightly lower level of
disaggregation, (and thus suitable for broad policy
purposes), by injecting the latest information of
the Fourth Plan and working out its implications
within a very short period of time and with minimum
arbitrary assumptions. But to make use of this operational nature of the model, its basic parameters
should be revised, say, every three to four years.

The primary objective of building these different
models is to assess the problems of resources allocation over sectors and over time. While formulating
these models, we obtain better insight into the
functioning of the economy as an organic whole. They
bring out very clearly the complexities of real life
and demonstrate the difficulties of drawing unequivo-
cal conclusions from the solutions of these exercises.
But, as Eckaus and Parikh have aptly concluded, "the
difficulties in basing judgements on evidence from
the model solutions are not a special feature of
the models but are intrinsic to the problems. The
models only force a greater awareness of alternative
possibilities by being more comprehensive and explicit
than less detailed models the structure of which permits a greater degree of ambiguity.[1] Indeed, it
should be made clear that no econometric models can
decide unequivocally whether a plan or program is
ambitious or not. It can bring out the extent of
the minimum "breakaway" from the past structure
(both in behavior and technology) that is necessary
in order to fulfill certain economic and social
goals. The level of tolerance of society for these
changes is very much a socio-political phenomenon

and cannot be decided in terms of pure economics.*

Hence, provided the figures are not read with prophetic precision, and provided the results are used as a general directive, such models have a very real usefulness, even allowing for these limitations.

For example, the operational value of the model is clearly indicated when applied to the Fourth Draft Plan in terms of the following features observed in its solution values.

The level of sacrifice or the degree of tolerance expected from the people for the execution of a plan depend very much on their physical capacity to postpone certain benefits together with their expectations for the future. In our present model, because it is phased annually, the plan allocations and sacrifices involved will be relevant over only a one-year period. In this light, the results of the model make it obvious that even a modest rise in living standards by 1975 would mean a tremendous sacrifice that would be concentrated in a few specific years of the plan. In fact, all the alternative versions of our model, irrespective of whether pessimistic and optimistic assumptions are used, show that any consumption benefit arising out of the plan efforts have had to be postponed until 1970. When translated in terms of fiscal efforts, it results in an average rate of taxation (direct) of 30-35 percent in few specific years. This should be regarded as extremely high, especially when one remembers the very low per capita income in India, together with a highly positively skewed distribution of income, and a base-period rate of taxation as low as 4 percent.

On the other hand, if we try to visualize the total tax effort needed for the whole plan period in a conventional way, it emerges as a comparatively low figure of 10-15 percent of additional taxation.

_____

*i.e., behavioral changes, assuming technological changes are autonomous or exogenous to the model.

Obviously, this way of looking at the problem is
likely to underestimate the ambitiousness of the
plan.

At this stage, one may suggest a more equitable
distribution of the consumption benefits of the plan
over time, even at the sacrifice of total consumption
benefit reckoned over the whole plan period. This
decision would relieve the severe strain envisaged
in a few specific years of the plan. In fact, this
is why it has been suggested that a sub-optimum
solution of the plan program might sometimes be
politically and socially less difficult to execute.
But this will not always be true, because it is possible to transfer resources from present to future
use, but impossible to transfer future resources to
the present use, when at present they are nonexistent.
For example, in alternatives one and five of the
planning model, the economy is seen to glide along
the consumption floor set by the planners during
the initial years of the plan in order to meet the
capital accumulation target set for the terminal
year of the plan. If we divert some of the resources
to consumption purposes in the early years of the
plan in order to relieve the strain in the consumer's
market, the above plan will become infeasible, and
the economy will fail to reach its capital formation
targets (i.e., the programme ends with the artifical
variables at the optimum base).

This is not to deny that there are also certain
circumstances under which an intertemporal transfer
of resources will be possible. But even that problem
needs to be solved in an optimizing framework, putting
all policy considerations explicitly into the system.
Absence of any optimizing criteria, irrespective of
the reasons offered, is a negation of planning.

Moreover, the present exercise gives an insight
into the problem of estimating the so-called trade
gaps of the economy. The popular approach is to
estimate the gap between the foreign-exchange requirements for imports and the foreign-exchange earnings
from exports of an economy, deriving these estimates
econometrically from past observations. Such functions

are basically behavioral and are not always the outcome of rational responses or the needs of technology.*
Rather, the justified need for foreign exchange to
bridge any trade gap must be based on an optimizing
framework, measured in terms of technological requirements and the highest efficiency, and subject to the
import substitution possible under the influence of
possible technical changes.

By using our "policy-oriented" concepts of consumption and import propensities we demonstrate that
nearly 80 percent of the present need for foreign
aid could be economized.

The treatment of foreign aid in the model can
be divided into three parts: The aggregate level
of foreign aid, calculated over the whole plan period;
the annual phasing of foreign aid; and the nature
and composition of foreign aid.

In practice, the decisions at all the three
levels are governed mainly by negotiations based on
politics and international relations. In economic
model-building, the common practice is to place the
major emphasis on the level of aid. But our present
model shows quite unmistakably the importance of the
phasing of foreign aid as distinct from its level.
Also, from the study of shadow price of foreign exchange given in these models, it is clear that given
full freedom of choice, any intertemporal allocation
of foreign aid in India should be preferably positively skewed. That is to say, the different versions
of the model prove between them that the constraining
effect of foreign aid measured in terms of shadow
prices declines with the increase in the prosperity
of the economy and with improved phasing of aid.
The concept of shadow price referred to above is not

---

*Also, this behavior is largely influenced by
a saving constraint over the sample period, and
hence is likely to overestimate the trade gap, if
over this period the saving-investment gap was the
larger constraint.

the conventional one, which is usually measured in
terms of marginal productivity of foreign exchange.
Rather, it is related to the concept of discounted
consumption stream subject to several plan constraints,
like monotonicity of per capita consumption over the
plan period. But by way of qualification it must be
recognized that the above results may be partly influence by the nature of our assumptions, for
example in the projection of export earnings, the
predetermined nature of the phasing and level of the
servicing cost of foreign aid, and the time profile
of gestation in the investment projects.

For the sake of comparability with other studies,
an alternative measure of productivity of foreign
aid, more akin to the conventional definition, has
been computed. Finally, as the sensitivity analysis
of the requirement vector of the program shows, there
is scope even in the present circumstances for economizing in foreign aid to India without destroying
the basic structure of the plan.

Another notable feature of these exercises is
the light they cast on the popular debate over the
choice of discount rates in the evalution of the
social time-preference for consumption. The model
demonstrates that in an economy running at subsistence
level and with an ambitious goal in its development
program, the debate on discount rates will prove to
be largely academic. The plan layouts in the present
model are sensitive to the choice of discount rates
used, but the effects of these changes over the
normal range are found to be insignificant in the
sense that they are less than the normal observational
and rounding errors associated with these plan variables.

Further, it is obvious from our findings that
if one wants to reduce the ambitiousness of the
plan, the following would be some of the alternatives:
To lower the targets of output and consumption; to
increase the export targets; and to increase the
expectation of aid.

The Planning Commission of India has recently

published the report on the Fourth Plan covering the
period 1969-74. Unfortunately the information given
in this document is too sketchy to be fed into our
model in a comparable form for checking its detail
consistency and feasibility. Hence, a comparatively
aggregated and generalized attempt has been made in
the Appendix to test the feasibility of the macro
structure of the Fourth Plan. We have preferred to
keep this exercize separate from the main body of
the book because of its exploratory character. But,
in general, the official plan has attempted to reduce the ambitiousness of the initial draft by ex-
ploring all the aforesaid alternatives.

                          NOTES

     1. Eckaus and Parikh. Multi-sectoral Intertem-
poral Planning Model of India. M.I.T.

1

THE
BASIC
PROBLEMS
OF
PLANNING

Planning is best defined as an exercise which attempts to harmonize the activities of different economic units of society, (e.g., households, institutions, and the government), with a given objective in view. In programing terms, it therefore means maximizing the value of a function subject to limitations set by nature, institutions, knowledge, and time.

Accordingly, the first important step in constructing a planning model is to make a decision regarding the disaggregation of the activity sectors representing the different decision units. This, in practice, is seen to depend largely on the details of the operational mechanism available in connection with the implementation of the plan (in theory, the problem of aggregation is too well known in economic literature). For example, it will be of little use to attempt to enumerate all the different types of soaps in a planning model if there is a single homogeneous treatment for all kinds of soaps in its fiscal tools. At this point, however, it should be emphasized that the level of aggregation adopted in a plan might sometimes exceed that needed for its implementation, in order to enable the secondary and tertiary effects of planned-resources allocation to be taken into account. For example, the plan might be extended purely for indicative purposes to cover activities that would be outside the direct

control of the planning authority. In a developing
country, however, the most important constraint in
determining the level of disaggregation of the
activity sectors is the availability and reliability
of data, although it should be remembered that the
degree of accuracy needed in any plan estimate
differs considerably from sector to sector, depending
on the implementation mechanism and broad strategy
of the plan.

The second most important step in building a
planning model is the introduction of intertemporal
elements into its variables; this is done primarily
to accommodate leads and lags of time in economic
activities. Indeed, as it is of the nature of constraints to have a time dimension, the plan scheme
itself must also incorporate time dimensions, e.g.,
perspective plans, five-year plans, or annual plans.

Perspective plans normally cover a wider time
span, and they are essentially demand-oriented.
Over a very long period, supply restrictions are
conceptually very low. At the other extreme, annual
plans or short-term plans are highly constrained by
supply or capacity considerations, including labor,
land, and capital. Medium-term plans enjoy some
flexibility on the supply side, subject to gestation
of investment or capacity generation, and hence can
accommodate some alternative choice on the demand
side. The above difference in the intertemporal
strategy of a plan became increasingly distinct in
later plans in India.

The above discussions, in brief, bring out the
inherent complexities of any plan formulation. This
complexity increases further when the problems of
regional allocation and income distribution are
brought into the model. In most of the existing
models, however, the above complexities are reduced
to some extent in either of the two following ways:

1. By disintegrating the total structure of
the plan, (intertemporal, intersectoral, and inter-
regional), into several blocks of almost independent
groups of activities at different convenient levels

of disaggregation. These blocks are initially treated
in isolation, and subsequently an attempt is made
to achieve some logical consistency between them
by a process of iteration or trial and error.

2. By tackling them in totality as a system
of simultaneous equations, but in lesser detail.

The advisability of adopting the former or the
latter approach, or both, depends very much on the
structure of the economy and the stages of development,
and will be discussed in detail in subsequent chapters,
using illustrations from Indian plans. But it should
be repeated that planning conceptually in any form
other than totally or comprehensively is bound to
be an exercise in approximation. Hence the justifi-
cation for using any of the partial or aggregative
techniques would depend to a large extent on the
degree of error they are likely to introduce into
the solutions. This again depands largely on the
interdependence of the activities within the system
and the extent of its structural changes.

2

THE FORMULATION
OF PERSPECTIVE PLANS
IN THE
PLANNING MODELS
OF INDIA

FIRST FIVE-YEAR PLAN

The basic plan frame of the First Five-Year Plan was formulated primarily on the Harrod-Domar growth model. The model was set out basically in the form of the following equation:

$$1 \times \frac{1}{\alpha} = 1\sigma \qquad (1)$$

where 1 represented the amount of investment in a given period, α represented the marginal savings ratio, and σ represented the marginal output capital ratio. In the original Harrod-Domar model, growth g was equal to $\frac{S}{K}$ where S denoted the average propensity to save and K denoted the marginal capital output ratio. This modified version was necessary in order to accommodate any difference that might be present between average and marginal propensity to save.

The above equation, however, assumed a gestation lag of only .5 years between net investment and output. To be used for the First Plan, further sophistication was needed, since the plan assumed a gestation lag of two years between investment and output.

The First Plan made several exercises with alternative assumptions about marginal capital/output

ratios (strictly speaking, investment/incremental
income ratios), initial-savings propensities, and
marginal-savings propensities. The planners, however,
admitted that unfortunately all these parameters
were illustrative and mostly derived from the experiences of other countries. Directly below are the
explicit assumptions that formed the basis for the
perspective framework of India's First Plan:

> α_0, Average propensity to save, i.e., investment/
> income ratio at the base period, (1950/1),
> = .05.

> β_1, Marginal propensity to save between 1950/1
> and 1955/6 = 0.20.

> β_2, Marginal propensity to save between 1955/6
> and 1968/9 = 0.50.

> β_3, Marginal propensity to save from 1968/9
> onwards = 0.20.

> "b" Investment divided by income = 3/1.

> In addition, the model assumed:

1. The marginal propensity to save between the
years 1948/9 and 1950/1 to be equal to the average
propensity to save over the same period.

2. Provisions for foreign aid, apparently
implied by the assumption of a comparatively ambitious
propensity to save of the community (i.e., domestic
saving supplemented by foreign resources.)

3. Population increase of 1.25 percent over
the entire period of projection.

The Likely Algebraic Fomulation
of the Growth Model

X_i = National income in "ith" period.

α_0 = Average propensity to save at the base period (0).

β_1 = Marginal propensity to save over the next five-year period (1950/1 to 1955/6).

b = Investment/income ratio.

Therefore, output in the base period, and subsequent periods are:

$$X_0 = X_{-1} + X_{-2} \; \alpha_0 \; b^{-1}$$

$$X_1 = X_0 + X_{-1} \; \alpha_0 \; b^{-1}$$

$$X_2 = X_1 + X_0 \; \alpha_0 \; b^{-1}$$

$$X_3 = X_2 + \left(x_0 \; \alpha_0 + (x_1 - x_0) \; \beta_1 \right) b^{-1}$$

when $b^{-1} = \dfrac{1}{b}$

and so on.

On the basis of the above relations, the movements of national income, consumption, and saving were formulated over the years 1955/6, 1960/1, and 1967/8.

For the year 1950/1, national income was estimated at Rs.90,000 million; for the year 1955/6 it was calculated at Rs.100,000 million, and hence a rise of 11.1 percent over 1950/1 was visualized.[1]

SECOND FIVE-YEAR PLAN

Similar exercises were repeated during the Second and Third Plans, but they were supplemented in places by an expanded and comparatively more detailed account of major plan activities. To begin with, in the Second Plan, the estimates based on the aforesaid macro-structure of the plan were revised in the light of a more optimistic assumption regarding the capital/output ratios to be used, a more pessimistic assumption towards the community's likely propensity to save, together with a revision in the estimates of the rate of growth of population over the plan period. The ex-post "aggregate" incremental capital/net output ratio in the First Plan was estimated at 1.8

as against 3:1 assumed for the Second Plan period
(in the First Plan model). This very favorable
capital/output ratio during the First Plan was
attributed partly to certain favorable conditions
(e.g., weather) contributing to the growth of income
in this period, and the planners took it to be a
sufficient reason for postulating a more favorable
capital/output ratio for the future plans. For the
second plan, therefore, it was revised to a ratio
of 2.3:1. This was based partly also on the calculations of the estimated increases of net output
in a number of individual sectors which were selected
in the light of the investments proposed in the
plan, coupled with the basic assumption that with
industrialization, the capital/output ratio would
be expected to increase over time. These ratios
were re-estimated at 2.6, 3.4, and 3.7 respectively
for the Third, Fourth, and Fifth plans. Thus, these
ratios must again be regarded as to some extent
illustrative and indicative. Savings propensities
were again clouded in vagueness, since the investment
coefficients were allowed to go up during this period,
without specifying in the model what portions of
these investments were expected to be financed by
foreign saving. The investment/national income
ratio was raised from about 7 percent in 1955/6 to
11 percent in 1960/1, then rising to 14 percent in
1965/6 and ultimately to 16 percent in 1970/1.
These revised projections suggested a much lower
investment/income relation than that postulated in
the First Plan (20 percent in 1970/1).

Regarding population growth rate, the assumption
of a flat rate of growth of 2.25 percent per annum
over the whole perspective plan period (1951-70)
was revised to 2.25 percent per annum between 1951
and 1960, 2.33 percent per annum between 1961 and
1970, and 2.40 percent per annum between 1971 and
1980. These estimates were in fact intermediate
between the upper and lower limits put forward by
the Census Commission in the census report of 1951.

In the official plan document of the Second
Plan, the layout for perspective plan included, in
addition to the presentation of the Harrod-Domar

type of growth, a special emphasis on the role of
heavy and capital-goods industry, especially in the
long-run strategy of its planned growth. The logic
of this was presumably derived from the Mahalanobis
model[2]. Mahalanobis' model exhibited two major aspects, one of which was more relevant to the long-term
growth strategy developed in the Second Plan. The
other one referred more directly to the short-term
investment allocations over the Five-Year-Plan
horizon. In this present chapter, I am concerned
with the former aspect, while the latter aspect is
discussed in later chapter.

In brief, Mahalanobis' model can be described
as follows: The economy consists of two sectors,
the investment-goods and the consumption-goods
sectors. Conceptually all industries producing raw
materials for consumer-goods industries are included
in the consumer-goods sector, whereas all industries
producing raw materials for the investment-goods
sector are included in the investment-goods industry.
No separate sector for intermediate goods is created.

Quite often criticism is made of the limitations
and unreality of the two-sector classification of
an economy and the strategy built on it. Evidently
this raises the familiar problem in economics of
aggregation and disaggregation, but in my opinion
the objection becomes a minor one provided the
strategies built on the basis of such a model are
also read at an aggregative level. The investments
in the Mahalanobis model at a point of time are
divided between (i) investment in capital-goods
industry and (ii) investment in consumer-goods
industry. Conceptually, the income generated by
the former is considered to be cumulative, written
up by its relevant output/capital ratio, (i.e.,
expanding capacity), whereas the latter would lead
to an increase in income once and for all and maintain
that level throughout (assuming the life of an asset,
once created, is infinite.)

Let the fraction of total investment in a period
devoted towards producing more capital goods be
denoted as λ_i. Then $\lambda_i + \lambda_c = 1$. Let also the

original ratio of investment to income ratio be as α_0, then

$$\frac{I_0}{Y_0} = \alpha_0$$

$$I_t - I_{t-1} = \beta_i \; \lambda_i \; I_{t-1} \qquad (1) \quad (\beta_i = \text{output/capital investment-goods sector})$$

and $$C_t - C_{t-1} = \beta_c \; \lambda_c \; I_{t-1} \qquad (2) \quad (\beta_c = \text{output/capital in consumption-goods sector})$$

Equation (1) could be presented as

$$I_t = I_0 \; (1 + \lambda_i \; \beta_i)^t \text{ when } I_0 = \text{investment in t=0 (i.e., Base)} \quad (3)$$

or

$$I_t - I_0 = I_0 \left((1 + \lambda_i \; \beta_i)^t - 1 \right) \qquad (4)$$

From equation (2) it could be deduced that

$$C_t - C_0 = \beta_c \; \lambda_c \; I_0 \left(\frac{(1 + \lambda_i \; \beta_i)^t - 1}{\lambda_i \; \beta_i} \right) \qquad (5)$$

Adding (4) and (5)

$$Y_t - Y_0 = I_0 \left\{ \left((1 + \beta_i \lambda_i)^t - 1 \right) \frac{\beta_c \; \lambda_c}{\beta_i \lambda_i} + 1 \right\} \qquad (6)$$

If we now put $I_0 = \alpha_0 \; Y_0$ when α_0 is a fraction less than one, then we would have:

$$Y_t - Y_0 = \alpha_0 \; Y_0 \; \frac{\beta_c \; \lambda_c + \beta_i \; \lambda_i}{\beta_i \; \lambda_i} \left((1 + \beta_i \; \lambda_i)^t - 1 \right) \qquad (7)$$

or

$$Y_t = Y_0 \left[1 + \alpha_0 \frac{(\beta_c \lambda_c + \beta_i \lambda_i)}{\beta_i \lambda_i} \left((1 + \beta_i \lambda_i)^t - 1 \right) \right] (8)$$

It therefore follows that the rate of growth of national income is dependent on α_0, λ_i, β_i, β_c, and t. Now α_0 is an initial condition, β_i and β_c are technical factors, hence λ_i becomes the decision variable in the growth process of the model.

With illustrative values of α_0, β_i, β_c, Y_0, and λ_i, Mahalanobis tried to develop the following two basic strategies of a perspective plan: (1) the importance of the problem of investment allocation in a planning decision, and the role of heavy industry, and (2) the basic choice involved in the decision-making process of a perspective plan between a high rate of growth in the immediate present (with corresponding consumption benefits) with a relatively low future rate of growth, and vice versa. This choice element was made clear with detailed numerical illustrations by Mahalanobis in Sankhya (1955).[3]

The entire argument in the model runs as follows: If a high value of λ_i is chosen, then in the beginning the system would move at a somewhat slow rate, whilst it would gain in acceleration with the passage of time. The reason for this is that a high value of λ_i would increase the magnitude $(1 + \lambda_i \beta_i)^t$ whilst lowering the value of the ratio

$$\frac{\beta_c \lambda_c + \beta_i \lambda_i}{\beta_i \lambda_i}$$

Now the reduction of

$$\frac{\beta_c \lambda_c + \beta_i \lambda_i}{\beta_i \lambda_i}$$

would always be the same and independent of time, whereas the increase of $(1 + \beta_i \lambda_i)^t$ would be the function of time and would increase as time t

increased. Hence the reduction in the above ratio
brought about by a rise in λ_i could be larger than
the increase in the expression $(1 + \beta_i \lambda_i)^t$ for
small values of t. With the passage of time, however,
$(1 + \beta_i \lambda_i)^t$ would tend to dominate the whole process
of expansion, so that a higher value of λ_i would
mean a higher rate of growth in the future. But it
is worth noting the fact that the role of the capital-
goods industry, and as such the importance of λ_i
given in the above model, is based only on the
assumption of a closed economy. In an open economy,
it would be always advantageous to invest where
productivity of capital is highest, irrespective
of the values of λ_i. The necessary expansion of
capacity (or, for that matter, the necessary expansion
of consumption) could be satisfied in that case by
exchanging domestic goods for imported capital goods
(only few goods are not importable).

But any extreme assumption of a complete openness
or a complete closedness of the Indian economy is
unreal. Given the period under consideration,
Mahalanobis' model can be defended as closer to reality
if one admits the presence of a comparatively stagnant
market for Indian export.

Two other models, the Harrod-Domar model and
the Feldman model, have a close similarity to that
of Mahalanobis. The Mahalanobis and the Harrod-
Domar models are similar in that both emphasize
capital/output ratio and propensity to save as the
two major determining factors in the growth process
of the country. In the Harrod-Domar model, with a
single activity sector, the estimates of the capital/
output ratio are purely technical, whereas in the
Mahalanobis model they are subject to product mix.
The role of the propensity to save in the Mahalanobis
model is not as explicit as in the Harrod-Domar model.
α_0 of Mahalanobis' model represents the average
propensity to save of the base period in a closed
economy. $\lambda_i \beta_i / \lambda_i \beta_i + \lambda_c \beta_c$ represents the
marginal propensity to save, which is assumed to
remain constant over the plan period. This is
because $\lambda_i \beta_i + \lambda_c \beta_c$ represents the productivity
of new investment, i.e., the incremental outputs.

Thus, $\lambda_i \beta_i / \lambda_i \beta_i + \lambda_c \beta_c$, strictly speaking,
indicates the proportion of incremental income that
takes the form of investment. Since investment
equals saving in a closed economy, the above ratio
is taken as an estimate of marginal propensity to
save. This proves that the selection of the value
of λ_i in the Mahalanobis model (the only instrument
variable) is not unconstrained. If savings propensities have behavioral character, then the selection
of λ_i must be influenced by the habit of the society.

As to its comparison with the Feldman model,
both of them are guided predominantly by the objectives
of long-term planning and a high rate of industrialization. Further, both these models have two-sector
classification and both, following Marxist tradition,
assume a closed economy and emphasize that investment
in capital goods should be the principal source of
generating increments in national income. Both again
neglect the demand aspect of the market in terms of
propensities to save and invest. This neglect of
the demand aspect in these models might be less
objectionable in a totalitarian state, but it is
definitely a serious omission in a democratic state
such as India.

THIRD FIVE-YEAR PLAN

At an early stage in the work of the Third Plan,
a sustained rate of growth of 5 percent per annum
was visualized. Given the assumed population growth
rate of 1.2 percent, this implied an increase in
per capita income of a little less than 4 percent
per annum. However, as it was anticipated by the
planners that over the next fifteen years the
population would be likely to increase at more than
2 percent per annum, the development of the economy
over the next fifteen years should be conceived in
terms of a revised cumulative rate of growth of
approximately 6 percent per annum.

These considerations accordingly influenced
the formulation of the physical programs and targets
for the Third Plan.

Taking a broad view of the development of the
Indian economy, it was reckoned that at 1960/1
prices, the national income should rise from about
Rs.145,000 million at the end of the Second Plan
to about Rs.190,000 million at the end of the Third
Plan, about Rs.250,000 million at the end of the
Fourth Plan, and about Rs.330,000-340,000 million
at the end of the Fifth Plan.

Allowing for the increase in population on
these estimates, income per head was stipulated to
go up from around Rs. 350 at the end of 1960/1 to
about Rs. 384, Rs. 450 and Rs. 530 in 1966, 1971,
and 1976 respectively.

The above picture was formulated in the context
of a severe domestic restraint, an intensive savings
drive, a high level of exports, full utilization
of resources and manpower, and a considerable improvement in technology. Net investment as a percentage
of national income was estimated to rise from 11
percent in 1960/1 to 14-15 percent at the end of
the Third Plan, 17-18 percent at the end of the
Fourth Plan and 19-20 percent at the end of the
Fifth Plan. Domestic savings were also stipulated
to rise in corresponding fashion from about 8.5
percent in 1960/1 to 11.5 percent, 15-16 percent
and 18-19 percent in Third, Fourth and Fifth Plans
respectively.

It was also implied that external aid would
form a diminishing proportion of the total investment
and that by the end of the Fifth Plan, the economy
would be strong enough to develop at a satisfactory
pace without dependence on external assistance (outside the normal inflow of foreign capital).

So far, we notice that the exercises for the
Third Perspective Plan were very similar to the
First and Second Plans. There were, however, a
number of differences. Thus, the First Perspective
Plan tended to emphasize the role of saving, the
Second Plan the role of the capital-goods sector,
and the Third Plan, for the first time, tried to
work out in a disaggregated sector analysis the

tentative targets of capacity for the year 1970/1,
as against the "two-sector exercise" of the Second
Plan.

The sectoral approach of the Third Plan was
regarded as an improvement in technique.[4] To quote
the plan document:

> In recent years considerable progress has
> been made in developing new techniques
> and concepts for the formulation of the
> long plans of development. . . . It is
> particularly required for analyzing the
> complex relationships and correct propor-
> tions between different branches of the
> developing economy, covering consumer
> study and steady inter-industrial rela-
> tions.[5]

In this connection it is interesting to note
further that the Second Plan strategy of a closed
model was replaced by a vigorous export promotion
philosophy in the Third Plan. However, because of
the limitations of data and information, the exploita-
tions of the above technique were not very satisfactory
in the Third Plan projections, and were confined
to several specific material balances only.

To summarize, the Third Plan brought forward
for the first time an explicit recognition of the
need for disaggregated planning schemes (sectoral
and regional) in its perspective framework. In a
paper entitled "Certain Dimensional Hypotheses
Concerning the Third Plan," circulated within the
Commission in November, 1958, by the Perspective
Planning Division of the Indian Planning Commission,
a list of 67 commodities and their targeted outputs
for 1960, 1965, 1970, and 1975 was drawn.

Unfortunately, this commodity-balance model was
integrated rather loosely with the broad intersectoral
allocation pattern used in the plan.

More generally, these exercises identified the
Third Plan very clearly with the concept of a planning

model (i.e., plan targets based largely on requirement
considerations of the economy), whereas the First
and Second Plans did not bring out explicitly that
character as "planning models" and could be interpreted
to a large extent as types of projection models.

THE DEMONSTRATION PLANNING
MODEL FOR INDIA

At this stage, it is useful to examine the model
developed in 1960 by Jan Sandee[6] under the auspices
of the Indian Statistical Institute (ISI), a semi-
official research body in India. This perspective
planning model of India can be regarded as theoretically very satisfactory and fairly well ahead of its
time. While its methodological influence is conspicuously noticeable in later exercises on plan formu-
·lation in India, especially during the time of the
preparation of the Fourth Plan, it did not significantly influence the formulation of the Third Plan.
This applies especially to its numerics, although
it is fair to point out that it was probably not
formulated with that end in view. To begin with,
the model was based on an assumed (slightly hypothet-
ical) economic situation in 1960. The author himself
presented the report as a "model" to demonstrate
the possibilities of planning models in India. Of
course, the report admitted that "for this demonstration to be convincing the model had to be realistic. . . . too much realism would have made detatched
judgment difficult, however, and for this reason
the model treats long-term problems rather than
the more pressing questions of the day." The model
is essentially of a Leontief "static and open type,"
its primary purpose being to study the problems
relating to comparative statics. However, it does
have certain dynamic elements. The investment
requirements of the plan in the terminal year were
made endogenous by assuming (a) linear growth of
investment in all sectors, and for all its commodity
components, (b) zero gestation lag, and (c) an
unchanged capital output ratio for all the sectors
of the economy. Furthermore, it should be noted
that all the estimates of the Sandee model are made

in terms of incremental changes using constant
marginal coefficients. However, there is no provision
for idle capacity or replacements, and the feasibility
considerations, other than the purely technical ones
are overlooked. No behavioral equations are built
into the system, and the export and import assumptions
are of a very crude nature.

The model employs conventional capital input/
output relations in studying the intertemporal interdependence of the economy, although for the agricultural sector it has a different approach, which
skillfully avoids the problem of paucity of data,
especially relating to capital, by developing this
sector on a time-trend basis. The 1953/4 inter-
industry table prepared by the Indian Statistical
Institute, is used for current flow relations. The
model then develops a system of underdetermined
equations with few degrees of freedom. This is used
later on in the exercise for the formulation of a
linear programming model. Instead of assigning the
estimates of exogenous vector arbitrarily (as is
done in the conventional input-output model), Sandee
tried to obtain them by maximizing the consumption
in the target period. Additional constraints were
also brought in, e.g., the import-export balance,
and fixing upper limits for exports, for steel imports,
transportation, etc., in the system of inequalities.

The methods used in Sandee's planning model are
regarded as far superior to those used in the Third
Plan formulation. The material balances or supply-
demand equations formulated during the Third Plan
were much less integrated than they were in Sandee's
model. In fact only recently, in connection with
the formulation of the Fourth Plan, have methods
almost similar to Sandee's been employed.

But in spite of the sophistications of the
Sandee model, it still appears rather premature,
particularly when one remembers the problem of
availability of data in India at that time. Moreover, it lacks one of the most important elements
of a dynamic planning scheme--namely, an intertemporal
phasing of investment, output, and consumption.

DRAFT FOURTH PLAN

The layout of the perspective plan given in
connection with the preparation of the Fourth Plan
was unequivocally explicit and conforms satisfactorily
to the standard programming concepts. It is well
known that the supply constraint to an economic
system always decreases with an increase in the time
span (time horizon) of a plan. Accordingly, the
planners in India quite justifiably assumed the
perspective plan, i.e., the picture of the economy
in the distant future, to be of a demand-oriented
nature. On the other hand, the feasibility of a
perspective plan is to be judged in the light of
the supply constraints appearing in the context of
medium- and short-term plans. To quote the official
Draft Fourth Plan in this context: "Constraints
which loom large in the immediate present, tend to
diminish or even disappear given timely decision
and prompt action" in the long run.[7]

This approach to perspective plan targets was
further substantiated by the commission's reluctance
to lower the sights of the perspective plan below
the targets previously proposed in the initial draft,
except in terms of "minimum changes," despite the
many unforeseen and adverse happenings affecting
the economy viewed against the poor performance of
the Third Plan. This implies greater sacrifices and
efforts during the Fourth and Fifth Plans.

The aforesaid "minimum changes" were visualized
mainly in the foreign trade sector, in connection
with the balance-of-payments problems; in the
population sector, in terms of a need for reduction
in the population growth; in the consumption sector,
emphasizing the needs for mass-consumption goods,
leading to a higher priority for agriculture; and
in the field of income distribution, by asking for
a reduction in inequalities in income and property,
between rural and urban areas and backward and
advanced regions.

After setting the objectives and issues of the
perspective plan in a comparatively satisfactory

programming framework, the official document unfortunately presented the plan targets (as the
solution values of the model) in very broad macro-
economic terms, in the same oversimplified fashion
that had been used in the earlier plans. Only by
closely examining the different technical papers
associated with the formulation of the Fourth Plan
was it possible to realize the sophisticated nature
of the exercises performed during its preparation.

The most important point to notice at this
stage is that the difference in the techniques of
formulation of the perspective plans and of the
five-year plans had been considerably reduced.
Both the physical and the financial balances were
attempted for the whole of the perspective period
and at five-yearly intervals. The detailed stages
of formulation will be discussed in later chapters.

Coming to broad strategy, from the First Plan
to the Third Plan, the main objective of long-term
strategy had been to accelerate the rate of capital
formation, and through this the rate of growth of
national income. These plans contained no mention
of the distribution of national income, nor any
detailed layout of the anticipated consumption
standard of the people. However, in the light of
the experience of a decade of planned development,
and the general impression that higher-income groups
had perhaps benefited more than lower-income groups
during this period, it was felt necessary at the
beginning of the Fourth Plan period to adopt a long-
term strategy that would ensure a minimum level
of income, within a decade or so, for the lower-
income groups in the country.

The Perspective Planning Division of the Planning
Commission therefore prepared a preliminary paper
in 1962 on the minimum level of living that should
be taken as a target variable in the plan.[8] The
starting-point was the pattern of income distribution
in 1960/l. It was then postulated that the share
of each income group, as a proportion of the total
national income, could not be radically changed
within the next decade or so. The next step was

to fix the minimum level of per capita income to be
ensured to the lower-income groups within such an
assumed pattern of income distribution. To set the
minimum level of per capita income, a distinction
was made between what might be called the minimum
desirable level and the minimum feasible level of
per capita income. The former was the ideal standard
set by objective study of the minimum requirements
per person in terms of food, clothing, education,
etc. The latter approximated to what appeared
capable of being achieved with the resources available,
within a period of approximately fifteen years.

The minimum desirable level of per capita income
was set at Rs.35 per month, or Rs.420 per year,
for 1975/76. This was based, among other factors,
upon food requirements as indicated by the Nutrition
Advisory Committee. It was then proposed that the
level of per capita income of the third poorest 10
percent of the population should be raised to the
above level by 1975. Since the total population
estimate for this year was 625 million, the amount
of income required for this decile of the population
could be estimated and was placed at Rs.26,250 million.
The pattern of income distribution in 1960/1 indicated
that the income of this group constituted 4.5 percent
of total income. Hence, according to the postulated
hypothesis, the required level of national income
for 1975/6 could also be estimated and was placed
at Rs.582,750 million. Later on, having taken into
account the present level achieved, it was considered
too high, and the per capita income target was
accordingly reduced to Rs.25 per month, (i.e., per
capita consumption at Rs.20 per month), or Rs.300
per year for the same decile. Hence the corresponding
national income target was reduced to Rs.416,660
million. To achieve this target, a required growth
of 7 percent per annum was necessary during the
Fourth and Fifth Plans.

In the final draft of the Fourth Plan document
on the material and financial balances, the population figure was revised to 630 million, national
income to Rs.323,000 million, and per capita income
to Rs.512, taking the population as a whole and
valued at 1960/1 market prices.[9]

In this document a certain income/consumption
(i.e., savings ratio) relation was assumed, (although
it seemed to be derived arbitrarily), and per capita
consumption in 1975 was accordingly placed at Rs.409
for private consumption and Rs.72 for government
consumption.

The projections for gross output were computed
for 1975/6 from the estimates of consumptions given
in the Perspective Planning Division's exercise,
by the use of an interindustry model. (In the
official Draft Fourth Plan these projections were
shown only for the year 1970/1.)

Thus, the Perspective Planning Division's
estimates of national income for 1975/6 seem to have
had a "requirement" basis, although the presentation
in places is so unsystematic that it is very difficult
to say with confidence that in no cases have the
estimates been based on supply considerations (i.e.,
calculated mainly on a mechanical extroplation basis,
from the time-series data on income and output),

Basically, the final-demand vector was computed
as follows: (1) Estimated were made of the per
capita income and expenditure on the basis of some
minimum standard, (2) demand elasticity was derived
from the National Sample Survey (NSS) data to convert
the scalar estimate of per capita consumption into
a vector; (3) export targets were computed, based
mainly on the study of the export estimated made by
the Ministry of Commerce and relevant organizations
(these estimates were generally the outcome of a
series of deliberations and conferences, although
at times based on exercises developed from mathematical
models); (4) imports were treated as partly endogenous
to the system, and public consumption as wholly
exogenous (5) the investment vector was postulated
on the assumption that the ratio of saving of national
income would be raised by 21 percent by 1975/6.

On the basis of the official estimates of
population growth, per capita consumption was worked
out at Rs. 409 in 1975/6 (at 1960/1 prices). The
the consumption vector for 1964/5 was calculated

using the commodity-flow method. Subsequently, the
following equations were used for method. Subsequently,
the following equations were used for calculating
the consumption vector for 1975/6:

$$C_{it} = C_{io} \left(\frac{x_t}{x_0} \right)^{Qi}$$

$$C_{it} = P_t \ C_{it}$$

C_{io} = ith element of consumption vector at the
period "o" and C_{it}, the same for the year t; x_0 and
x_t referred to per capita consumption for period
0 and t period. P_t was population in period t and
C_{it} was total consumption of ith element in period
t; Qi represented the expenditure elasticity of
ith element of the consumption vector.

For the purpose of the Fourth Plan projections,
the expenditure elasticities estimated on the basis
of the tenth round of the National Sample Survey
(December 1955-May 1956) were used.[10] The elasticities
of the rural and urban areas had been averaged, the
weights being the total expenditure on each commodity
in rural and urban areas respectively; in a few cases
independent adjustments were made in the light of
more recent and current information. The choice
went in favor of this earlier round, since later
rounds of the survey contained much less detail.

The above estimated items, which were based
on the stated demand elasticities, covered about
75 percent of total expenditure in the year 1955/6.

Details of the commodity composition of the
remaining 25 percent, a major part of which was
expenditure on services, were not fully available.
It was, therefore, taken to be the difference between
aggregate personal consumption and the total expenditure on all the specific items for which demand
was computed, thus implying that the elasticity of
the residual together with the other calculated
elasticities would sum to unity.

The next important stage was the conversion
of the commodity classification, used in the demand
projections, into an input/output classification.

The public consumption in this exercise was
defined as current government expenditure minus
transfers and subsidies. For 1975/6, these were
arbitrarily assumed to be outside the model, and no
explicit mention was noticeable regarding the
methods of estimating them. To quote the Perspective
Planning Division: "The level of public consumption
has been projected on the basis of targets of
expansion in education, health, and social services,
the likely increase in current expenditure on other
development activities, and past trends in the case
of civil administration."[11]

The capital formation for 1975/6 was also
determined in a rather arbitrary manner, by assuming
a rate of investment of 18.2 percent of national
income (as against 17.5 percent in the draft outline
of the Fourth Plan) in the lower alternative and
20.3 percent in the higher alternative. In addition,
replacement investment in 1975/6 was assumed to be
exogenously determined and was made equal to one-
tenth of the sum of net investments over the last
fifteen years prior to the period under consideration
(i.e., prior to 1964/5).

The scalar estimate of investment was converted
into a vector, assuming the 1964/5 commodity composition of investment to remain unchanged. This
commodity composition of investment in the base year
was again derived from an analysis for that year
of the absorption of construction materials and
specified categories of machinery and equipment in
a few specific investment projects.

The estimates of all intermediate imports (other
than P.L. 480 imports* and imports of machinery,
which did not require further processing within the
country), were attempted from the demand angle. The
demand for these imported commodities was estimated
on the basis of input requirements per unit of output

---

*Imports under the U.S. Agricultural Trade
Development and Assistance Act of 1954.

in the using sector, less the supply of these inputs
from domestic sources.

Project Imports. The estimates were again mainly
the outcome of discussions and deliberations between
different ministries and technical committees, rather
than of an econometric exercise conducted in the
light of a general framework of the model. To quote
the Perspective Planning Division documents: The
model treats imports as being specified exogenously.

     Last of all, a conventional static input-output
model, embodying a current flow coefficient matrix
for the year 1964/5 (details of which will be discussed
in connection with the five-year plans) was presumed
to have been used to derive a set of production
targets for 1975/6 in conformity with the consumption,
investment, and export estimates already derived.

     Over and above the sectoral balances thus derived
for the year 1975/6, greater detail was attempted
by trying to develop material balance at specific
commodity levels, as had been done in the Third Plan
exercise. For this approach, demands for specific
commodities, absorbed mainly as intermediate products,
were arrived at essentially by the application of
the end-use analysis. The successive stages were:
(a) Identification of the major consuming sectors
and their subsectors, and their current production
targets; (b) determination of input norms on the
basis of observed data, and adaption of them for
the future in the light of relevant technical information; (c) calculation of the material-input
requirement for the targeted production of the using
sectors; and (d) estimation of additions and depletions
to stock and other uses.

     Considered along with the macro-economic
assumption of the plan and the broad interindustry
balances, these material balances provided a basis
for fixing a more detailed set of output targets
for the principal commodities in the plan and testified
to the plan's balance and consistency.

     The intersectoral relations revealed at this
level of disaggregation were claimed to have

contributed to the improvement of the technological
concepts used in the input-output tables. Unfortunately, however, the draft plan contained no explicit
information as to the precise method by which these
material balances were grafted into the sectoral
balances. As has already been mentioned, the final-
demand vector thus computed was used to calculate
gross output for the year 1975/6 by using an input-
output table for 1964/5 of the order of 77 x 77,
prepared by the Planning Unit of the Indian Statistical
Institute at 1960/1 factor cost. This obviously
demonstrated that the model used for the Fourth Plan
was static, and was intended mainly for checking
the consistency of output levels for 1975/6. The
treatment of investment in this model was not
explicitly specified in the "material and financial
balance" document of the Fourth Plan, was assumed
to be exogenous, and, unfortunately, was rather
arbitrarily determined.[12] However, some mention
of a likely method of estimation of the investment
requirements for the year 1975/6 was made by Alan
Manne and A. Rudra, in Sankhya, 1965, and it seems
likely that their paper gave a reasonably realistic
picture of the likely method adopted in the plan
for the estimation of investment for 1975/6.[13] The
limitations of their approach will be discussed in
detail in subsequent chapters, in connection with
the discussion of the Draft Fourth Plan.

                          NOTES

    1. See First Five-Year Plan, (Delhi: Government
of India Press, 1953).

    2. P.C. Mahalanobis, "The Approach of Operational
Research to Planning in India," Sankhya, Vol. 16,
(1966).

    3. P.C. Mahalanobis, "The Statistical Basis
of the Plan Frame," Sankhya, Vol. 16, (1955).

    4. The problems arising out of heavy aggregation
have been discussed exhaustively by Professor Paul
Streeten under two heads, "Misplaced Aggregation"

and "Illegitimate Isolation" in Gunnar Myrdal, Asian Drama. (London: Allen Lane, The Penguin Press, 1968).

    5. Third Five-Year Plan: Progress Report (Delhi, Government of India Press, 1967).

    6. Jan Sandee, A Demonstration Planning Model for India, (Calcutta: Indian Statistical Institute, Asia Publishing House, 1960).

    7. Fourth Five-Year Plan: A Draft Outline (Faridabad: Government of India Press, 1966).

    8. Planning Commission, Perspective Planning Division, "Perspective of Development 1961-76. (Implications of Planning for a Minimum Level);" (1962). Mimeographed.

    9. Planning Commission, Draft Fourth Plan: Material and Financial Balances, (New Delhi: Government of India Press, September 1966).

    10. Mainly, the expenditure elasticities computed by N.S. Iyenger, in the ISI Working Paper No.299, (December, 1964), have been used.

    11. Planning Commission, Economic Division, The Macro-Economic Hypothesis for the Fourth Plan, (Delhi: Government of India Press, 1964).

    12. Draft Fourth Plan: Material and Financial Balances, op. cit.

    13. Alan S. Manne and A. Rudra, "A Consistency Model of India's Fourth Plan," Sankhya, Series B, Vol. 27, Parts 1 & 2 (September, 1965).

3

Any attempt to describe the technique adopted
in the formation of a plan on the basis of the official plan document is bound to be conjectural and
indirect. This is because most of these official
plan documents present their objectives and priorities
in very general terms, except when quoting a few
stray and specific solution values of the underlying
planning models which were related directly to the
operational mechanism of the plan.

FIRST FIVE-YEAR PLAN

The formulation of the First Five-Year Plan
employed a growth model of the aggregative Harrod-
Domar type; in fact, the First Plan had the most explicit calculations, adhering to the letter and
spirit of the above model. These calculations, however, at first sight looked like estimates based on
simple forecasting. But one should remember that
many of its calculations had policy implications
with respect to foreign exchange and government
saving and could not, therefore, be regarded as of
a purely forecasting type.

What was conspicuously absent in the First Plan
was an integration between the plan allocations and
the macro-economic dimensions, formulated in the
growth model and described in the plan. Indeed, in

41

its operational framework it gave the impression of
a loose collection of plan provisions regarding a
few isolated semifinished projects. The impression
given was of an attempt to consolidate the existing
situation rather than an introduction of a well-
designed growth pattern. Credit is, however, due
for bringing forward, (in the chapter on "The Approach
to Planning"), almost all the basic items that have
been the guideposts to all subsequent plans in India.
The one interesting exception to note is that the
prime ideological element of later plans, namely,
the "socialistic pattern" of society, was absent
from this first plan.

The following are the broad objectives or aims
presented in the First Plan document:

(1) To restore the economy, which had
run down as a result of the war; to
resist the inflationary pressure that was
prevalent at the time; to build up the
transport system; and to ease the food
and raw-material position; (2) to formulate and execute program of development
which would be substantial in themselves,
while laying the foundation for larger efforts in the coming years; (3) to initiate
measures of social justice in a wide scale
thus taking the first step in the direction of the pattern of society placed
before the nation by the constitution in
the directives, and (4) to build up administrative and other organizations which
would be able to cope with a large program
of reconstruction wo which the nation was
committed.[1]

These objectives, however, were not fitted for-
mally into any comprehensive operational framework,
nor were they tested against any detailed set of
constraints representing the resource limitations
existing at that time within the economy. Indeed,
one is struck by the similarity of the First Five-
Year Plan to traditional government budgeting, dealing
with an assembly of discrete projects with no attempt
to examine the interdependence between them.

SECOND FIVE-YEAR PLAN

The Second Plan explicitly recognized the importance of the principle of a centralized consistency
in development design, for it was felt that the
traditional budgeting practice constituted an extremely
bad procedural model for those major portions of the
planning problems that required the balancing of
goals and expansion programs, of outputs and inputs,
of the output of one industry with that of others,
and of many other variables through time. It was
recognized that the practice of leaving the entire
initiation of the program design to the operating
agencies would not work and that, instead, the
initial design would have to be formulated by a
central group who viewed the economy as a whole, and
then tested and modified in consultation with the
operating agencies, before the whole program was
submitted for political approval. The official plan
document on the Second Plan, like the First Plan,
started with the simple aggregative Harrod-Domar
growth model.

The detailed resources-allocation pattern of
this model over the five-year horizon was presumably
based on the general strategy built into the two-sector
model of the perspective plan, and again was formulated by Prasanda Mahalanobis in a four-sector model.
One should be very clear at this stage that the
official plan carried no mention of its association
with the Mahalanobis four-sector model. However,
since the resources allocation of the official plan
document matched very closely the allocation pattern
of the Mahalanobis four-sector model, and since
Mahalanobis was at that time Statistical Adviser to
the Indian Cabinet, it is tempting to conclude that
they are in fact closely related to each other.

Thus, the total investment and the allocation
coefficient of investment in this plan between capital
goods and consumption goods were decided by the
interaction of the propensity to save and the long-
term growth considerations. But analysis of the
operational frame of the Second Plan reveals that it

gave a much more detailed sectoral allocation pattern. The supposed mathematical counterpart of the
detailed sectoral allocations was the Mahalanobis
four-sector model, although it should be admitted
that this operational plan frame was much more disaggregated than the model's four-sector division of
the economy. One would argue as a compromise that
the broad allocations in the plan were made on the
model's four-sector basis, whilst the detailed
allocations hung about this skeleton in a rather
loose and disjointed fashion.

     To quote Eckaus: "Though the sum total of
investment costs of these projects was subjected to
overall constraints derived from the aggregative
projections [including those from the four-sector
model]* there were nonetheless enough residual or
'buffer' sectors to reduce the constraining influence
of aggregate resource limitations of these projects."
Indeed, there was no visible explicit mechanism in
the Second Plan for coordinating the development of
the various sectors (especially in terms of gross
output) so as to avoid either bottlenecks or sur-
plusses. "To the extent that coordination and
scheduling was achieved, it was through the screening
procedures of the inter-ministerial committees and
working groups that met the Planning Commission
representatives. . . . As one of their tools these
committees apparently did prepare commodity balances
for the entire plan period, at least for particular
items and sectors, at discrete five-yearly points
of time."[3]

                THE MAHALANOBIS FOUR-SECTOR MODEL

     The four-sector model of P. C. Mahalanobis
attempted to solve the problem of allocating total
investment in such a way as to achieve certain overall
income and employment targets set for the plan period.[4]

_____

     *My brackets.

The allocation of investment between the capital-goods sector and the consumption-goods sector was determined exogenously in this model and derived from an earlier two-sector model. (See page 25.)

In the present model the consumption-goods sector was divided into three parts:

Sector 1.   Factories covering organized consumer-goods industries.

Sector 2.   Small-scale and household enterprises producing consumer goods.

Sector 3.   Service industries, including health, education, etc.

Finally, the investment-goods sector (as Sector i) was added to the list.

Corresponding to the four sectors, there were: four output/capital ratios, β_s; four capital/labor ratios, θ_s; and four allocation parameters, λ_s, showing the ratio of investment of each sector to the total investment.

The allocation problem was presented by the following system of equations:

$$Y_i + Y_1 + Y_2 + Y_3 = Y$$

$$N_i + N_1 + N_2 + N_3 = N$$

$$I_i + I_1 + I_2 + I_3 = I$$

in which Y, N, I, were assumed as arbitrary exogenous variables (in fact, Y and I being predetermined by the aggregate Harrod-Domar model, already discussed, whereas N was computed as a demographic variable, derived from population projections).

"Y_j"s represented sectoral increases in income, "N_j"s represented sectoral increases in employment, and "I_j"s represented sectoral increases in investment, and

$$\sum_j Y = Y, \quad \sum_j I = I \text{ and } \sum_j N = N$$

when j = sectors 1,2,3,i.

Hence the above system of equations could be rewritten as:

$$\lambda_i \beta_i I + \lambda_1 \beta_1 I + \lambda_2 \beta_2 I + \lambda_3 \beta_3 I = Y$$

$$\lambda_i I/\theta_i + \lambda_1 I/\theta_1 + \lambda_2 I/\theta_2 + \lambda_3 I/\theta_3 = N$$

$$\lambda_i I + \lambda_1 I + \lambda_2 I + \lambda_3 I = I$$

when βs represented the output/capital (income investment) ratios and θs the capital (investment)/labor ratios. The above system had three equations and four unknowns, λs, of which λ_i was determined by the two-sector model. Thus the remaining three unknowns, λ_1, λ_2, and λ_3 could uniquely be solved from the above system of equations.

It was stated in this model that from considerations of growth over a long period, the value of λ_i was to be fixed at one-third. This value was determined with the help of a two-sector model. Assuming the value of β_i equalled .20, and giving different plausible values to β_c, it was found by mathematical calculations that to keep pace with the fairly rapid increase in income over, say, about thirty years, it would be desirable that λ_i should have a value between .3 and .5. The value of λ_i equalling one-third was adopted because it was felt that "it would not be possible to go beyond this value under present conditions." With the value of λ_i thus fixed, the system of equations was solved.

It is obvious that accuracy in estimating these parameters was vital in order to obtain a correct solution to the problem. In this period in India, however, detailed statistical data were not available, and there is no convincing evidence to suggest that detailed exercises were attempted to estimate the

value of the parameters empirically. It was admitted
by the planners that most of the values used in the
model were determined on the basis of data from
foreign countries. The experiences of other countries during the same period showed that the overall
capital coefficients had in general varied between
.25 and .50. For the first plan it was assumed to
be .33, but the actual growth of income during the
plan period seemed to indicate that it should have
been higher. For example, the national-income
statistics available in 1955 for the six-year period
from 1948/9 to 1953/4 also gave a value of the capital coefficient as high as .5. Accepting this information, the overall capital coefficient was taken
at .5 in the Second Plan.

The next step was to estimate β_i, β_1, β_2, β_3,
and θ_i, θ_1, θ_2, θ_3, bearing in mind that in the final
solution (β), (aggregate capital coefficient), should
be equal to $\lambda_i\beta_i + \lambda_1\beta_1 + \lambda_2\beta_2 + \lambda_3\beta_3$. The estimates
of the values of these coefficients (i.e., β_i, β_1,
β_2, and β_3,) were based on national-income statistics
and on a few sample surveys carried out by the
Central Statistical Organization (CSO) of the United
Kingdom. However, these data could only give rough
figures, and adjustments had to be made on the basis
of informed guesses. The results of the estimates
were presented as follows:

Sector	Description	Parameters	
		(investment in Rs. per unit labor force)	
		β	θ
i	Basic investment goods	0.20	Rs.20,000
c_1	Factory consumer goods	0.35	8,750
c_2	Household indus- tries, including Agriculture	1.25	2,500
c_3	Services	0.45	3,750

The values of Y, N, and I were stipulated
wholly exogenously in the four-sector Mahalanobis
model. National income at the base year 1955/6 was
estimated at Rs.100,000 million. If an annual rate
of growth of 5 percent was to be achieved, the increase in income required during the plan was estimated at Rs.29,000 million. Given the rate of
growth of the population and the working force, an
increase in employment opportunities to absorb 11
million persons was considered essential in order
to prevent further deterioration of the unemployment
position.

With regard to investment, a target was estimated of Rs.56,100 million of total capital formation during the plan period, on the basis of an
average rate of investment of 9 percent of national
income and on the consideration of financial resources,
worked out in consultation with the Economic Division
of the Planning Commission and the Ministry of
Finance.

The solution values of the model in terms of
λs were:

Sector	New Investment (Rs. million)	Incremental Income (Rs. million)	Incremental Employment (millions)
i	18,500	3,700	0.9
c_1	9,800	3,400	1.1
c_2	11,800	14,700	4.7
c_3	16,000	7,200	4.3
Total	56,100	29,000	11.0

The allocation in the consumption-goods sector
(c_2) was further divided by another submodel, assuming
separate capital/output ratios and labor/capital
ratios for the agricultural and the small-scale
household-industry sector.

A striking similarity between the allocation of investment shown in the above table, and that in the official plan document, was noticeable in broad groupings, although the investment allocation contained in the official Second Plan gave a much more detailed breakdown. In this connection, Mahalanobis admitted that "this is as far as our simple model can take us. Further details must be settled from supplementary considerations."[5]

Hence, there is clearly no evidence to justify the belief that the "detailed" investment allocations given in the official plan were in any sense mathematically consistent.

In this connection, it should be noted that the Mahalanobis four-sector model provided no element of choice, in the sense that it gave a unique solution against the values of the parameters and exogenous variables assumed in the model, although Mahalanobis did introduce some degree of choice by assigning possible alternative values to the parameters and to policy variables.

R. Komiya has tried to develop a choice model in the same four-sector framework, in order to show that the Mahalanobis model gave a sub-optimum solution to the problem.[6] In Komiya's formulation, $1/\beta_i$ was denoted as a_i and $(\Theta_k \beta_i)^{-1} 10^6$ as b_i, 'i' referring to a sector in the model.

Accordingly, the parameters of the Mahalanobis model could be presented, per million rupees of income, (i.e. value added), as follows:

Sector	Capital (Million Rs.)	Labor (man-years)
1) Investment-goods sector	$a_1 = 5.00$	$b_1 = 250$
2) Consumption	$a_2 = 2.86$	$b_2 = 327$
3) Goods	$a_3 = .80$	$b_3 = 320$
4) Sector	$a_4 = 2.22$	$b_4 = 593$

Similarly, the data could also be reformulated as
follows: (1) The exogenous variable, in the nature
of total investment was equal to Rs.56,000 million;
(2) the increment of income, calculated at the end
of the period by 5 percent compound rate, was Rs.
108,000 million x $(1 + 0.05)^5$, (i.e., Rs.29,000 million, when the initial national income was equal to
Rs.108,000 million per annum); (3) the target or
policy variables was equal to 11 million new jobs
over five years.

Thus, according to Mahalanobis' formulation,
the investment allocation in Sector i (here Sector
1) would equal Rs.56,000 x .33 (i.e., Rs.18,500 million), and the increase in income would work out at
Rs.3,700 million.

Hence, the rest of the allocation problem would
boil down to the solution of a set of simultaneous
equations as follows:

$$Y_1 + Y_2 + Y_3 + Y_4 = \text{Rs.29,000 million}$$

$$a_1Y_1 + a_2Y_2 + a_3Y_3 + a_4Y_4 = \text{Rs.56,000 million}$$

$$b_1Y_1 + b_2Y_2 + b_3Y_3 + b_4Y_4 = \text{11 million}$$

When $\qquad Y_1 = \text{Rs.3,700 million}$

$$a_1Y_1 = \text{Rs.18,500 million}$$

$$b_1Y_1 = .9 \text{ million}$$

Hence $\quad Y_2 + Y_3 + Y_4 = \text{Rs.25,300 million}$

$$a_2Y_2 + a_3Y_3 + a_4Y_4 = \text{Rs.37,500 million}$$

$$b_2Y_2 + b_3Y_3 + b_4Y_4 = \text{10.1 million}$$

Thus three equations were formulated with three
unknowns and accordingly produced a unique solution,
assuming that the coefficient matrix of the system
was nonsingular.

The Solution Values*

Sectors

Items	1	2	3	4	Total
Increment Income (Rs. million)	3,780	3,400	14,700	7,200	29,000
Increment Investment (Rs. million)	18,500	9,800	11,800	16,000	56,000
Increment Employment (Million)	0.9	1.1	4.7	4.3	11.0

The above model assumed a 5 percent rate of growth of income. Yet if we accept that maximization of income was the goal, then a higher rate of income growth (relative to the rate contained in the Mahalanobis model) could have been attained, given the investment constraint, the employment target, and the structure of the economy. It is interesting to examine the logic behind this:

The problem, as presented by Komiya, could be placed in a programming form as follows:

$$\max \hat{Y} = Y_2 + Y_3 + Y_4$$

subject to $2.86 \ Y_2 + 0.8 \ Y_3 + 2.22 \ Y_4 = 37,500$

$$327 \ Y_2 + 320 \ Y_3 + 593 \ Y_4 = 10,100,00$$

Then the solution value would come as:

$$Y_2 = 5,998 \qquad Y_4 = 0$$

$$Y_3 = 20,348 \qquad Y = (Y_2 + Y_3 + Y_4) = 26,346$$

as against 25,300 in the Mahalanobis model.

---

*The same as on page 55.

In an alternative formulation, if one released the investment constraint as an inequality sign, then the problem could be restated as:

$$\overset{\Delta}{\max} \ Y = Y_2 + Y_3 + Y_4 \text{ subject to}$$

$$2.86 \ Y_2 \ + \ 0.8 \ Y_3 \ + \ 2.2 \ Y_4 \leqq 37,500$$

$$327 \ Y_2 \ + \ 320 \ Y_3 \ + \ 593 \ Y_4 = 10,100,000$$

with the optimizing solutions as

$$Y_2 = 0 \quad Y_4 = 0$$

$$Y_3 = 31,562.5 \qquad K_1 \text{ (slack vector)} =$$

$$1,225 \text{ and } Y = 31,562.5$$

which meant that the rate of growth could be further maximized even with less than full exploitation (i.e., economizing) of available investment funds.

In the context of the above discussions, it is obvious that if the activity levels derived from the Mahalanobis model cannot be regarded as otherwise sanctified, (say because of demand considerations, in the context of a completely closed economy), then there would be no reason to accept Mahalanobis' allocation pattern. But any such assumption as the closedness of the economy seems to be not unrealistic in the present case. Yet this assumption is unfortunately not made explicit, either in the Mahalanobis model or in the plan frame.

To sum up, the greatest limitation of Mahalanobis' two-sector model lies in its nonrecognition of demand considerations. Further, both the two-sector and four-sector models neglect the consistency requirements vis-à-vis the intermediate sectors and fail to give any optimality considerations. They contain no dynamic element, and even the four-sector classifications could be regarded as highly aggregative.

THIRD FIVE-YEAR PLAN

Insofar as the macro-economic projections are concerned, the approaches used in the Third Plan are similar to, but less explicit than, those used in the Second. However, the official plan document of the Third Plan period more clearly recognizes the importance, for planning purposes, of a realistic assessment of the value of the parameters of the macro-models. A valuable insight into the Third Plan model, adopted for this purpose, can be gained from examining some of the technical papers developed within the commission, especially the paper on "Certain Dimensional Hypotheses Concerning the Third Plan," prepared by the Perspective Planning Division of the Indian Planning Commission. Needless to say, in this paper there is no trace of any explicit mathematical model similar to the one prepared by Mahalanobis during the formulation of the Second Plan.

The only conceivable planning model that may hold the Third Plan variables in a formal way is that formulated by S. Chakrabarty in a paper "The Mathematical Framework of the Third Five-Year Plan," contained in Rosenstein-Roden's book.[7]

The Mathematical Framework

Definitions

$\sum\limits_{i} I_i$ = Sum total of net investment over the plan period, i.e. i = 1 to t.

$\sum\limits_{i} S_i$ = Sum total of net investment financed from domestic savings, i.e. cumulative saving over the plan period, i = 1 to t.

S_t = Saving in period t.

$\sum\limits_{i} F_i$ = Foreign aid or foreign saving over the plan period, i = 1 to t.

Y_0 = Base period national income.

$\dot{G}_n$ = Uniform rate of growth (compound) of national income over the plan period.

S_0 = Base period savings.

α = Uniform increment of saving in each period of the plan.

i = Time period of the plan.

ΔS = Increment of saving between the base level and final year of the plan (i.e. over 0 period).

ΔY = Increment of national income between the base level and the final year level of the plan, (i.e. t over 0 period).

m_1 = Average marginal propensity to save over the whole plan period.

$\dot{G}_p$ = Rate of growth of population (compound) per annum.

$(\dot{G}_n/G_p)$ = Rate of growth of per capita income per annum.

$\dot{D}_a$ = Rate of growth of agricultural demand per annum.

λ = Expenditure elasticity for agriculture.

β = Aggregate output/capital ratio.

$\dot{Y}_a$ = Rate of increase of agricultural production (income).

C_t = Consumption at the current period, (i.e., t period).

C_0 = Consumption at the base period.

$\dot{G}_c$ = Rate of growth of consumption per annum (compound).

$\dot{Y}_{na}$ = Rate of growth of nonagricultural production (income).

$\dot{T}_d$ = Rate of growth of derived tax revenue.

$\gamma_1, \gamma_2, \gamma_3$ = Elasticity of tax revenue to changes in "consumption" and "income" from nonagricultural and agricultural activities.

$\sum_i T_i$ = Total tax receipts over the whole period, i = 1 to t.

$\sum_i T_i^d$ = Total derived tax receipts over the whole period, i = 1 to t.

$\sum_i T_i^a$ = Total autonomous tax receipts over the whole period, i = 1 to t.

$\sum_i E_i$ = Total public expenditure, i = 1 to t.

$\sum_i E_{cti}$ = Public current expenditure, i = 1 to t.

pc = Proportion of investment made in public sector.

ΔD = Excess of public expenditure over public income and surplus of public enterprise.

$\sum_i R_i$ = Total surplus of public enterprise in whole of plan period, i = 1 to t.

T_t^d = Derived tax in period t.

The model contains the following equations (which differ slightly from those of S. Chakrabarty, and attempt to represent the mathematical version of the macro-plan prepared by the Perspective Planning Division of the Planning Commission):[8]

$$\sum_i I_i = \sum_i S_i + \sum_i F_i \qquad (1)$$

$$\Delta Y = \beta \sum_i I_i \qquad (2)$$

$$Y_0 (1 + \dot{G}_n)^t - Y_0 = \Delta Y \qquad (3)$$

$$\sum_i S_i = 5S_0 + \sum_{t=1}^{5} (S_i - S_0) = 5 \cdot S_0 + 15\alpha \tag{4}$$

$$\Delta S = \alpha t \text{ when } t = 5 \tag{5}$$

$$\Delta S / \Delta Y = m_1 \tag{6}$$

$$\dot{G}n - \dot{G}p = (\dot{G}n/\dot{G}p) \tag{7}$$

$$\dot{D}_a = \lambda(\dot{G}n/\dot{G}p) + Gp \tag{8}$$

$$\dot{D}_a = \dot{Y}_a \text{ (input/output ratio remaining constant)} \tag{9}$$

$$C_t = Y_t - S_t = (Y_0 + \Delta Y) - (S_0 + 5\alpha) \tag{10}$$

$$C_0 (1 + \dot{G}_c)^5 = C_t \tag{11}$$

$$w_1\dot{Y}_{na} + w_2\dot{Y}_a = \dot{G}_n \text{ (w_1, w_2 the weight of nonagri-}$$
cultural and agricultural output in the base)
$$\tag{12}$$

$$\dot{T}_d = \gamma_1\dot{G}_c + \gamma_2\dot{Y}_{na} + \gamma_3\dot{Y}_a \tag{13}$$

$$\sum_i T_i^d = T_0^d \sum_{n=1}^{5} (1 + \dot{T}_d)^n \tag{14}$$

$$\sum_i T_i = \sum_i T_i^d + \sum_i T_i^a \tag{15}$$

$$\sum_i E_i = \sum_i E_{cti} + Pc \sum_i I_i \tag{16}$$

$$\Delta D = \sum_i E_i - (\sum_i T_i + \sum_i R_i) \tag{17}$$

Thus the above system of equations had:

Exogenous variables as:

$$\text{(i)} \quad \sum_i I_i$$

$$\text{(ii)} \quad \sum_i F_i$$

$$\text{(iii)} \quad \sum_i T_i$$

$$(iv) \quad \underset{(i)}{\Sigma E} \, (ct)$$

$$(v) \quad \dot{G}_P$$

$$(vi) \quad \underset{i}{\Sigma R_i}$$

Initial values as:

$$(i) \quad Y_0$$

$$(ii) \quad S_0$$

$$(iii) \quad T_0^d$$

Parameters as:

$$(i) \quad \beta$$

$$(ii) \quad \lambda$$

$$(iii) \quad \lambda c$$

$$(iv) \quad \gamma_1$$

$$(v) \quad \gamma_2$$

$$(vi) \quad \gamma_3$$

$$(vii) \quad w_1 \text{ and } w_2$$

Unknown Variables as:

(1)	$\underset{i}{\Sigma S_i}$	(6)	m_1
(2)	ΔY	(7)	$\left(\dot{G}_n / G_P \right)$
(3)	$\dot{G}_n$	(8)	$\dot{D}_a$
(4)	α	(9)	$\dot{Y}_a$
(5)	ΔS	(10)	C_t

(11) $\dot{G}_c$ (15) $\sum_i T_i$

(12) $\dot{Y}_{na}$ (16) $\sum_i E_i$

(13) $\dot{T}_d$ (17) ΔD

(14) $\sum_i T^d$

Thus the model has 17 equations with 17 unknowns
and hence it can secure a unique solution. This
gives the five-yearly total of a few major variables,
some specific terminal variables, and a few principal
rates of growth of major plan magnitudes.

Numerical Illustrations

All the magnitudes in this exercise are in fact
based on the paper on the dimensional hypotheses of
the Third Plan, prepared by the Perspective Planning
Division of the Planning Commission.[9] In the final
plan document, many of the estimates contained in
this paper are much revised; but since I am more
interested in portraying the general framework and
logic of the plan, I prefer to use the figures
given in the paper for illustrative purposes.

The paper contains no information on the division
between agriculture and nonagriculture income.
Hence, in the present model, I have assumed the
ratio of rural and urban population to the total as
the revelant weights. Again,

$$(\sum_i T^d_i \; + \; \sum_i T_i)$$

are given as exogenous variables in the paper. In
order to accommodate the data given in the paper in
the above model, it was necessary to reduce the number of equations and unknowns to 15.

The following is a description of the solution
in iterative stages of the model. This differs
slightly from Chakrabarty's version.[10]

Exogenous Variables	Parameters

$\underset{i}{\Sigma}\underset{i}{I} = $ Rs.10,000 million

$w_1 = .19$

$\underset{i}{\Sigma}\underset{i}{F} = $ Rs.100,500 million

$w_2 = .81$

$\underset{i}{\Sigma}E_{ct} = $ Rs.86,000 million

$\beta = .45$

$\underset{i}{\Sigma}\underset{i}{R} = $ Rs.12,000 million

$\lambda = .75$

$\gamma_1 = .567$
$=$

$\dot{G}_p = .02$

$\gamma_2 = .323$

$\gamma_3 = .007$

$\underset{i}{\Sigma}\underset{i}{T^d} + \underset{i}{\Sigma}\underset{i}{T} = $ Rs.83,000 million;

$P_c = .67$

Initial Values

$Y_0 = $ Rs.125,000 million

$S_0 = $ Rs.10,500 million

Equation No. 1 $100,000 = \sum_i S_i + 10,000$

$$\sum_i S_i = 90,000$$

Equation No. 2 $\Delta Y = .45 \times 100,000$

$\Delta Y = 45,000$

Equation No. 3 $125,000 (1 + \dot{G}_n)^5 - 125,000 = 45,000$

$\dot{G}_n = .06$

Equation No. 4 $90,000 = 10,500 \times 5 + 15 \propto$

$\propto = 2,500$

Equation No. 5 $\Delta S = 2,500 \times 5 = 12,500$

Equation No. 6 $\dfrac{12,500}{45,000} = m_1 = .28$

Equation No. 7 $\dfrac{\dot{G}_n}{G_p} = .06 - .02 = .04$

Equation No. 8 $\dot{D}a = .04 \times .75 + .02 = .05$

Equation No. 9 $\dot{Y}a = .05$

Equation No. 10 $Ct = (125,000 + 45,000) - (10,500 - 5 \times 2,500) = 147,000$

Equation No. 11 $C_O (1 + \dot{G}c)^5 = 147,000 \quad \dot{G}c = .05$

Equation No. 12 $\dfrac{340}{420} \times .05 + \dfrac{80}{420} \times \dot{Y}_{NA} = .06; \quad \therefore$

$\dot{Y}_{NA} = .07$

Equation No. 13 $\dot{T}d = .567 \times .05 + .323 \times .07 + .007 \times .05 = .5$

Equation No. 16 $\sum_i E_i = 86,000 + .67 \times 10,000 = 153,000$

Equation No. 17 $\Delta D = 153{,}000 - (83{,}000 + 12{,}000)$
$$= 58{,}000$$

Equations 14 and 15 become redundant when the
total amount of receipts from autonomous and derived
taxes in the model are made exogenous.

A close scrutiny of the above mathematical
framework of the Third Plan convinces one that the
macro-economic exercise used is slightly more sophisticated than that contained in earlier plans. The
model's division between agriculture and nonagricultural output is demand-oriented, and a concept of
expenditure elasticity is introduced. This model
also contains a built-in tax-fiscal mechanism.
Viewed in its entirety, this Third Plan "macro-frame"
has less sophistication in calculating the logic of
sectoral allocation of investments, but has a more
elaborate structure for ensuring consistency between
target variables.

Unfortunately, however, like all its predecessors,
it lacks (1) proper checking of the consistency requirements, when the needs for intermediate inputs
are taken into consideration; (2) any attempt to
incorporate the dynamic element in the plan, in the
nature of an intertemporal phasing of investment;
(3) the explicit recognition of any optimizing test,
and (4) any attempt to formulate the fiscal implications against the objectives of the plan and the
behavioral responses (i.e., propensities) of the
society.

No doubt, in a limited sense, the need for plan
consistency is met in terms of input/output balances,
i.e., when national balances or commodity balances
are drawn up by the Perspective Planning Division
of the Planning Commission. But this approach unfortunately carries the risk of underestimating the
input requirements of specific outputs, because it
normally tends to ignore the feedback process between
sectors mutually interdependent. In addition,
these balance equations cover only the principal
producing sectors, and occasionally in heterogeneous
units; so it is impossible to integrate all of them

in the context of a totality of resources and the
overall objectives of the plan.

The final major objection centers on the fact
that this exercise is conducted only to depict the
picture of the last (i.e., terminal) year of the
plan. It completely overlooks the time path and the
process of adjustments throughout the whole plan
period. In addition, the breakdown involved in the
operational measures of the plan are given in much
more detail than the divisions provided in this
planning model, and hence this model loses a significant amount of its practical importance.

We shall now examine the basic logical framework
of the Indian Third Plan, and for this we shall rely
heavily on W. B. Reddaway's exercise.

THE REDDAWAY MODEL

Reddaway evolved two very important planning
tools, although in rather rudimentary form.[11] They
are the essence of backward planning and the need
for commodity balances to be incorporated in the
overall plan frame in a strict formal way, thereby
avoiding the many uncovered sectors, so common in
the official Third Plan formulation.

Backward planning essentially means a working
back of the major plan dimensions in the light of
a given final demand in the terminal year. "Final
demand" is defined in a conventional inter-industry
sense. Reddaway's model uses the backward planning
concept in a static sense when the relations between
the final demand and the gross output are formulated
for the terminal year only, and the intermediate
periods are ignored. Popularly, such planning
models are known as consistency models of the economy.

Strictly speaking, such models can not be
developed without the use of an inter-industry current flow matrix. Reddaway, however, in a rather
novel, but not very satisfactory way, tries to com-
pensate for the absence of such information in his

model. Although an inter-industry table prepared
by the ISI for the year 1955/6, was available at
that time, Reddaway does not use it. He probably
regarded it as unreliable for an operational planning
model. Many Indian planners would agree with him
on this point.

The great impact of Reddaway's model of the
Indian Third Plan is best seen if one examines some
of the preliminary exercises on plan formulation
conducted in India in connection with the formulation
of the Fourth Plan. Needless to say, significant
improvements on Reddaway's basic approach are made
in these later attempts by the use of a fully-fledged
inter-industry model and by the use of Leontief's
static approach.

Reddaway develops his planning model in nonmath-
ematical terms, but with strict mathematical logic.

As all other planning models in this study are
presented in a formal mathematical frame, I will
endeavor to treat Reddaway's model in a similar
fashion and with the minimum amount of distortion.
Mrs. P. Desai has made a similar attempt, but in a
most confused way; her criticism that the whole
system is underdetermined is entirely unfounded.[12]

The following is the attempted presentation
of Reddaway's model:

$$Q_i{}^t = \sum_{j=1}^{n} (Q_{ij})^t + C_i{}^t + G_i{}^t + I_i{}^t + N_i{}^t + X_i{}^t \quad (1)$$

$$Q_i{}^t = \sum_{i=1}^{n} (Q_{ji})^t + Y_i{}^t + M_i{}^t + T_i{}^t \quad (2)$$

$$S_i{}^t = \sum_{i=1}^{n} Q_{ji}{}^t + Y_i{}^t + T_i{}^t \quad (3)$$

$$\sum_{i=1}^{n} Q_{ji}{}^t = K_i . S_i{}^t \quad (4)$$

$$T_i{}^t = t_i (1960-1) \left(\sum_{i=1}^{n} (Q_{ji})^t + Y_i{}^t + M_i{}^t \right), \text{ for}$$

ith sector   (5)

$(I_i)^t = \lambda_i\ I_i\ (1960\text{-}6)^*$ (6)

$M_i{}^t = \alpha_i M_t$ (7)

$C_i{}^t = B_i\ S_i{}^t,^{**}\ i = 1$ to n; $t = $ time period   (8)

Unknown Variables

$(Q_i)^t = $ Total supply of ith commodity. . . Period t

$(I_i)^t = $ ith commodity component of total
         investment . . . .   "

$(Y_i)^t = $ Value added originating in ith com-
         modity sector . . . .   "

$(M_i)^t = $ Import of the ith commodity . . .   "

$(T_i)^t = $ Total indirect tax receipt in the
         ith sector . . . .   "

$\left(\sum\limits_{j=1}^{n} Q_{ij}\right)^t = $ Intermediate consumption of the
         ith commodity, i.e., row of the
         inter-industry sector. . . . .   "

$(C_i)^t = $ Consumption of the ith commodity .   "

$\left(\sum\limits_{i=1}^{n} Q_{ji}\right)^t = $ Material input for the ith sector "

The Exogenous Variables

$(G_i)^t = $ Government expenditure in ith sector   "

---

*The investment allocation of sectors was con-
verted into commodity classifications, assuming the
base-period proportions and, in a few cases, making
independent changes.

**The B's were base-period relations. But in
most cases they are either 0 or 1 in the base period
and, therefore, the formulations of equation 8 were
not as heroic as they appeared.

$(Ni)^t$ = Inventory holding in the ith
       sector . . . . Period t

$(Xi)^t$ = Export in the ith sector . . . . .   "

$(Si)^t$ = Domestic output of the ith sector. "

Ii (1960-6) = Total investment over the
            plan period in terms of the
            ith commodity component. . . "

M^t = Total import for 1965/6.   "

Parameters

Ki = Material input coefficient to total gross domestic output.

ti = Base period tax rate per unit of supply in the
ith sector.

λi = The fraction of total investment over the plan
period in terms of the ith commodity component,
applied to the last year of the plan.

$\propto i$ = Proportion of imports in sector i to the total
import.

Bi = Proportion of total gross output of ith sector
allocated to consumption (base period ratio).

The above shows clearly that there were 8 equations and 8 unknowns, and hence the system is uniquely
determined, quite contrary to the apprehension of
Mrs. Desai.[13]

FOURTH PLAN FORMULATION

A study of the process of plan formulation
during the Fourth Plan would clearly demonstrate
again the enormous multiplicity of decision-stages,
of views, and of techniques that normally precede
the formulation of a plan. The approach and methods
adopted the formulation of a plan for a country such

as India become increasingly diverse, since the plan
is for a democratic country which is geographically
very large and contains states that are semi-autono-
mous in their plan decisions and have different
vested interests.

Basic differences in the formulation of the
Fourth Plan compared to earlier plans are: (a) The
recognition of the need for sectoral balances as a
check on overall consistency of plan targets; (b)
the backward planning principle with a well-defined
objective specified at five-yearly and fifteen- to
twenty-yearly intervals; and (c) the room for an
explicit treatment of the Indian foreign-trade sector.

In a work of the present size, it is difficult
to cover the huge variety of techniques adopted by
the different units or divisions of the Indian Planning Commission and other government ministries.
For the present I shall confine my analysis to two
distinct exercises, conducted within the Commission,
which were instrumental in the formulation of the
basic planning model--itself the foundation for the
Fourth Plan. The first is the attempt made in the
Economic Division of the Planning Commission, and
the second is the exercise conducted by the Perspective
Planning Division of the same Commission.

In all the earlier plans, the Economic Division
of the Planning Commission, working in collaboration
with the Economic Division of the Ministry of Finance,
confined itself mostly to the assessment of the
resources, availability, and the financial framework
of the respective plans (to be discussed shortly).
However, during the formulation of the Fourth Plan,
the Economic Division, for the first time, formulated
a formal quantitative plan frame, tracing the real
flows embodied in the plan alongside the exercise
conducted by the Perspective Planning Division. The
two approaches by the two different divisions of the
Planning Commission were identical in some respects,
in others significantly different.

THE ECONOMIC DIVISION'S EXERCISE

The Economic Division's approach is summarized
in the paper "The Macro-Economic Hypothesis for the
Fourth Plan," circulated on 18 April 1964. This
paper demonstrates well how an operational plan
normally inherits its initial frame in the context
of the broad economic directions supplied by the
legislature and political plan agencies. The initiation of the Fourth Plan frame started in a macro
setup with highly simplified assumptions and under
very broad and distinctly identifiable objectives.
The macro-frame thus formulated was subsequently
fitted into the sectoral and more disaggregated framework, and ultimately translated into specific plan-
decisions at the micro level.

The broad alternative assumptions put forward
by the National Development Council of India, the
supreme planning body, in 1962/3, can be summarized
as follows:

1. A growth rate of 5 percent in agriculture
and 12 percent in industry, on the basis of one
billion dollars (net) of foreign aid per annum up to
the year 1970, and a reduction of foreign aid to
half a billion dollars (gross) per annum thereafter,
in the Fifth Plan. Further, there was the implicit
assumption of a comparatively faster rate of growth
in the rural standard of living than in the urban
area.

2. A growth rate of 4 percent in agriculture
and 12 percent in industry, on the basis of one
billion dollars (net) of foreign aid per annum during
the Fourth Plan and a gradual reduction thereafter.
In fact, the above were presented only as ad hoc
examples; in practice quite a large number of alternatives were attempted.

Due to the broad nature of the indicators, and
the difficulties involved in matching them with the

standard concepts normally adopted in India, for an
analysis of the plan in terms of national-income
analysis and inter-industry classifications the planners were forced to redefine their terms. This they
attempted in the aforementioned paper.

In addition, the presentation of problems in
the original form was incomplete, in the sense that
the objectives to be attained in terms of per capita
consumption, faster rate of growth of national income
in the post-plan period, the extent of government
responsibility in investment, the general pattern
of income distribution acceptable in society, and
so on, tended to be all rather vague. I have tried
to formulate as rigorously as possible the presentation of the Economic Division's paper in a mathematical framework.

The plan formulation in this paper has two
distinct stages: (a) Macro, i.e., in terms of national
income aggregates; and (b) Sectoral, i.e., in terms
of inter-industry production classifications. The
former has four major sectors and the latter has
twenty-nine individual sectors. In both stages the
implications of the following two alternative growth
assumptions are calculated:

Sectors	Assumption (a)	Assumption (b)
1. Agriculture	4.0	5.0
2. Mining and fac- tory establishments	12.0	12.0
3. Small industries	4.0	4.0
4. Services	6.0	6.0

These growth rates are brought in the model as
exogenous variables. Their calculation is not completely arbitrary. They are estimated from past
performances and future requirements computed in
the perspective plan framework.

The foreign aid assumptions are taken on the
basis of the negotiations with donor countries at

the time. With regard to their intertemporal phasing,
it is assumed that net foreign aid in the last year
of the Fourth Plan will be less than average, since
by the year 1975/6 a complete elimination of the
dependence on foreign aid is recommended.

Regarding the import-surplus assumptions in
1970/1, the paper states:

> In recent assessments [in the Consortium
> meetings] the likely import surplus in
> 1965/6 has been estimated at Rs.5,500-
> 6,600 million, nearly all of which will
> have to be financed from disbursements of
> foreign aid. Since many of the Third Plan
> investments which could have a significant
> role in the import substitution or export
> enlargement, are expected to bear the full
> fruit only by about 1967/8; hence it is
> unlikely that the foreign aid requirements
> in the first two years of the Fourth Plan
> will not be any lower than the 1965/5
> level.[14]

Restrictions of the import surplus would therefore require a virtual halving of net foreign aid
during the final three years of the Fourth Plan.

As in all the previous plans, elaborate sectoral
allocations and output targets are calculated only
for the final year of the plan. The choice of techniques in production activities, the problems of
income distribution, regional allocation, etc., are
not explicitly treated in this preliminary stage of
the plan formulation.

Another basic problem normally met with in any
plan formulation appears very prominently in this
exercise--the computation of the initial conditions
of the model, the picture of the base period of the
plan. This problem arises because, although the
Fourth Plan was to commence from 1965/6, the prepar-
atory work regarding its formulation started as
early as 1962/3. This aspect is solved in the Fourth
Plan by making alternative pessimistic and optimistic
assumptions regarding the base-period conditions of
the plan.

The estimates of net capital formulation in
these models have both an endogenous and an exogenous
counterpart. The gestation lag between investment
and income is taken to be two years, and it is assumed
that the post-terminal rates of growth of output
beyond the five-year plan horizon will be the same
as those prevailing on average over the intra-plan
(five-year plan) period. The allocation of total
investment is made only for the terminal year of the
plan, and is rather arbitrary. Unlike the perspective plan exercise, there is no mention of any mathematical relation used in this process.

Public consumption is assumed to rise by a certain rate, but no definite rationale is built to
support this assumption. With regard to private
consumption, the estimate for total consumption as
a scalar concept is derived on a residual basis.
The consumption estimate as a vector is calculated
on the basis of individual expenditure elasticities
from the rural and urban sectors separately, together
with a few normative considerations, such as the
provision for a higher rate of growth in rural per
capita consumption than in urban per capita consumption. Since the estimates of the propensity to save
are unfortunately treated as a residual, it becomes
impossible to calculate an implication in terms of
the behavioral functions. It is also emphasized
that in considering the real consumption standard
of the people, both private and public expenditure
must be taken together.

An inter-industry table for the year 1959 is
computed for this purpose and is used for the
sectoral allocation in the Draft Fourth Plan. Of
course, at every stage the coefficients or parameters
computed from this table are readjusted in the light
of the likely changes in the production techniques
available in the economy.

For the foreign-trade sector, exports are predicted by a combination of extrapolation and value
judgements. Imports of capital and consumption
goods (after having fixed the base-period norms for
the noncompetitive and intermediate imports, which

are to remain unchanged) are subject to three alternative assumptions, namely: (1) Imports of electrical,
nonelectrical, and transport equipment industries
should bear the same proportions to the total domestic output as was the case in the base year 1959;
or (2) the category of other imports should maintain
the same aggregate level and pattern as in the base
year 1959; or (3) both the level and pattern of
other imports are adjusted so as to permit larger
imports of equipment than under category 2.

The implications of the three assumptions can
be seen from Table 3.1.

In brief, the entire analysis aims at a consistent level of output for 1970/1, stressing that the
scope for supplementing consumption goods with imports by 1970/1 would seem to be very remote, and a
rise in industrial output would be inevitable if
agriculture grew by 4 percent. In Table 3.2, the
growth assumptions of the macro-model are matched
with the macro-aggregations derived from the solutions
of the inter-industry model.

TABLE 3.1

Distribution of Domestic Outputs in
Broad Groups of Manufacturing Industry for
Alternative Import Assumptions
(Rs.million)

Industrial groups	Assumption 1	Assumption 2	Assumption 3
1. Consumption-goods industries	61,820	61,460	61,540
2. Intermediate-goods industries	30,990	32,540	32,730
3. Capital-goods industries	18,050	24,740	23,380
TOTAL	110,860	118,740	117,050

TABLE 3.2

Comparisons of the Growth Assumptions
of the Macro-Model and the Macro-aggregates
Derived from the Inter-Industry Model
(Percent)

Sectors	Macro-growth assumptions	Growth implications in sectoral model
Agriculture	4.0	4.0
Mining and factory establishments	12.0	10.0
Small-scale industries	4.0	4.2
Services	6.0	7.2

Source: Planning Commission, Economic Division,
"The Macro-Economic Hypotheses of the Fourth Plan,"
(April, 1964). Mimegraphed.

Algebra of the Model

Exogenous Variables

(1) Sectoral growths, referring to value-added growth
    rates, for ith sectors when i = a, m, e and s,
    when a = agriculture, m = mining and manufacturing,
    e = small-scale industries, and s = services.

(2) (a) Total aid = A
    (b) The fraction of aid allocated in the final
        year = λ

(3) Export in the final year = E_t

(4) Value added, of the ith sector in the base period
    (o) i ranging from 1 to 4 = NI_o^i

(5) Depreciation in period $t = D_r^t$

(6) Capital formation in tth period (exogenous) = Capt (exo)

Initial Conditions

(1) Urban population at the base = Pu_0

(2) Rural population at the base = Pr_0

(3) Per capita gross-consumption expenditure in rural sector = Hr_0

(4) Per capita gross-consumption expenditure in urban sector = Hu_0

(5) Indirect tax at the base = I_B

Parameters

(1) Current flow coefficient matrix = (A) (29 x 29)

(2) Investment/income ratios for four sectors = (ci/o), i = a, m, e and s.

(3) Expenditure elasticity for rural and urban sectors for jth commodity = $\hat{er}(j)$ and $\hat{eu}(j)$.

(4) Rates of growth of rural and urban population = Pl.r. and Pl.u.

(5) Rate of growth of indirect tax = I_r

(6) Proportion of public consumption to domestic expenditure = $\propto$

(7) Rates of growth of public-consumption coefficient per annum = $\propto_r$

(8) Proportion of jth element of capital-goods imports to total = $mj/\Sigma mj$

(9) Proportion of jth element of "other imports" to total = $oj/\Sigma oj$

(10) Proportion of jth element of public consumption to total = $pj/\Sigma pj$

(11) proportion of capital-goods imports to total gross domestic output at the base = w.

(12) Proportion of jth element of exports to the total = $\alpha_j/\Sigma\alpha_j$

(13) Fraction of capital formation made in period t to the total plan period = Q; (t ranging from 2 to t + 2).

(14) Proportion of jth element of capital in period t to the total $pj^t/\Sigma pj^t$.

(15) Proportion of private-consumption expenditure in the rural sector to the total = k.

(16) Intermediate import coefficient vector = $|a|$

Endogenous Variables

(1) National income at period t (i.e., final year)
$$= \sum_{i=1}^{4} NI_t^i$$

(2) Total domestic gross expenditure at period t
$$= \sum_{i=1}^{4} NE_t^i$$

(4) Capital formation over the whole period (inc. w.c.) (endogenous)

$$= \Sigma\ cap^W\ (end)$$

(5) Capital formation total in period t = $Cap^t(T)$

(6) Public expenditure in tth period = public expenditure^t.

(7) Private consumption in tth period = private consumption^t.

(8) jth element of capital formation in tth period = $cap^t(T)_j$.

(9) Private-consumption vector total = |(Pri. Con. total)|.

(10) Consumption vector for the rural sector = $|(C_r)|$

(11) Consumption vector for the urban sector = $|(C_u)|$

(12) Per capita expenditure, rural and urban, in period t = Hr_t and Hu_t

(14) Total import in tth period = Im_t

(15) (i) Intermediate imports in period t = $Im(inter)^t$
     (ii) Capital-goods imports in period t = $Im(cap)^t$
     (iii) Other-goods imports in period t = $Im(others)^t$
     (iv) jth element of capital goods import = $Im(cap)_j$
     (v) jth element of other goods import = $Im(other)_j$

(16) Gross-output vector in period t = $|x^t|$

Flow-Chart of the Model

(1) $\sum_{i=1}^{4} NI_t^i = \sum_{i=1}^{4} NI_O^i (1 + v_i^r)^t$; i, referring to a, m, e and s (all total four in number)

(2) $\sum_{i=1}^{4} NI_t^i = \sum_{i=1}^{4} NI_t^i + I_B (1 + I_r)^t + A + D_r^t$

(3) $\Sigma Cap^W (end) = \sum_{i=1}^{4} (NI_{t+2}^i - NI_2^i) Ci/o$

(4) $Cap^t (end) = Q\Sigma Cap^W (end)$

(5) $Cap^t (T) = Cap^t (end) + Cap^t (exo)$

(6) $(Public\ Expt)^t = \alpha \sum_{i=1}^{4} NE_t^i (1 + \alpha_r)^t$

(7) $Private\ cons^t = \sum_{i=1}^{4} NE_t^i - Cap^t (T) - (Public\ Expt.)^t$

Vector Conversions

(8) $\text{Public Exp}_j^t = (\text{Public Exp}^t)\ pj/\Sigma pj$

(9) $\text{Cap}^t\ (T)_j = \text{Cap}^t\ (T)\ ptj/\Sigma ptj$

(10) $|\text{Pri Con Total}| = |C_r| + |C_u|$

(11) $C_r(j) = \text{Pr}_0\ (1 + Pl_r)^5$

$$\left\{ \text{Hro}(j) \begin{bmatrix} \text{Hr}_t & - \text{Hr}_0 \end{bmatrix} (\hat{e}r\ (j) + \text{Hr}_0\ (j))\ j=1 \right\} \text{ to 22 (j refers to commodity component of consumption)}$$

(12) $Cu(j) = PU_0(1+Pl_u)^5$

$$\left\{ \text{HTo}(\mu) \begin{bmatrix} \text{Hu}_t & - \text{Hu}_0 \end{bmatrix} \hat{e}u\ (j) + \text{Hu}_0\ (j) \right\} j=1 \text{ to } 22$$

(13) $\text{Hr}_t = \dfrac{\overset{4}{\underset{i=1}{\Sigma}}\ \text{Private Cons}^t K}{\text{Pr}_0\ (1 + Pl_r)\ t}$

(14) $\text{Hu}_t = \dfrac{\overset{4}{\underset{i=1}{\Sigma}}\ \text{Private Cons}^t\ (1 - K)}{\text{Pu}_0\ (1 + Pl_u)\ t}$

(15) $(E)\ _j^t = Et\ (\theta j/\Sigma \theta j)$

(16) $\text{Im}_t = E^t + \lambda A$

(17) $\text{Im}_t = \text{Im (inter)}^t + \text{Im(cap)}^t + \text{Im(other)}^t$

(18) $\text{Im(capt)}^t = \sum\limits_{i=1}^{4}\ NI_t^i\ W^*$

(19) $\text{Im(other)}^t = \text{Im}_t - (\text{Im(inter)}^t + \text{Im(cap)}^t);$
      $(\text{Im}_t = \text{Total imports})$

---

*Type 1 (Page 66).

(20) $\text{Im(inter)}^t = a' \,|x\ t|$

(21) $\text{Im(cap)}_j^t = \text{Im(cap)}^t\ mj/\Sigma mj$

(22) $\text{Im(other)}_j^t = \text{Im(other)}^t\ ej/\Sigma ej$

(23) $|x\ t| = (I-A)^{-1} \Big(|Cr^t| + |Cu^t| + |\text{Public Exp}^t| +$

$|\text{Cap}^t\ (T)| + |E^t| - |\text{Im(Cap)}^t| - |\text{Im(other)}^t| \Big)*$
when (A) matrix was 'net' of intermediate imported
elements.

Finally, an attempt is made to match the "initially
assumed" sectoral growth rates with the sectoral
growth rates derived from the above inter-industry
exercise (by calculating fx when x represents gross
output and f represents diagonal matrix of value
added per unit of gross output). The degree of import substitution in the capital- and consumption-
goods industries in this exercise is used as the
adjustment mechanism. Subsequently, the policy
implications and the technical feasibility of the
suggested import substitution, calculated by the
model, are considered.

THE PERSPECTIVE PLANNING
DIVISION'S EXERCISE

The second major independent exercise on the
formulation of India's Fourth Plan was conducted by
the Perspective Planning Division of the Indian
Planning Commission. This was conducted in two major
stages: one keeping the perspective plan in view,
(this was developed in a technical paper under the
heading "Notes on Perspective of Development - India,
1960-1 to 1975-6," in April, 1964) and the second
keeping the Draft Fourth Plan particularly in view.
This appeared in another document: "Draft Fourth
Plan: Material and Financial Balances, 1964-5,
1970-1, and 1975-6," in September, 1966.

---

*Estimated by iteration.

We have already discussed the former document
in an earlier chapter. In this section, we will
deal mainly with the second document.

The purpose of this technical paper could be
summarized in its own language as "being intended
for the public at large, to deal in nontechnical
terms with the details of the proposed program and
policy of the Fourth Plan as given in the draft outline." For example, in the draft outline the rationale
of the program is explained in rather broad terms,
and the basis for arriving at particular targets is
not very explicit. No attempt is made to show in
detail the internal consistencies and balances of
the plan in their different aspects. The second
paper claims to bring out this underlying logic of
the plan. In other words, it tries to check the
balances between different activities in the economy,
both in physical terms and financial terms. In addition, it attempts to probe into the operational
feasibility of the plan. At the same time the paper
admits quite justifiably at the outset that "as the
work on plan formulation started nearly four years
ahead of the date of commencement of the plan when
thinking went on simultaneously in so many different
government and non-government agencies, any attempt
to locate exactly the origin of a plan frame, must
be regarded as of doubtful validity."

This paper could be divided into four major
stages:

1. Formulation of a macro-plan;

2. Allocation of resources in an inter-industry
    consistency model;

3. An attempt to build up material balances
    for specific commodities;

and

4. Assessment of the scheme of mobilization
    of financial resources of the plan.

In my opinion, stages 1 and 4 in this paper are satisfactorily integrated. Stage 2 is reasonably well related to stage 1. Stage 3 is well formulated when taken in isolation, but is rather less satisfactorily integrated with stages 1 and 2 in particular. Indeed, in many places it would be regarded as rather confusing in its relation to the other stages.

Starting with stages 1 and 2, this part of the paper bears a close resemblance to the earlier described exercise conducted by the Economic Division of the Planning Commission.

Stage 1:   The Macro-Model

For a large number of aggregated sectors, including agriculture and allied activities, mining, large-scale industries and power, railways, road transport, and communications, the output estimates are based on the production targets indicated in the official Draft Fourth Plan. The government estimates on income are derived from both budgetary data and the Fourth Plan projections of the Planning Commission. The estimates for the remaining sectors, which include small-scale industries, construction, commerce professions, liberal arts, etc., contain a large margin of error, and in many cases have been computed from a few broad indicators. The physical-output targets in agriculture for major crops in the draft plan are estimated for the year 1970/1 by fitting log-linear relations from past observations between area or yield and time. These gross outputs are then converted into value-added concepts. They are first of all converted into value terms from which material inputs, such as seeds, manures, fuel, electricity, are then subtracted. The manufacturing sector receives similar treatment. The targets for physical gross outputs are converted into value-added concepts by assuming unchanged ratio of value-added to total output based on the Annual Survey of Industries of 1960.

The estimates of national-income growth in sectors like construction, small-scale industries,

and transport are rather shaky and are mainly computed
in terms of "trends" in gross earnings less material
outputs.

As the above description shows, the rationale
of macro-projections of national income is not very
explicit nor convincingly stated in this paper. In
the next stage, the net domestic product at (factor
cost) 1960/1 prices is derived by adding to the
national income the net factor payments to the rest
of the world. The figures relating to net factor
payments for 1970/1 are based on the projections
made by the resources working group and the finance
departments of central and state governments. Later
on, the estimates of income generated by the local
bodies are also incorporated. In the majority of
cases, these estimates are made on a mechanical extrapolation basis, from a detailed sector classification, adjusted by individual value-judgements at
all stages. Next in priority comes the estimation
of the depreciation provision. In brief, the depreciation provision is calculated separately for construction and machinery, and is based on the perpetual
inventory method. In respect of construction, the
average life is assumed to be fifty years. In
respect of equipment and machinery, different rates
of depreciation are supplied, depending on the life
of the machinery in the different sectors.

The estimates of imports and exports in the
macro-analysis are computed by different ministries
and departments, almost all of which use the mixed
approach of extrapolation and value judgements. No
evidence is available to substantiate any claim that
a formal econometric exercise was conducted for this
purpose. The excess of imports (of goods and services)
over exports is calculated by adding the nonfactor
payments to the estimate of commodity imports, and
deducting from exports any nonfactor receipts on current account, for the Fourth Plan period. The next
major stage is the estimation of gross domestic expenditure at market prices. For this purpose the
following flow relations are formulated:

1. National income plus net factor payments to
the rest of the world plus indirect taxation and

miscellaneous receipts (net of subsides) is equal
to net domestic product at market prices.

2.   Net domestic product at market prices plus
depreciation provision is equal to gross domestic
product at market prices.

3.   Gross domestic product at market prices
plus excess of imports of goods and services over
their exports is equal to gross domestic expenditure.
The gross domestic expenditure in the economy is
further subdivided into private consumption, public
consumption, and private and public gross capital
formation, including working capital.

The estimates of gross capital formation are
based upon a separate calculation of the requirements
of net investment and replacement investment.
Replacement investment is derived by the perpetual
inventory method, whereas net investment is assumed
to be 17.5 percent of national income in the year
1970/1 (the figure given in the draft outline).
The rationale of this probably lay in the Harrod-Domar
macro-projections made at the time of the earlier
perspective plans.

Public consumption is treated as a genuine exogenous element in the model.   The projections of non-
plan expenditure of center and states prepared by
the Planning Commission for the Fourth Plan are taken
as the starting-point.   The rough estimates of
revenue outlay of local bodies made from their own
resources and the revenue plan expenditure of the
center and states is added to this.   From the total
current expenditure thus derived, certain expenditures
are deducted; these include interest payments, appro-
priation and other transfers from income to capital,
transfer payments, and subsidies.

The increases in consumption due to revisions
in pay scales of the government employees and increases
in allowances have also been deducted when converting
the consumption expenditure to 1960/1 prices.

Finally, private consumption at the macro level
is treated as residual.   Population in the model is

taken as exogenously determined. The macro-dimensions
thus derived are subsequently fed into the detailed
inter-industry framework.

Stage 2: The Inter-Industry
Consistency Model

    This model has 77 sectors and is formulated
exclusively for checking and setting up a consistent
set of gross output targets for the year 1970/1,
within the boundary conditions set by the macro-model.
For this purpose, an exercise is attempted on the
lines of Leontief's static inter-industry model, in
the form $X = (1 - A)^{-1}F$, where F denotes the final
demand vector, X denotes the gross output vector
and A denotes a coefficient matrix of input/output
technology.

    At this stage of the calculations, it should
be noted that the whole of the final demand (defined
as consisting of private and public consumption, net
capital formation, replacement investment, stock
changes and exports, less imports) is treated as
exogenous in this paper.

    The macro-dimensions of these variables are
borrowed from the macro-models already discussed.
The vector conversion of the scalar values are computed in the following manner:

(a) Private consumption. The consumption pattern
of the base year, i.e., 1964/5, is estimated by the
commodity-flow method. The volume of a given consumption item entering into final consumption is
obtained from the following relations: final consumption = (production plus imports) - (intermediate
users + capital formation + exports + increases in
stocks).

    The value of consumption at market prices is
then obtained by multiplying the quantity consumed
by the retail prices for 1960/1. The limitations of
data at this stage are acutely felt and explicitly
recognized in the aforesaid documents.

(b) On the basis of macro-estimates of private consumption in 1970/1 and official estimates for population growth, the per capita consumption expenditure
for the year 1970/1 is computed. This is given as
Rs.342 per capita in 1970/1 at 1960/1 prices.
(c) The expenditure elasticities of the major expenditure of heads of households for rural and urban sectors
are estimated separately by N.S. Iyengar on the basis
of the tenth round, December 1955-May 1956, (National
Sample Survey household consumption data).[15] This
round is selected because the information obtained
in it is much more detailed than that found in earlier,
rounds. All these elasticities were used as the concept of "income" elasticities, and to use these elasticities to compute the demand pattern for 1970/1
entails a heroic price assumption. No special consideration is given to this fact in the Perspective
Planning Division paper. The combined elasticities
for the population as a whole are obtained as a
weighted average of the elasticities of different
groups, the weights being the total expenditure on
each commodity in the rural and urban areas respectively.
(d) The exact relationship used for the consumption
projections for each item in 1970/1 is as follows:

$$c_{it} = c_{io} \left(\frac{x_t}{x_o} \right)^{Q_i}$$
$$C_{it} = P_t \, c_{it}$$

where c_{it} is the per capita consumption of ith item
in t period and c_{io} is the consumption of the ith
item at the base period; Q_i is equal to expenditure
elasticity of the ith item, and x_t and x_o are the
aggregate per capita private expenditures in period
t and period o. P_t is equal to population in the t
period. C_{it} is the total consumption of the ith
item in the consumption vector in the period t. The
most difficult task encountered in these exercises
is the problem of conversion of the NSS classification
to the standard inter-industry classification adopted
in this sectoral model.

The input/output table used in this model is
formulated for the year 1964/5 by the Planning Unit

of the Indian Statistical Institute and has 77 activity sectors. For the purpose of projections, independent changes in the coefficients are made in this paper to accommodate a few predictable changes in technology.

(e) Public Consumption. The vector conversion of the scalar estimate of public consumption for the year 1970/1 is calculated by assuming that the pattern of expenditure in 1960/1 holds good in 1970/1.

(f) Capital formation (net). The model assumes five elements in the capital formation vector--construction, electrical equipment, nonelectrical equipment, transport equipment, and metal products. The total volume of capital formation is defined by the macro-model and the capital-formation vector is built up by assuming that the commodity (by their industry of origin) component of net investment of 1964/5 holds good in 1970/1.

(g) Exports and Imports. The macro-model gives estimates of the global values of exports and imports and their differences. The commodity breakdown for exports is borrowed from the draft outline. Hence for the purpose of the present model, it may be assumed as exogenous. Treatment of imports has already been described in earlier paragraphs.

Stage 3: The Material Balances

In the third stage, the paper presents the specific material balances both in physical and money terms in the majority of cases for quite a large number of sectors. To be more precise, it enumerates for all particular commodities the consuming sectors, the target of production in the consuming sectors, the consumption norms, the requirement in each consuming sector, and the total requirement aggregated over all the sectors. In most cases, this total requirement is further multiplied by the unit price of the specific commodity to give a value figure for that production sector. Unfortunately, these individual sectors are never integrated with the inter-industry flow matrix of 77 x 77.

THE FINANCIAL COUNTERPART
OF THE DRAFT FOURTH PLAN

The procedures adopted in formulating the financial balances in India's five-year plans are more or
less standardized and uniform in all the plans.
They have no rigorous mathematical frameworks at
their base. They could be regarded as the outcome
of a mixture of mechanical extrapolation of past
trends and the individual value-judgements of planners. But these estimates are in general made in a
very detailed sector classification before they are
combined under broad aggregative heads. They are
normally made for the entire plan period. For the
first time, however, in the Fourth Plan document,
separate figures for the financial variables are
shown for the terminal year of the plan. This makes
the task of a marriage between the physical and
financial planning rather easy. The link between
the macro-plan (in physical terms with national income categories) and the financial plan (which is
more or less defined in the flow of fund classifications) is established by matching the needs for
investment with the source of supply of investment
finance in the plan-frame.

To elaborate, the investment provisions (net)
as a percentage of national income in the macro and
inter-industry models for the year 1970/1 are estimated on the basis of the growth requirements for
the short-term and perspective plans. But the
feasibility of the investment provisions are tested
in terms of the sources of supply of investment,
e.g., private, public, and corporate saving, plus
the availability of foreign aid. But the estimates
of the total supply of domestic savings, and their
phasing over time in the financial plan, could not
be regarded as independent of the macro-magnitudes
like national income and its rates of growth, and
hence could not evidently precede the formulation
of the macro-model. Indeed, in practice one would
always observe a simultaneity between the two planning schemes. How far the formulation prescribed
in this paper is ensured in the actual plan is

anybody's guess; however, the paper gives a satisfactory balance between the two approaches in the final
solution. But strict comparisons between the two
approaches for the year 1970/1 are complicated by
the different price concepts used by the planners
for the valuation of financial variables and of the
national income aggregates used in the macro-model.[*]

Conceptually, a marriage between the physical
flows and the financial flows is desirable. Indeed,
it is extremely desirable for India, where the technical considerations for production must be matched
with the behavioral responses of the different production and consumption units of the free market
economy, under the broad influence of a given fiscal
framework. But the financial pictures developed in
the Perspective Planning Division paper fail to
inform us just how far the behavioral relations of
the economy are taken into account in the formulation
of the relevant balances.

Table 3.3 shows the financing of the net capital
formation for the Fourth Plan as a whole, whereas
Table 3.4 gives the statements of finance for gross
investment for the years 1965/6 and 1970/1, all at
1965/6 prices.

Table 3.5 presents the accounting balance of
the derivation of the government saving which went
into Table 3.4. Table 3.6 is an accounting presentation of personal income, and Table 3.7 gives the
scheme of financing of capital formation for the
three plans annually and brings out the standard
pattern followed in all the plans.

THE MANNE MODEL

Any discussion of the alternative planning
models attempted for the Fourth Plan will remain

_____

[*]For example, the former estimates were valued
at 1965/6 purchaser's prices, whereas the latter
were valued at 1960/1 producer's prices.

TABLE 3.3

Fourth-Plan Investment and its Sources of Finance
(Rs.million at 1965/6 prices)

Sources of Finance	Public Sector	Private Sector		Total	Percent of National Increase
		Household	Corporation		
Total investment financed out of:	136,000	35,000	42,500	213,500	16.1
Public savings	52,500			52,500	4.0
Household savings	36,500	32,300	14,900	83,700	6.3
Corporate savings		2,700	20,750	23,450	1.7
Total domestic saving	89,000	35,000	35,650	159,650	12.0
Foreign saving (postde-valuation)	47,000	6,850		53,850	4.1
National increase (cumula-tive total)				1325,000	100

Source: Planning Commission. Draft Fourth Plan: Material and Financial Balances, 1964/5, 1970/1, and 1975/6, (New Delhi: Government of India Press, September, 1966).

TABLE 3.4

Statement of Finance for Gross Investment, 1965/6 and 1970/71

(Rs.million at current prices)

	1965/66	1970/71		1965/6	1970/1
Net investment	27,500 (13.8)	51,700 (17.5)	Foreign capital	6,600 (3.3)	8,000 (2.7)
Replacement outlay	7,500 (3.7)	13,000 (4.4)	Depreciation provision	10,000 (5.0)	18,000 (6.1)
			Corporate savings	1,900 (1.0)	3,200 (1.1)
			Private savings	13,300 (6.6)	19,800 (6.7)
			Government savings	3,200 (1.6)	15,700 (5.3)
Total	35,000 (17.5)	64,700 (21.9)	Total	35,000 (17.5)	64,700 (21.9)
National Income	200,000	295,000	National income	200,000	295,000

Note: Figures within brackets are percentages of national income.

Source: As for Table 3.3.

TABLE 3.5

Government Current Account
(Rs.million at current prices)

Expenditure	1965/6	1970/1	Revenue	1965/6	1970/1
Goods and services	25,600	33,700	Corporate taxes	3,300	4,900
Transfers and subsidies	4,500	7,000	Other taxes	26,150	39,700
Saving	3,200	15,700	Other receipts	3,450	3,600
Net interest payment	1,000	3,500	Additional taxes (Fourth Plan)	-	9,200
			Surpluses of enterprises	1,400	2,500
Total	34,300	59,900.	Total	34,300	59,900

Source: As for Table 3.1.

TABLE 3.6

Personal Income

(Rs. million at current prices)

Source	1965/6	1970/1	Destination	1965/6	1970/1
Gross domestic product	235,000	356,600	Personal savings	13,300	19,800
Deduct depreciation	10,000	18,000	Personal taxes	4,000	7,200
Deduct indirect taxes and miscellaneous receipts	23,800	40,100	Consumption	179,800	262,700
Deduct income earned from abroad	1,200	3,500			
National income	200,000	295,000			
Add national-debt interest	2,000	4,650			
Add transfers	3,000	4,500			
Deduct income accruing to government	2,100	8,000			
Deduct corporate savings and corporate taxes	5,200	8,100			
Add private donations from abroad	300	300			
Discrepancy (-)	900	1,350			
Personal income	197,100	289,700	Personal income	197,100	289,700

Note: All figures for 1965/6 are at current prices of that year. For 1970/1, income and other related magnitudes are at 1965/66 prices, and investment and balance-of-payment estimates are in postdevaluation rupees.

Source: As for Table 3.1

90

TABLE 3.7

The Financing of Public-Sector Outlays: 1951-6 (First Plan),
1956-61 (Second Plan), and Annual Estimates for Third and Draft Fourth Plan
(Rs. million at 1965/6 postdevaluation prices)

	1951-6	1956-61	1961-6	1961/2	1962/3	1963/4	1964/5	1965/6	1966-71	1966/7	1967/8	1968/9	1969/70	1970/1
Total current expenditure of which:									200,700	36,280	38,180	40,040	42,040	44,160
Non-developmental									142,680	25,330	26,610	28,420	30,210	32,110
Developmental									54,820	10,950	11,570	11,610	11,830	12,050
Total current revenue receipts of which:									234,140	39,680	43,100	47,020	50,320	54,020
Direct taxes									42,480	7,550	7,790	8,380	9,030	9,730
Indirect taxes									146,110	24,480	27,070	29,610	31,400	33,550
Non-tax revenue									45,550	7,650	8,240	9,030	9,890	10,740
Balance from current revenue	3,240	110	-4,730	1,630	560	-1,560	-1,630	-3,730	33,450	3,410	4,930	6,980	8,280	9,850
Surplus from public enterprise	1,150	1,670	6,960	750	780	1,760	1,300	2,370	13,450	2,520	2,420	2,610	2,820	3,080
Capital receipts	6,840	14,390	21,390	3,400	3,860	3,820	5,470	4,840	38,800	5,770	6,540	7,510	8,750	10,230
Budgetary receipts (external assistance)	1,890	10,490	24,550	2,620	4,060	4,970	5,720	7,180	47,000	9,000	10,000	10,500	9,500	8,000
Deficit financing	3,330	9,540	11,510	1,840	1,830	2,110	1,880	3,850	-	-	-	-	-	-
Additional taxation	2,550	10,520	26,600	1,040	2,760	6,000	7,570	9,230	27,300	1,550	3,650	5,550	7,300	9,250
Total resources	10,600	46,720	86,280	11,280	13,860	17,090	20,310	23,740	160,000	22,250	26,540	33,150	36,650	40,410
Public Sector (plan) outlay of which:	19,600	46,000	86,300	11,300	13,850	17,100	20,300	23,750	160,000	22,250	27,550	33,150	36,650	40,400
Public investment (excl. current outlay)	15,600	36,500	71,800	9,600	11,650	14,400	17,000	19,150	136,000	19,250	23,650	28,350	30,950	33,800
Private investments	18,000	31,000	41,900	7,150	7,400	8,550	9,850	8,950	77,500	13,100	14,350	15,550	16,700	17,900

Note: Slight discrepancies could not be accounted for.

Source: As for Table 3.1.

incomplete unless a reference is made to an unofficial
planning model formulated by the Indian Statistical
Institute in collaboration with the Center of International Studies, M.I.T., New Delhi, and the Perspective Planning Division of the Indian Planning Commission.[16]

The main reason for attaching such importance
to this work is its powerful influence on the methods
of plan formulation adopted by the Perspective
Planning Division of the Planning Commission.

The resemblance between these two exercises
is almost perfect insofar as their inter-industry
exercises are concerned. However, the source of
data and the period of reference in the two papers
are different. Besides, the scope of Alan Manne's
planning model is narrower, as it completely excludes
the financial counter/part of the plan. The base
period in the Alan Manne model is 1960/1, whereas
in the Perspective Planning Division's exercise it
is 1964/5. The basic production and input parameters
are also different. The coefficients in Alan Manne's
paper are based on the 1960/1 ISI inter-industry
table. The Perspective Planning Division's estimates
are from their new inter-industry table, compiled
for the year 1964/65.

The most important difference between the two
approaches, however, appears in their treatment of
capital formation for the final year of the plan.
In the Perspective Planning Division's exercise,
the phasing of investment and the allocation for the
year 1970/1 are rather arbitrarily and lossely
integrated with the total investment requirements
over the plan period, which are developed in the
macro-model. Alan Manne, however, is calculates
it from a model based on "a functional behavior
of investments in relation to time."

The model is based on a thirty-sector classification of the economy. Its main purpose is to
examine the effects on output and imports of altern
native assumption regarding the growth of aggregates
consumption and ivestment over the plan.

The Model*

Unknowns

X_j = Annual rate of domestic production, process j, target year.

Y_i = Annual import rate, item i, target year. ($Y_i = Y_i + M_i$).

Z_i = Demand for investment goods i, induced by output increase, total for the whole decade. (i = four sectors).

w = Annual rate of deficit on merchandise, target year.

Coefficients

a_{ij} = Current account output (+) on input (-) item i, process j, target year.

b_{ij} = Capital coefficient (fixed) for item i process j; (induced cumulated fixed investment per unit of annual output) (only four non-zero positive rows).

c_{ij} = Import of item i required per unit of process j, target year, for $i \neq j$.

c_{ii} = Import of item i per unit of domestic output of item i.

Exogenous Variables

M_i — Exogenous part of the import.

p_i = The total of private consumption, public consumption, and exogenous fixed investment for the target year.

E_i = Export in the target year.

Constants

x^o_j = Annual rate of domestic production process j base year then $a_{ij} x_j + y_j = (P_i + E_i) + .17Z_i + 0.04 (x_i - x^o_i)$ ... set (1)

---

*The presentation here differs slightly from that of the original paper.

$$Z_i = \sum_j b_{ij} (x_j - x_j^o) \qquad\qquad \text{set (2)}$$

$$\sum_i M_i + \sum_i Y_i = \sum_i E_i + w \qquad\qquad \text{set (3)}$$

Now

$$Y_i = \sum_j c_{ij} X_j \text{ (a known variable)} \qquad\qquad \text{set (4)}$$

Thus, in the above model there are altogether 65 equations and 65 unknowns, and it is therefore possible to obtain a unique solution provided the Simon-Hawkins conditions are fulfilled.

In the above system of equations, b_{ij} represents the ith capital component for unit change in output in the jth sector of the economy. Hence $\sum_j b_{ij}$ $(X_j - X_o)$ represents the capital formation in terms of the ith commodity for the whole plan period needed for the "planned" output changes in all the sectors. How much of this should be allocated to the final period of the plan will depend on the pattern of investment phasing. The fraction of total investment (net) allocated in the target year is defined in the paper as the stock flow conversion factor.

This approach is based upon the assumption that the volume of investment will rise smoothly from the base of the target year; (in unusual periods like war, it would, of course, be quite incorrect to assume that the investment flow keeps rising steadily from year to year).

If it is assumed that the rate of growth per annum is "r," then
$$r_t = \text{ index of } \underline{\text{gross}} \text{ annual investment rate at t}$$
years after the base dates, with annual growth rate r.

therefore

$$_c10r = \text{ index of gross investment rate at}$$
the target date

Also $\displaystyle\int_{t=0}^{10} e^{rt} dt$ = index of accumulated gross investment over decade.

Therefore

$$\frac{e^{10r}}{\displaystyle\int_{t=0}^{10} e^{rt}\, dt} = \frac{r}{1 - e^{-10r}} = \text{Target year's stock flow conversion factor at growth rate r for a decade.}$$

Now, assuming investment is growing at 8.7 percent per annum, the above stock flow conversion factor is estimated at 15 percent. The above formula is then adjusted for a gestation lag of investment of two years (θ) and is present as

$$\frac{e^{10r}}{\displaystyle\int_{t=0}^{10-\theta} e^{rt}\, dt} \qquad \frac{re^{\theta r}}{1 - e^{-10r}}$$ and has been estimated in the neighborhood of .17, i.e., 17 percent.

Similarly, a stock flow conversion factor for inventory holdings has been calculated as the product of the stock flow conversion factor for fixed investments and the ratio of inventory to gross annual output, i.e., 17 x .25.

The above description of the model shows that it is static and open, without a financial counterpart.

All the parameters in the model, such as aij's and bij's, are estimated from the base-year data (and not from a time series), and independent checks and corrections are made in individual cases from technical and other up-to-date information before they are used for projection purposes. In this paper, the above model is used for two alternative projections, one containing an ambitious and the other a conservative assumption regarding the rates of growth, together with provisions for different degrees of import substitution.

The three major exogenous vectors described are
household consumption, public consumption, and exports.

Household Consumption

The projection for 1970/1 is based on expenditure
elasticities calculated from NSS rounds (13th round,
June 1957 to May 1958), and the base-period consumption
vector is derived from the inter-industry table for
1960/1 and is calculated by a residual flow method.

The mimeographed paper "Studies Relating to
Planning for National Development" gave estimates
of the expected volume of exports for India's principal
agricultural commodities for 1970/1. These projections were made, in general, in two steps: The first
step was to estimate the possible world import demand
for these commodities by 1970/1; the second was to
arrive at the Indian share in world import demand
by 1970/1 by studying Indian export trends. These
export projections are given in physical quantities,
are translated into value equivalent at 1959/60
prices, and are allocated to different sectors to
match the inter-industry classifications. The export
projections for nonindustrial goods are rather crude
and arbitrary in this study.

Public Consumption

The aggregate estimate of government consumption
is borrowed from the Perspective Planning Division's
paper and is divided into sectoral components based
upon the 1960/1 pattern of public consumption.

Imports are divided into the noncompetitive
(treated as endogenous) and competitive. The breakdown of total imports into sectoral components is
somewhat arbitrary.

Exogenous capital formation has two parts:
replacements and net investment. The replacement
requirements of each sector are set equal to a rough
estimate of investments for the period (1965/6-t)
and 1970/1-t), where t is the expected life of capital
goods in question (t = 15 years in this paper).

It is claimed in the paper that two alternative exercises were conducted in the following contexts: (a) Ensuring that minimum consumption of the entire population by the end of the Fifth Plan was Rs.20 per capita per month and that the amenities of life in the rural areas would be improved; (b) ensuring that the economy would be capable of sustaining an average annual rate of growth of the order of 7 percent, even after 1975/6, without depending on foreign aid; (c) achieving a significant increase in employment opportunities during the next decade; and (d) promoting a social order which would provide equality of opportunity and which, at the same time, would prevent excessive disparity of income and wealth.

Of the four, no provisions for (b) and (c) are explicitly noticeable in the model. The omission of (b) is a very grave limitation, whereas the omission of (c) merely limits the scope and coverage of the plan.

NOTES

1. First Five-Year Plan, (Delhi: Government of India Press, 1953).

2. R.S. Eckaus, "Planning in India," in National Economic Planning. Edited by Mr. F. Millikan. (New York: National Bureau of Economic Research, 1967).

3. Ibid., page 38.

4. P.C. Mahalanobis, "The Approach of Operational Research to Planning in India," Sankhya, (December, 1955).

5. Ibid.

6. R. Komiya, "A Note on Professor Mahalanobis's Model of Indian Planning," Review of Economics and Statistics, Vol. XLI, (1959), p. 20.

7.   P.N. Rosenstein-Rodan, Capital Formation and Economic Development, (London: George Allen and Unwin, 1964).

8.   S. Charkrabarty, "The Mathematical Framework of the Third Five-Year Plan," in Rosenstein-Rodan, op. cit., and Planning Commission, Perspective Planning Division, "Certain Dimensional Hypothesis Concerning the Third Plan," (November, 1958). Mimeographed.

9.   Ibid.

10.   Chakrabarty, op.cit.

11.   W.B. Reddaway, The Development of the Indian Economy, (London: George Allen and Unwin, 1965).

12.   Padma Desai, "The Development of the Indian Economy: An Exercise," Oxford Economic Papers (N.S.), Vol. 15 (1963).

13. Ibid., page 59.

14. Planning Commission, Economic Division, "The Macro-Economic Hypothesis for the Fourth Plan," (April, 1964). Mimeographed.

15.   N.S. Iyenger, Some Estimates of Engel Elasticities, Based on National Sample Survey Data, (London: Royal Statistical Society, 1967).

16.   Alan Manne and A. Rudra, "A Consistency Model of India's Fourth Plan," Sankhya, Series B, Vol. 27, (September, 1965).

The main functions of both the five-year and
the perspective plans formulated in India are to
specify the government's intentions. One-year plans,
on the other hand, have the task of presenting the
measures required for implementing government policy.
Indeed, the development plan is regarded as the
master document, while the working document for the
planners is the one that provides specific directions
year by year. Hence, the annual plans are drawn up
almost in conjunction with the budget estimates,
and together they form an obligation for the government. Since it is essential that these intentions
(assuming the administration intends to implement
them) be stated as "concrete investment projects"
or as "proposed legislation," they must be shown
in the one-year plan in a concrete form. Besides,
it is impossible to plan to this degree of detail
over a longer period of, say, five years, especially
when the resources of the plan, like the public
revenue, are reckoned and administered annually.
On the other hand, the full statement of the plan,
in the sense of intentions, efforts, and outcomes,
requires a period of not less than three to five
years, which would normally constitute the gestation
period of any plan project. Indeed, in this sense,
a considerable proportion of the expenses of the
annual plans are predetermined, i.e., committed.
One-year plans might thus be regarded as extensions
of the budget to the whole national economy. As

for the operational jurisdiction of the annual plans,
it does not have the same binding force for the
private sector as it would have on the government
sector. However, it does act on the private sector
indirectly through budgetary measures.

In the Indian context, annual plans have brought
to the forefront two other important aspects of
planning: the federal and state financial relationship, and the achievement of flexibility in the
five-yearly plans in the light of the experience of
plan implementation.

To summarize, the bulk of the formulation of
the annual plans runs in terms of a series of discussions and conferences between the central government and the states to work out the agreed details
of the scheme of plan execution--namely, the plan
administration and the phasing of central assistance,
the assessment of the resources realization and the
day-to-day phasing of investment activities, limited
by the global constraints of the five-yearly sectoral
aggregates.

Very recently, the annual plans in India have
become significant in yet another way. The annual
plan for 1966/7 was initiated separately and independently of the Fourth Five-Year Plan, and stood in its
own right (the Fourth Plan was to commence, subject
to normal circumstances, on 1 April 1966), Subsequently, another annual plan for the year 1967/8
was brought into operation, and the fourth was
further postponed until 1969. Presumably this was
necessitated not only by certain unforeseen incidents
that might have changed the basic underlying assumptions of the Draft Fourth Plan (the work on which
started as early as 1963/4), but by the very uncertain
situation prevailing at that time. This uncertainty
had made any formulation of a five-yearly picture
extremely difficult, and sometimes heroic. This
shows how the annual plans in India provide planners
with a greater degree of flexibility and maneuverability.

It is believed that the main purpose of these
ad hoc plans was to use the existing limited resources
in the changed context of drought and war with China
and Pakistan, to preserve the existing plan projects,
and to make a renewed assessment of resource availability, in light of which a fresh constellation of
projects with longer time horizons could be formulated.
Indian planners have, however, repeated in the Final
Fourth Plan that the maximum number of objectives
of the perspective plans for the year 1975/6 have
been preserved, and that both the present annual
plans and the ensuing Fourth Plan have been used as
a transient state to readjust and rebuild the economy
accordingly.

5

**MANPOWER
PLANNING
IN
INDIAN
PLANS**

A typical example of sectoral planning is the
exercise on manpower planning attempted in the Indian
plans. In the <u>First Plan</u> (1951-56) the need for
matching the manpower needs, as a key element of
economic input, with the manpower supply is explicitly
recognized. The plan emphasizes the need for col-
lecting and disseminating information regarding--

(a) manpower resources,

(b) organization of an efficient employment
     service,

(c) appraisal of types of skill required, and

(d) training facilities needed.

As to specific strategy, it expresses special
concern about the provision of employment opportunities
for additions to the labor force during the First
Plan, and about ways to deploy effectively the large
reserve of idle rural manpower. Unfortunately, no
such program is proposed, nor is any quantitative
exercise undertaken to measure the extent of demand/
supply disequilibrium.

It was sometime in 1955 that the Planning Commission for the first time appointed an Engineering
Personnel Committee to assess, among other things,

the shortage of supervisory and higher grades of
engineering personnels expected by the end of the
Second Five-Year Plan. But the exact techniques
used for this assessment are not spelled out in the
plan.

The Second Plan relies heavily on the findings
of the Engineering Personnel Committee, and devotes
much attention to devising a proper organizational
setup for solving any likely shortages of manpower
in the engineering industry. With regard to unskilled
unemployment, its strategy resembles that adopted
during the First Plan, namely, that "in determining
the program for the next five years, the prime consideration is that at least the deterioration in
the unemployment situation should be arrested."[1]
But apart from building a general strategy and suggesting a few organizational changes, (such as the
Cabinet Committee on Manpower), the Second Plan
failed to provide any formal model structure to cope
with manpower issues. As a preliminary to the
formulation of the Third Plan, the Perspective
Planning Division of the Planning Commission published
a series of manpower studies dealing with the educational characteristics and employment pattern of
various professional groups. The primary intention
of these studies was to collect and compute norms
of manpower needs in different sectors, for the
purpose of assessing future requirements of each
type of technical and nontechnical personnel over
the plan period. It subsequently attempted a few
tentative forecasts, based on these norms, of the
demand for engineering manpower over the Third Plan
period. Further, the Third Plan, like its predecessors, contained recommendations for extending
the organizational establishments of manpower planning.
The Institute of Applied Manpower Research (1962),
and the Steering Group on Manpower (1965) are two
notable examples. The Draft Fourth Plan presents
a more systematic review of supply/demand position
for the various categories of high-level manpower
and asserts confidently that "the Fourth Plan starts
with the distinct advantage that in most fields,
especially in engineering, acute shortages except
in certain specialised lines have largely been

eliminated." It recommends that "therefore emphasis
on education, particularly technical, should hence-
forth be more on quality rather than quantity."[2]
Unfortunately, however, the official draft of the
Fourth Plan document contains no explicit mention
of the technique used or model adopted for the
compilation of these manpower estimates. But it
does appear that the technique adopted was very
similar to that described in the paper "India's
Manpower Requirements--Some Preliminary Estimates
(1968-69 to 1978-79)" by the Directorate General of
Employment, January 1969. This estimated the demand
for the manpower vector and its supply by using two
separate and independent models before their balance
was checked.

DEMAND MODEL

If I, P, and E denote income, labor productivity,
and employment, and r_I, r_p, and r_E the annual percentage rates of growth in these three variables
respectively, in any particular sector, then the
following relations will hold true, assuming a
geometric growth:

$$I_t = I_o \left(1 + \frac{r_I}{100} \right)^t$$

$$P_t = P_o \left(1 + \frac{r_P}{100} \right)^t$$

$$E_t = E_o \left(1 + \frac{r_E}{100} \right)^t$$

$$I_t = E_t \cdot P_t$$

$$I_o = E_o \cdot P_o$$

$$\text{then, } 1 + \frac{r_E}{100} = \frac{100 + r_I}{100 + r_p}$$

$$\text{or, } r_E = \frac{r_I - r_P}{100 + r_P} \cdot 100$$

Then if in the ith sector the base period employment is W_B^i, then in the tth period it will be

$$W_t^i = W_B^i (1 + r_E)^t.$$

In the second stage, the industry breakdown of manpower needs has been converted into an occupational classification by passing it through an industry/ occupation matrix (L). This industry/occupation matrix is computed basically from the 1961 population census and is subsequently adjusted in the light of information regarding the likely impact of technological changes on the composition of the labor force.

In calculating the need for additional manpower in any sector over a period, provisions are made for replacement needs arising out of retirement and deaths. This need is placed at 2 percent per annum over the plan period for all occupations comprising the total labor force employed. This percentage is calculated on the basis of birth rates, age and sex composition, mortality rates, retirement age, and rate of migration of the population.

Thus $\Delta O = L \cdot \Delta E + S_e \cdot 0.02$

when ΔO = additional requirement of labor vector, occupation-wise, over the relevant period,

ΔE = vector of additional manpower, industry-wise,

L = industry/occupation matrix, and

S_e = vector of occupation classes employed.

Because of the paucity of data, however, the above
approach is adopted only in terms of a highly aggregated sector classification. Furthermore, this
approach is pursued only in the nonagricultural
sector. In the agricultural sector, the requirements
are estimated from norms quoted in an ad hoc manner
in these documents, and no details as to how they
are formulated are available.

As has already been mentioned, the norms of
the occupational component of industrial labor are
based on the 1961 census with adjustments for any
change over time. The categories to which special
attention was paid were engineers and scientists,
since it was feared that they might act as constraining elements during the Fourth Plan. But fortunately
enough, the findings of the above report convincingly
show that there will in fact be a surplus both of
engineers and scientists in relation to demand over
the Fourth Plan period.

This brings us to a very useful survey by R.G.
Agarwal and P.N. Mathur[3] on the methods of estimation
used within and outside the commission. This survey,
which deals with the forecasting of demand for
engineering personel in India, divides the problem
into three parts-- approach, basis, and method.

We shall now discuss each of these in turn.
Although the sectoral approach is now becoming
fashionable, both the global and sectoral approaches
were adopted by the various planning bodies in
earlier exercises.

As to the basis of calculation, the manpower
requirements of engineers were made a function either
of investment or output or the total workforce.
Obviously, the assumptions behind these three
approaches are rather different. Unfortunately, no
systematic attempts were made to check the validity
of these assumptions. Of course, sufficient care
was taken to allow for any possible changes in price,
in technology, and in the scale of production.

With regard to the method of estimation, the engineering coefficients related to output or investments were usually assumed to be constant. However, in recent years, regression models on time series data were attempted by the Institute of Applied Manpower Research (IAMR) for estimating the function relations of engineering coefficients. Unfortunately, they used only a few observations, and these observations were very much biased, being subject to heavy supply constraints.

SUPPLY MODEL

The supply of a given category of skilled manpower in any period is estimated as the total number of entrants into schools, colleges, or technical institutions (as the case may be), l years ago, adjusted for normal rate of dropouts. l in this case is defined as the "gestation" or training period of the respective labor force. For engineers, it is assumed to be five years, and for scientists three. To illustrate, here is a typical demand/supply flow pattern for engineers and scientists, calculated over the Fourth Plan period.

Categories	Additional requirements during Fourth Plan	Supply	Surplus
Engineers	113,500	244,000	1,30,500
Scientist	37,000	94,750[*]	57,750

[*]Planning Commission, Education Division, "Estimated Cost of Programs of Higher Education in the Fourth Plan."

A CRITIQUE OF THE THEORETICAL FRAME-
WORK OF THE MANPOWER MODEL

Manpower needs can be treated both as a problem
of supplying a form of current intermediate inputs
(as labor services) and as installing a capital-
capacity potential, in the nature of creating a stock
of human beings, endowed with certain virtues and
a period of active life. The manpower-producing
sectors (for skilled personnel) are to be identified
with educational and training institutions. In the
same line of logic, the supply of unskilled manpower
is governed primarily by demographic considerations
such as births, deaths, the age composition of the
population, and also by social laws such as school-
leaving age and the age of retirement. The rate of
migration and immigration will appear as another
major determining factor.

The current inputs of manpower service-rendering
sectors can be identified with the consumption of
households. Thus, in a closed model, manpower
activity should be treated as similar to all other
activities, and as such must be solved in a simultaneous scheme. But in the existing models, manpower
problems have been treated separately in two submodels. The demand for manpower is dependent on the
level of activities in different sectors and is
determined exogenously by a production model. The
supply of manpower is determined again exogenously
by a separate submodel of the education sector.
This approach neglects the feedback of manpower
requirements by the education sector. But the
advantage of an approach such as this is that it
avoids the most difficult problem of formulating
a stable functional relationship between the input
of household and the level of manpower services
rendered. It also avoids the problem of relating
the level and pattern of manpower-generating activities (as stocks) to the categories of manpower
services to be created in the future. The former
appears normally in much more aggregated form than

the latter (i.e., scope of some alternative uses of
manpower stocks). Lastly, as the gestation lag in
manpower generating services is very large, the
assumption of manpower supply, exogenously determined
from the model, may be quite realistic in a medium-
term plan horizon such as the five-yearly plans; but
in a longer-term model it is advisable to build a
manpower model within the fold of a comprehensive
model frame, in order to take full account of the
mutual interdependence of all economic activities.

                            NOTES

    1. Second Five-Year Plan, (Delhi: Government
of India Press, 1956).

    2. Fourth Five-Year Plan: A Draft Outline,
(Faridabad: Government of India Press, 1966).

    3. R.G. Agarwal and P.N. Mathur, "Develop-
ment of a Sectoral and Multi-Factor Approach to
Estimation of Demand for Engineering Manpower."

6

Any discussion of the techniques of formulation
of micro-plans in India would be extremely difficult,
since neither the official plan documents nor any
of the major technical papers on plan formulation
prepared by the Planning Commission contain any
significant reference to the problems of plan formulation on a plant basis. Some references to micro-
plans in the industrial sector, in a rather sketchy
and superficial form, are available in the document
on the industrial development program issued by
the Planning Commission.[1] In addition, some minor
discussions regarding the choice of investment in
the different annual plan programs are noticeable
in the "notes" prepared by the Program Administration Division of the Planning Commission during
negotiations with the state governments on the grant
of financial assistance. Programs are here defined
as a rather homogeneous complex of project activities.
For example, the whole of the extension service in
the agricultural sector is regarded as a single
program. The element of choice in these programs
normally expresses itself as a choice of the "mix"
of the different operational schemes (or projects)
which will provide similar outputs or benefits,
although, strictly speaking, choice of techniques
(in a purely engineering sense) should be relevant
only at a project or plant level.

On the question of integration of the micro-plans
with the global plan, no definite reference can be
located in the official plan documents or any associated papers as to how it is done. Conceptually,
any definite sequence between macro, sectoral, and
micro plans would be impossible because the sequence
might work either way. Indeed, before a choice of
"mix" of a program or the choice of technique of
production of a project would be finalized, neither
the coefficients of the capital flow matrix nor the
coefficient of the current flow matrix used in
conventional macro or inter-industry plans could be
assumed as given in the programing scheme. Similarly, no absolute choice of any type is possible
on the macro level, unless it is considered in the
perspective of the sectoral or global pattern of
the plan, especially since the scarcity and prices
of the primary factors can be evaluated only at the
national level (i.e., taking total supply and demand
into consideration). Hence the need for simultaneity
and totality in a plan.

A further complication is introduced into the
plan-frame when sectoral choices are brought into
the picture. The element of these choices will increase in proportion with the openness of the economy,
or in inverse proportion with the freedom of choice
in buying by the final consumers. Similarly, the
scope of choice will be less if the projects are
complementary, and greater if they are substitutable.
Lastly, the greater the aggregation under the activity
heads, the larger the scope of choice of techniques.

However, in the Indian context, although the
exact procedures regarding the integration of micro
and macro plans are not very explicit, a study of the
macro and sectoral plan formulation by the Central
Planning Organization in India will convince one
that almost always a given pattern of final demand
vector is assumed when setting production targets
in all the plan exercises. This is presumably due
in part to the assumption of stagnant exports and
in part to the implicit overconfidence of Indian
planners, who feel that fiscal measures will always
take full care of all the supply/demand balances
in the market.

Consequently, planning at the micro level in
India is seen to have been conducted under the
sectoral or global investment constraints of the plans
with only one-way sequences, and without any consideration for a feedback process.

In this chapter will be described the broad
outline of the investment criteria supposed to have
been adopted in India in most of the micro-plans
in the public sector. The private sector is normally
assumed to be guided by profit-making considerations,
both realized and expected, and to be influenced
only at times by fiscal and monetary measures (a type
of accounting-price correction).

In the public sector, on the other hand, the
private-profit maximization principle is replaced
by social considerations. The familiar techniques
of benefit-cost analysis are applied in some form
in almost all public sector projects, even though
the exact method varies from project to project and
from time to time. I will try here briefly to develop
the general concepts and methods used, and give a
few specific examples from the Indian context.

The goal of benefit-cost analysis, and of economic
choice in general, can be stated as the maximization
of certain objectives (benefits) subject to the
existing constraints (costs) imposed by the economic
and political environment of society. The objectives
may be singular or multiple. For example, the objective of a steel project may be minimization of the
unit cost and fulfillment of a targeted output, and
may at the same time include the fulfillment of aims
related to the regional allocation of employment.

To list the objectives, however, is not to set
them in the sense required for derivation of the
operational criteria. The relative importance of
the various objectives must be specified if they are
to be reflected in planning, and the specification
must be quantitative. One method is to select only
one major objective, and to set the others as a
system of constraints. For example, the regional
objective of the Indian national plan made itself
felt only at the level of the selection of project
sites.

The following are the conceptual considerations
in the project and program evaluation schemes adopted
in the Indian plans: (They are not always stated
explicitly in the official plan literature.)

1. The allocation of sectoral investments in
the light of a _fixed_ final demand pattern.

2. The choice of projects or programs subject
to sectoral investment constraints and other technical
and behavioral limitations, and in the light of one
or more specific objectives.

The objectives of the second category are translated in terms of the benefits accruing from these
projects. Hence, for that purpose, different benefits
are combined with different values (weights), mostly
in the context of social considerations formulated
by the planners.

The benefits of public sector projects can be
classified in this context as primary and secondary
The primary benefits can be further subdivided into
direct and indirect. For example, with regard to
the consequences for income, these subdivisions could
be defined as follows: "Direct-income increases"
are those within the sector of the project; "indirect-
income increases" are those in sectors vertically
connected with that sector through direct technological links. Secondary effects relate to consequences.
In a similar way, savings, employment, and other
effects of a project can be evaluated. Effects can
also be subdivided into those felt during the period
of construction (gestation) and those which occur
after the project is in operation.

The most accurate method of estimating the
economic impacts of any program would be to use a
detailed econometric model. This would bring out
all the relationships existing between the projects
and the economy as a whole. Such a model, however,
would be highly complex and would require a wealth
of information. Hence, in India, approximative
methods were adopted; this seems, indeed, the only
feasible solution.

The benefits of each project can be reduced to
a common denominator in the light of the multiple
objectives of the economy by using a system of
notional weights. For the cost, different weights
can be applied to the different elements of cost,
such as the private and social cost of a project.
The cost, again, might refer to one or more scarce
factors (factors which are abundant could be regarded
as free gifts and might be assigned as having zero
opportunity cost). This means that evaluation must
be introduced not only for the product market, but
also for the factor market. Accordingly, a set of
weights is needed to reduce all cost elements to
a common denominator. In development literature
these weights are normally called "accounting prices"
or "shadow prices." Market prices of commodities
and factors can be alternatively employed, provided
the project will not call for large-scale economic
decisions. But if investments decisions are so large
relative to an economy (e.g., a major dam project
in a small country) that they can alter relative
outputs and prices over the whole economy, the
standard, partial-equilibrium technique of cost-
benefit is likely to fail.

A further complication arises when the benefits
or costs of the programs are distributed over time.
In the case of benefits, the usual method is to use
"discount" rates for assessing contributions from
future income or employment. Discounting of individual contributions may be avoided altogether if a plan
exists in which years and sectors are differentiated.
The projects may then be chosen by trial and error,
so as to finally provide for the rise in income and
employment envisaged annually in the plan.

The time element will also enter if the gestation
period is very long and the effects during the gestation periods are quite different from those during
the period of operation.

With regard to the distribution of costs, the
different elements of cost do not have to be combined
by their market valuation, but can be combined by
the accounting prices. Accounting prices, as already

defined, are fictitious prices which may be assigned
to some cost elements or products to give a better
approximation of the relative importance of these
elements in the economy. Evidently accounting
prices are a global concept in an optimization setup.
In practice, for the sake of convenience, accounting
prices are normally calculated by sub-models, like
the accounting price of foreign exchange derived
from a foreign trade econometric model. Finally,
the benefit-cost ratios for all projects translated
into homogeneous concepts and brought to a point of
time are compared and chosen on the basis of the
highest benefit-cost ratio. The total investment
expenses in the different projects thus selected
are adjusted under the aggregate global constraint,
(in terms of the amount of investment), allocated
in the respective sectors. Then a stage will come
when the feedback process (already discussed) will
begin in the light of this selection of projects.
(This, unfortunately, was not done in an explicit
way in India.) Revision of the input columns of the
inter-industry table will take place, and the sectoral
scheme will be modified in the light of the new capital
coefficients. In this chain of adjustments, even
the broad framework of the macro model may be affected.
Accordingly, the translation of macro to sectoral
and to micro may again be repeated, and this to-and-
fro movement will continue until a consistency will
finally be attained between all three stages of the
plan.

THE INDIAN CASE

"Where a theoretically more satisfying approach
was found difficult to follow in practice, either
due to lack of data or difficulties of computing, a
less accurate but simpler approach was adopted."[2]
At this stage it should be noted that an exercise
on the choice of technique in India has been confined
mostly to productive sectors rather than to service
sectors.

As has already been discussed, in the national
plan the choice of sectoral allocation of resources,

and to some extent the choice of techniques of production, are introduced through a back door in terms
of choice between several alternative plan objectives
under alternative assumptions. At the micro level--
i.e., on the project level--no discussion of the
choice of technique is noticeable in the official
plan documents. However, Dr. S.R. Sen, the Program
Advisor of the Indian Planning Commission, discusses
in his book a few rather simple methods that were
supposedly used in the Indian plans at the micro
levels.[3] They are, in brief: surplus criteria, value
added criteria, foreign-exchange criteria, and basic-
and defense-industry criteria. However, as has
already been mentioned, the micro choices are always
considered under the "aggregate sectoral" investment
constraints.

The surplus criteria can be explained as follows:

S (Surplus) = annual value added (V) net of
depreciation and salary and wages (WR).

K = capital invested.

S/K is the surplus criterion which is net of depreciation but gross of amortization, interest, taxes, etc.
K is composed of three parts-- Kf (fixed capital),
Ki (working capital), and Ka (ancilliary Capital).
Ka covers part of the investment in roads, townships,
etc., which is neccesary for any project, although
not shown against the project.

According to Sen, when it is a case of choice
of technique, the attempt to estimate complementary
and supplementary investment is redundant, since they
can be assumed to be more or less the same in alternate
projects and will therefore cancel out in a comparison.*

---

*Complementary investment refers to extra invest-
ment needed for supplying incremental current inputs
to the projects under consideration. Supplementary
investment refers to extra investment needed in

In the Indian context, almost all discussions on
choice of technique regard foreign-exchange availability as a major constraint and incorporate it in
the project evaluation scheme more or less as follows:

F_k = foreign exchange component of capital
investment.

F_o = foreign exchange component of output.

P = additional premium given to foreign
exchange.

S' = Adjusted surplus after a premium is
given to the foreign exchange component.

Then $$S' = \frac{S - F_o P}{K + F_k P} \cdot 100$$

The wage rates, the foreign-exchange values,
the interest rates, etc., will be translated in
terms of national values rather than market values.
However, their calculation is likely to involve
heavy guesses, since conceptually they are also
to be determined in the light of a general equilibrium analysis.

Apart from the foreign-exchange considerations,
the gestation lags need special treatment. To
accommodate the gestation of investment and different
lifetimes of the projects, time profiles of the
fruitful life of alternative projects are estimated,
and the surpluses are added over the fruitful time
horizon less the period of gestation; (in fixing
the time horizon of a project, such factors as
depreciation, the engineering life and the economic
life of the project, including allowance for obso-
lescence, must be taken into consideration).

'other' sectors to give a final shape to the output
of the projects under consideration (i.e., conceptually, the rows of a conventional inter-industry table).

Future income that will originate from a project should be estimated on the basis of the technical concept of plant capacity. For this, neither a very small nor an unusually large unit should be selected, so as to conform to the concept of marginal extension. The surplus ratio can be calculated from more or less similar projects, not too old to evaluate the likely productivity of alternative projects. It is very difficult to guess how far the latter sophistication penetrates into the evaluation scheme in India.

Lastly, it should be noted that although Indian planners admit that a uniform method of choice of projects would be desirable on theoretical grounds, in practice uniformity is not maintained and, in their view, is not always possible. In fact, the formulas used for different types of projects are sometimes very different. In many projects, for example, the need for time discounting is totally overlooked, and any use of the accounting-price concept is not explicit.

The choice of technique criteria is also largely confined to productive sectors such as steel, fertilizer, etc., where evaluations of benefits are comparatively easy to formulate.

NOTES

1. Planning Commission, Program of Industrial Development, (Delhi: Manager of Publication, 1962).

2. S.R. Sen, The Strategy for Agricultural Development, (London: Asia Publishing House, 1962).

3. Ibid.

A study of the existing planning models in India
will convince one of their glaring limitations.
However, it should be admitted that the methods of
planning have been much improved since the inception
of the first five-year plan in the early 1950's.
Detailed specific criticisms have already been made
in earlier chapters: This chapter will present a
broad general cristicism of the Indian planning
models.

(1) None of the planning models are of the
optimizing type. They are formulated basically to
ensure a consistency between targeted variables.

(2) These models mainly attempt to lay out the
configuration of the terminal year of the plan at
five-year intervals.

(3) Even where the post-terminal conditions
of the economy are specified in these planning models,
they are very aggregative and rather loosely integrated with the perspective plan-frame. Indeed in
all these models the perspective plans and the five-
year plans are formulated in rather a disjointed
way.

(4) The annual phasings of the plans are normally
done in macro-economic dimensions only and lack the
detailed specifications in which the plan's

operational mechanisms are formulated. They are
normally presented with much less detailed specifications than those of the terminal conditions presented
in the plans.

(5) The manpower model has been developed in
much aggregated form, and completely outside the
principal plan structure, ignoring the simultaneous
effect between the two.

(6) The detailed plan allocations (those published
in the official plan documents) are never expressedly
fitted in an exact and formal manner with the macro-
economic dimensions of the plans.

(7) The inter-industry specifications given in
the Fourth Plan (earlier plans have no inter-industry
exercises) are never matched with the specifications
of the material balances, given separately for major
specific commodities in value and quantity terms.

(8) The pricing in the plan is implicit and
is never geared to the physical or financial outlays
of the plan. Indeed, the pricing assumption in all
these plans seems to be one of wishful thinking.
The balances between the financial resources and the
physical outlays of the plans are extremely poor.

(9) All the plans apparently ignore many of
the very important behavioral responses of the
economy both in terms of the household and of institutions.

(10) The tax-fiscal feasibility and the capacity-
technology feasibility of the plans are based separately and are never consider together.

(11) There is a complete lack of systematic
investigation into the problems of project evaluation
and choice of technique in the context of the global
objectives, and no standardized project evaluation
schemes are evolved.

Lastly, there is the universal complaint that
the parameters used in Indian plans are mostly

illustrative and bear little relation to reality.

They are mainly in the field of:-

(a) Import coefficients

(b) Export elasticities and import propensities

(c) Capital coefficients

(d) Input norms, especially in agriculture and services

(e) The gestation pattern of investment

(f) Consumption propensities

(g) Tax incidences

(h) Regional differences in the parameters

(i) Idle capacity and underemployment of labor

(j) Availability of skilled personnel.

From the list of the limitations cited above, I have deliberately kept aside the limitations that pertain to the actual implementation of the plan.

PART

II

A NEW
THEORETICAL
AND COMPUTABLE
FRAME

Model-building in economics refers to formaliza-
tions of the functional relationships existing between
the different economic activities of a community.
The functional forms used may either be exact or may
contain stochastic elements. Or, again, they may
either be quantitative or of loose ordinal nature.

Broadly speaking, models in economics can be
divided into four classes: (i) They may be descriptive,
describing structural relationships; (ii) they may
serve the purposes of forecasting; (iii) they may
test the implications of alternative policy measures,
or (iv) they may be used for planning. The differences
between these types, especially between the last
three, are only differences of degree and are not
very firmly demarcated. For example, the forecasting
models would either be completely closed or open
with exogenous variables uniquely pre-assigned,
whereas in policy models these exogenous variables
are policy-oriented. The difference between a planning model and a policy model normally lies in the
fact that the former carries the elements of choice,
decided endogenously from within the system, in the
light of optimizing criteria, whereas the latter has
the elements of choice decided from outside the
system, i.e., not specified within the model.

In an Economic Commission for Europe (ECE)
study, these models have been classified from a

different angle: "Optimal policy models" are those
"based on precise knowledge of medium- and long-term
economic aims, which are mathematically expressed in
the form of a preference function," whereas growth
models "reflect the initial conditions of the economy
(including economic policy measures already proposed)
and show the most probable path of the economic
development."[1]

Alternatively, models can be classified as
partial, total (aggregative) or intersectoral (sometimes called sectoral). Choice between these classes
is normally guided by operational needs; the structure
of the economy, especially its "block nature"; the
availability of data and computational facilities;
the urgency (i.e., the need for quick implementation)
of the plan; and the assumed political and social
framework. Indeed, it has often been admitted that
the choice of a model should not be influenced solely
by the size of the model, measured, say, by the
number of sectors it covers, because in some circumstances, especially when data are scarce, a more
aggregated model may be equally informative and
accurate, and at the same time easier to solve.
Moreover, to quote the ECE, "experience has proved
that simple econometric models adapted to the accuracy
of data are usually a more efficient tool than the
unformalised elaborate models."[2]

NOTES

1. United Nations, Economic Commission for
Europe, Development in the Construction and Use of
Marcro-economic Models, (New York: 1968).

2. Ibid.

Our suggested planning model belongs to the multisectoral, intertemporal group. R.S. Eckaus attempted something similar, but time coverage and sectoral divisions were different. Very recently Alan Manne computed a similar model. Again, the details of the present model are very different from Manne's. His model ignores almost all behavioral or fiscal aspects of the economy and any limitations set by manpower availability. Besides, the preference function of his model differs from that of the present one.[1]

Before discussing the basic structure of our model, we shall examine a few familiar problems connected with the estimation of parameters. The model has three broad types of structural system:

1. A conventional open input/output type of transaction flows, with observations for only one, or at the most two years.

2. A behavioral equation system purporting to approximate to the economic behavior of consumption, inventory holdings, imports, etc., based on time series or cross-section data.

3. A set of inequality restraints and boundary conditions, either on the target and the instrumental

variables or on the individual coefficients and the relations between them.

Now the problems of estimability in the above three types of structural system can be enumerated as follows: In type 1, the difficulty of applying the conventional concept of statistical estimability to the structural coefficients is well known. Different research workers have developed indirect criteria for testing the workability of an input/output model and its performances, relative to other methods that make use of GNP projections or final demand projections by sectors over time-series data. The estimate of error in the predictability by input/output and other methods could be indirect tests of the workability of the input/output model, provided a critical level of the error of prediction to be tolerated is pre-assigned. Two basic questions can be posed at this stage. First, to what extent can an input/output system be combined with a set of behavioral relations to form the basic structure of a policy model or planning model in its short- or medium-term framework? Second, what role can standard statistical methods play in improving the workability of an input/output system as a part of a general policy model?

The first question can only be answered when one has some empirical idea about the sensitivity of the coefficient structure to the level of allocation of industries--hence, some idea as to what is meant by structural change of relationships within an input/output model compared to that of a behavioral model.

In answer to the second question, it should be noted that intercountry cross-section data, based on a uniform classification of industries, might provide a small sample in the statistical sense, although the data-collection problem would be tremendous and complicated. Of late, the need has been felt to delve behind the input coefficients of Leontief's input/output model, in order to obtain a better estimate of the structural coefficient in this context

Next, we move to the estimation problem relating to the behavioral equations. In this connection, it should be emphasized that the problem of specification of an econometric model is so essential to model-building for policy purposes that it transcends, in many cases, even the need for applying a complicated technique of estimation.

The problem of estimation in this field is one too vast to deal with here; it could be referred to in any standard econometric textbook.

The third type, inequality constraints, appear to play a double role in relation to the econometric estimation, typical to those of the behavioral equation system: On the one hand, they minimize the apparent unreality of the catch-all term "residual equational error" in the statistical estimation of behavioral equations, by explicitly allowing extraneous estimation and/or a priori information; on the other hand, by emphasizing the optimization objective of a policy model, one allows estimation to be viewed as a part of decision-function theory.

THE STRUCTURE OF THE MODEL

Our present computable planning model of India regards capital and skilled manpower as the major constraining factors in the process of her growth. This approach does not exclude the role of other factors such as social institutions and planning organization in the process of any economic growth. Indeed, all our experience with development problems and development planning has amply demonstrated that economic development is not a simple matter of generating enough capital investment. It is a far more complex problem of generating the right spirit and institutions required for working and managing the capital and manpower, and this in turn requires a transformation of the economic, social, legal, and cultural environment. The above approach is based on a conviction that the other factors will not act as the constraining elements in India's

growth process over the next decade or so, and
that an adequate level of capital formation and
skilled manpower will be indispensable as a catalyst
to generate all the other forces of development.

In this model, the capital constraint has been
made to work in terms of (i) the capacities of the
initial period, and (ii) the supply of savings. The
concept of capacity has been used mainly in an
engineering sense, defined as the optimum output
realizable from a capital stock when employed against
2.5 shifts of labor, (8 hours a shift), although
in many cases the prevalent practice of existing
shift work in the given industries has been accommodated. The supply of savings to finance the new
investments has been constrained by the behavior of
households and institutions together with national
policy regarding what is a desirable and a tolerable
level of living standard to be guaranteed.

The potentiality of generating public saving
is largely constrained by the social, political,
and financial responses of savers and investors as
taxpayers. Furthermore, as the model has been
formulated on a disaggregated basis, it is not only
the level but also the composition of saving that
becomes the effective constraint, in all the above
cases. This is because saving acts as a constraint
by restraining the availability of investible surplus
for capital formation. Hence, if capital formation
is calculated in disaggregated terms, the supply of
saving is also to be reckoned in disaggregated terms.

The demand for capital formation (i.e., investment) has been estimated in this model in terms of
needs for the expansion of capacity, given the prevalent gestation lag of investment. The demand for
investment in the "market" sense has not been explored
in this model. Like all other similar models, it has
been assumed that any shortfall in the private sector
from the desired level of investment can always be
replaced from the public sector. A consideration
for the quality of capital acting as a constraint
in economic development has appeared in this model
in the form of nonsubstitutable imported capital

goods required in the development process. They are
nonsubstitutable in the sense that they contain
quality which domestic skill cannot produce (or cannot produce in sufficient quantity). But skill can
be imbibed with time. Hence, the model makes provision for import substitution in the light of past
performance. Indeed, this is one of the goals of the
plan. It is at this stage that the constraint arising
from the potentiality of export expansion becomes
effectively felt. Without surplus export earnings,
indispensable imports cannot be financed. Foreign
capital and aid have been assessed as the constraint-
releasing factors in this model frame.

On the side of primary inputs, the restraining
effect of labor may act both in an aggregative and
a sectoral sense. In underdeveloped countries, an
overall shortage of labor is normally ruled out.
Therefore, in familiar planning models, manpower
does not appear as an explanatory variable affecting
the growth and development of the economy. But in
a disaggregated model the picture will be much different. In most of the developing countries, skilled
manpower of different types will be in short supply.
The growth of the economy is therefore likely to be
constrained by the growth of the skilled manpower
supply. Finally, in many popular planning models
the constraining role of the technical factors have
been overemphasized, whilst those arising from the
behavior of households, institutions, and government
have been underestimated or even overlooked. This
arises from a common belief, prevalent among planners,
that technology presents a more rigorous constraint
than the habits of the people. But this has been
challenged in many countries from planning experiences.
Hence, in the present model, the constraining effect
of social, behavioral, and fiscal implementability
has been built-in. It should be remembered that
the purpose of planning is not only to maximize
certain objectives subject to certain constraints,
but also to release these constraints over time.
This brings time, as the last set of constraints,
into the system. Therefore all variables and parameters of the planning model must carry time suffix.

The structure of the present planning model can be broadly divided into (1) an objective and (2) a set of limitations or constraints.

Any planning scheme will normally include a multiplicity of objectives. To accommodate these objectives in a programming frame, the common practice is either to combine them into a single objective, using different weights between them, or alternatively to place some of the objectives in the form of constraints. It is evident that any goal or objective imposed in a plan via a constraint is equivalent to one that has an infinite weight in the objective function until it is satisfied, and a zero weight after it is satisfied.

In the present model, the major alternative objectives, such as balance-of-payments considerations, guarantee of a minimum level of consumption, and reduction of idle capacity and wastage, are all accommodated in the system of equations representing the set of constraints; whereas the maximization of consumption over the plan period is placed as a preference function.

The present model is a finite time-period one, and spreads over ten years. Its objective function belongs to the Ramsey Group. Broadly speaking, the preference function of a model with finite time horizon can be divided into two groups: (i) Turnpike, when the final or terminal-period configuration (e.g., the consumption or capital stock at the terminal year of the plan) becomes the objective of optimization, without paying any attention to the comparative attractiveness of the time path that leads from the initial to the terminal situation; (ii) Ramsey, when the consumption stream over the whole time period becomes the objective of maximization.

Trunpike theorem has, as its objective, the optimization of the terminal-period configuration of the economy. It is indifferent to the state of affairs existing between the initial and the terminal year of the plan. It may, for example, aim at maximizing the total weighted sum of capital stock

at the end of the plan period. It sets no condition
as to the behavior of consumption or production
during the intervening period. It has few alternative formulations. It may assume a completely closed
model; in which case, it will prescribe a Von Neumann
equiproportional growth of all the sectors of the
economy. Alternatively, it may be constrained by
the supply of labor or foreign exchange, determined
exogenously from the model. In this version, the
model will recommend no consumption but only accumulation over the intervening plan period. Such a
picture is, however, highly unrealistic.

Regarding the Ramsey model, there are broadly
three groups. The first is illustrated by the
requirement that consumption in all sectors grow at
the same exponential rate up to the relevant time
horizon. To quote Chakravarty, "if the preference
function is specified in this way and all capacity
is assumed to be utilized, then for specified initial
and terminal conditions there exists only one solution, if at all, which will provide for such a rate
of growth."[2] It might be argued that this problem
admits of no choice at all. This view, however, is
not totally correct, since in a slightly different
formulation elements of choice can be explicitly
introduced in setting the rates at which consumption
of various items are allowed to grow, and also in
the establishment of the terminal production levels.
The second group is more complicated; an attempt is
made to minimize the time needed to move from the
specified 'initial' to the desired 'terminal' situation. The third group is where the preference
function, to be maximized, is an integral of utility
of consumption, consumption being treated as a vector
subject to the requirement that instantaneous
efficiency conditions are observed. Of these, the
last one bears the greater resemblance to the objective
function used in the present model.

It can be shown quite easily at this stage that,
assuming a preference function which is linear in
consumption and devoid of all discrimination between
present and future consumption, the optimum solution
to a problem with a Ramsey type of preference function

will be almost the same as the optimum solution for
a problem of the Turnpike type, inasmuch as all
consumption over the plan period will be postponed
until the tail-end of the plan is reached. This
means that during the plan period, activities will
be entirely confined to capital accumulation. Obviously, this correspondence will hold good only for
plans of large but finite time horizons. Over very
short periods, a Ramsey model might under certain
conditions even prescribe all consumption and no net
investment. Alternatively, like the Turnpike theorem,
it will prescribe a Von Neumann path in a "commodity-
producing commodity" scheme.

The preference function used in the present
model, although of the Ramsey type, is much more
simplified.

To begin with, a constraint relating to a
terminal capital stock has been added. Without this,
the investment in the terminal period would have
been zero. The rationale of post-terminal stock of
capital is to ensure a desired rate of growth of
consumption in the post-terminal period. This is
discussed in detail in connection with the steady-
state formulation of the model.

Secondly, it was decided in this model to use
an element of time discounting in the evaluation of
the consumption stream over the plan period, in
order to avoid a consumption profile very much humped
at the tail-end of the plan period. Such a profile
seems very unrealistic and impracticable in any
planning scheme. For the sake of simplicity, it is
assumed that society would like to maximize the total
discounted value of consumption (estimated at the
price relatives of the base period) over the whole
plan period. This means that the planners do not
want to make any discrimination between the different
elements of the consumption vector (i.e., equal
utility for all the items of consumption), at any
given point of time, although assuming a diminishing
utility over time.

With regard to the rates of discount of time
preference with respect to consumption, an equal

discounting for all items of consumption over time is assumed and an attempt is made to trace the sensitivity of the plan allocations to changes in the discount rates. In the present exercise, the discount rates are pegged at three alternative levels: 10 percent, twenty percent, and thirty percent per annum; and the ranges of their sensitivity are also explored. Finally, a lower floor, which is assigned to consumption and which will work against any (absolute) fall in the average real wage of the population per capita compared to the base, is pegged into the system of constraint. In addition, there is equation ensuring a monotonicity of consumption rise per capita of the population.

Evidently, under the above scheme, the solution values of the consumption vector may not always balance with the consumption vector, derived from the income-consumption behavior of the people. Fiscal provisions in terms of tax subsidy are built into this model to take account of the problem of balance between demand and supply of all goods and services in the economy.

Broadly, the present model can be divided into two stages, the steady state and the transient state. The flow charts of the steady state and the transient state are presented in Charts 9.1 and 9.2.

THE STEADY STATE

The steady state consists of a principal model and five separate submodels. Many variables, which are exogenous to the principal model, are endogenously determined by the submodels. The basic supply/demand balance and the savings/investment balance of the economy are presented in diagram from as follows:

Total supply = Home output + all imports.

Total demand = Home final demand + Export + Intermediate demand.

Supply of saving = Domestic income - Demand for consumption + Import - Export.

CHART 9.1
Flow Chart of the Steady State

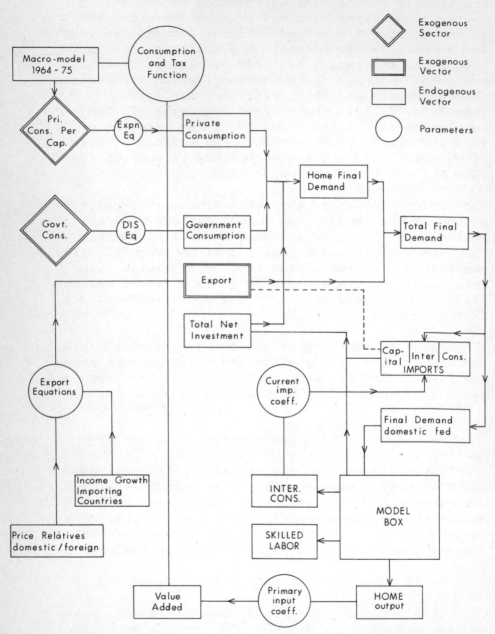

Exogenous Sector

Exogenous Vector

Endogenous Vector

Parameters

Demand for saving = Production of investment goods.

Incremental demand for skilled labor = Incremental labor input arising from an expansion of output plus demand for replacement.

Increase in the supply of skilled labor = Enrollment in education and training institutions L years ago, L being the gestation of manpower investment.

Data from seven separate submodels are fed into this steady-state model at different iterative stages of its solution, in order to arrive at the final result. The final result is given in terms of (i) gross outputs, (ii) fixed and working capital, (iii) replacement investment, (iv) imports, (v) value added, (vi) requirements for skilled manpower, (vii) intermediate demands, and (viii) saving investment gaps, with their fiscal implications.

The seven submodels are the following: (a) Export submodel, (b) import submodel, (c) consumption/income submodel, (d) public-expenditure and tax submodel, (e) marco-economic model, (f) skilled-manpower model, and (g) tax model.

Of the seven submodels, model (e) is borrowed from the exercise of the Perspective Planning Division of the Planning Commission, conducted during the formulation of the Fourth Plan. The export model is developed primarily to derive the income and price elasticity of Indian exports in disaggregated form. This submodel is used to derive export forecasts under alternative assumptions regarding the effects of devaluation. These alternative assumptions are ultimately fed into the basic steady-state model.

The import submodel mainly develops the parameters of import propensities for different categories of import.

The consumption/income submodel develops the parameters of saving propensities and expenditure elasticities.

The public-expenditure and tax submodel calculates
the expenditure pattern of the public authorities
during the plan. Similarly submodel (g) estimates
the tax propensities and other fiscal implications
in the financing of the plan. (All these submodels
will be discussed in detail in Part III of this
book.)

The steady-state flow chart (Chart 9.1) starts
from the left-hand corner with the per capita consumption assured in the plan for 1975/6, and derived
from the macro-economic model. Then it is passed
through the consumption-income submodel to get the
detailed composition of consumption goods for the
community. The estimates of government consumption
(derived from the public sector submodel), exports
(derived from the export submodel) and capital formation (derived from the principal model in iterative
stages), are added to it in order to derive to total
final demand. This total final demand, less capital-
goods and consumption-goods imports, gives the total
final demand to be satisfied from domestic sources.
This vector is then passed through the model box
(containing production coefficients) to give domestic
gross output and intermediate demands. In solving
the above within the main model, two major policy
variables are introduced. They are (i) Balancing
of imports with exports, and (ii) ensuring prescribed
sectoral rates of growth of consumption over the
post-terminal year of the plan. The gross and net
national income are subsequently derived from the
production relations given in the main model. The
tax/subsidy implications of the model are estimated
by evaluating the gap between the desired level of
consumption and the actual level of consumption from
parameters derived from the consumption/income
submodel. The manpower model in the end attempts
to estimate the skilled manpower requirements for
1975/6. The supply/demand balance is checked by
comparing it with the estimate given by the official
sources.

The steady-state formulation has a 22-sector
classification of the activity sectors. The
variables of this model have the following notations:

Notations

$|\ Q\ |$*   = output vector (n x 1), n = 22.

$|\ C_i\ (Pr)\ |$ = Private-consumption vector with only ith element positive and rest zero, i ranging from 1 to 22.

$|\ C_i\ (Pu)\ |$ = Public-consumption vector with only ith element positive and zest zero, i ranging from 1 to 22.

$|\ E_j\ |$ = Export vector with jth element positive, rest zero, j ranging from 1 to 22.

$|\ I_m(cap)_m\ |$ = Imports of capital goods with mth element positive, rest zero, m representing sectors 16, 17, and 20.

$|\ I_m(con)_m\ |$ = Imports of consumption goods with mth element positive and rest zero, m representing sectors 4, 14, 21, and 22.

$|\ I_n(int)K\ |$ = Imports of intermediate goods by sector K; K = 1, 2, 3, 4, 13, 17, 18, 21, and 22.

$|\ r_i(pr)\ |$ = rate of growth of ith element of private consumption, i ranging from 1 to 22.

$|\ r_i(pu)\ |$ = rate of growth of ith element of public consumption, i ranging from 1 to 22.

$|\ r_j\ |$ = rate of growth of jth element

---

*A vector is indicated by the symbol $|\ \ |$.

(Notations continued)

of export, j ranging from 1 to
22.

$| r_m |$ = rate of growth of mth element
of capital and consumption-goods
imports, m ranging from sectors
4, 14, 16, 17, 20, 21, 22.

The following are the variables in the model:

Endogenous

(a) Gross outputs ($|Q|$)

(b) Replacement-investment vector ($|RQ|$)

(c) Vector of commodity component of net fixed
investment (K Δ Q)

(d) Vector of commodity component of working
capital ($|S \Delta Q|$)

(e) Imports of capital goods ($| Imp(Cap)m|$)

(f) Imports of consumption goods ($| Im(Con)m|$)

(g) Imports of intermediate goods ($| Im(int)k|$)

Exogenous

(a) Exports ($| Ej |$)

(b) Private consumption ($| Ci(pr) |$)

(c) Public consumption ($| Ci(pu) |$)

(d) Rate of growth of ith element of private
consumption (ri(pr))

(e) Rate of growth of ith element of public
consumption (ri(pu))

(f) Rate of growth of jth element of export (rj)

(g) Rate of growth of mth element of capital-goods and consumption-goods imports (rm)

Parameters

$[a_{ij}]$ = (A);   (22 x 22) (current flow matrix)

$[K^*_{ij}]$ = (K);   (22 x 22) (fixed-capital flow matrix)

$[S_{ij}]$ = (S);   (22 x 22) (working-capital matrix)

$[R_{ij}]$ = (R);   (22 x 22) (replacement-capital matrix)

i'_j = Vector of noncompetitive intermediate import component of domestic output

A_i = Constant of the linear equation relating the imports of capital goods to net fixed-capital formation and time.

b_i = Regression coefficient of the above, with reference to net fixed-capital formation.

a'_j = Referring to constants of the regression equation relating total capital goods imported to imports of individual items. j = 16, 17, and 21.

b'_j = Corresponding regression coefficients of the former equations.

D_j = Constants in the regression coefficients relating imports of all consumption goods to individual items. j= 4, 6, 14, 21, and 22.

d_j = The corresponding regression coefficients of the former equation.

c_i = Regression coefficients relating linearly the import of capital goods to a time trend, (and to net fixed-capital formation as a second variable).

Mr = Manpower requirement for unit of output in rth sector.

Equations

$$|Q_{c1}| = \sum_{i=1}^{n} \left[\left\{ 1 - (A+R) - r_i \, (pr) \, (K+S) \right\}^{-1} |C_i \, (Pr)| \right] \tag{1}$$

$$|Q_{c2}| = \sum_{i=1}^{n} \left[\left\{ 1 - (A+R) - r_i \, (pu) \, (K+S) \right\}^{-1} |C_i \, (Pu)| \right] \tag{2}$$

$$|Q_{E3}| = \sum_{j=1}^{n} \left[\left\{ 1 - (A+R) - (r_j) \, (K+S) \right\}^{-1} |E_j| \right] \tag{3}$$

$$|Q_{m4}| = \sum_{m=1}^{n} \left[\left\{ 1 - (A+R) - (r_m) \, (K+S) \right\}^{-1} |I_m \, (cap_m) + I_m(con_m)| \right] \tag{4}$$

Thus required output $|Q_n| = |Q_{c1}| + |Q_{c2}| + |Q_{E3}| - |Q_{m4}|$ where $|Q_{c1}|$ is the hypothetical output vector with a given private consumption vector and post-terminal differential rates of growth r_i (pr). Similarly $|Q_{c2}|$ is the hypothetical output vector with public consumption as the only demand element in the final demand vector, $|Q_{E3}|$ the output vector for export, $|Q_{m4}|$ the output vector that need not be produced domestically because of the imports of corresponding items and their post-terminal rates of growth.

The system of equations referred to in (1) can be solved uniquely, since C_i (Pr) is exogenous to

the model. The same is true for the system of
equations referred to in (2) and (3). In the fourth
equation, the variables representing the import of
capital and consumption goods are exogenous from
this system, but dependent on the total output by a
special constraint built into this model in the form
of $[(i'|E| - i'_j |Q| + A] = [i'|Im (cap)_m| + i'|Im$
$(con)_m|]$. The import of capital goods is subject
to another constraint which makes it dependent on
the total fixed-capital formation of that period.
The scalar concept of consumption and capital-goods
imports are converted into vectors by assuming linear
relation of each element of the vectors to the total.

The four systems of equations are solved by
iterations, being based on the principle of convergence
when $(|Q_n| = |Q_{n-1}|)$, where $|Q|$ refers to the gross-
output vector and n refers to the number of iterations.
The skilled manpower requirement is estimated as $M_r Q$.

THE TRANSIENT STATE

The transient state of the model comprises four
submodels and one principal model. Its main purpose
is to layout the intertemporal movements of the relevant economic variables in the context of the objectives of the plan. Each of these variables, therefore, has a "time" reference. The four submodels--
(i) the export submodel, (ii) the import submodel,
(iii) the public-expenditure submodel, and (iv) the
consumption-income submodel--supply information to
the main model, derived from their solution values,
at each period of the plan. (The details of these
submodels will be discussed in Part III of this
book.) In brief, the export submodel works out the
estimates of demand for Indian exports abroad. The
import submodel, on the other hand, formulates the
parameters as import propensities for the different
categories of import. The public-expenditure model
again is borrowed from the exercise of the Perspective
Planning Division of the Planning Commission. The
above four submodels of the transient-state model
are the same as those of the steady-state model.
The only difference is the sectoral disaggregation

adopted in them. The principal model of the steady-
state formulation has twenty-two sectors and the
transient six sectors. The maximum sector classification that can be adopted in all the submodels is
accordingly constrained by the number of sectors of
their respective principal models. It is unfortunate
that far fewer sectors are adopted in the transient-
state than in the steady-state formulation, but
this is necessitated by our computational limitations. However, maximum care has been taken while
aggregating the sectors, bearing in mind all the
familiar problems of aggregation. (This problem
will be discussed in detail in Part III, as a problem
of estimation of parameters of the model.)

The transient state has again a theoretical
and computational framework. In its computational
form, the manpower problem of the principal model
is treated separately in another submodel. There
are two main reasons for this: the comparative paucity
of data, both in terms of details and in terms of
reliability, is much more serious for the manpower
sector of the economy than the rest; the parameters
for the education sector, with long production
gestation and with diversity of classification, are
conceptually very difficult to formulate. Assuming
the gestation lags in training for the scientists
and engineers are as long as three to five years,
our assumption of an exogenous supply of skilled
labor over a medium-term plan is not very heroic.
Hence, in the computational part of the transient-
state model, the sector classification is reduced
to four, and manpower is treated separately in a
submodel.

Lastly, in both the transient-state and steady-
state models, the service sector, including banking
and insurance, and the labor-service component of
public consumption and construction (both public
and private) are treated outside the model. There
are two main justifications for this. Firstly, the
1959 inter-industry table, which was prepared by the
Indian Government Planning Commission and which
supplies the basic production information for the
model, contains no activity sectors on the aforementioned services in its classifications. But in

estimating national income from this table, the wage
and non-wage payments of these sectors are included,
having been derived from other sources.[3] This
approach evidently assumes that the material (intermediate) input consumption of these sectors is
negligible. If this is not so, then the estimate of
gross output will be understated, although the
estimate of net value remains unchanged. But in our
opinion, the above assumption is not too unrealistic;
at the same time, a treatment such as the above helps
to reduce the load on the computer considerably.

The following are the assumptions made in
estimating net outputs in these sectors during the
plan period:

1.   The amount of per capita services rendered
by banking and insurance that cater mainly for final
consumers will remain constant.

2.   The salary component of public administration
will remain constant compared to its material component part, as in the base year.

3.   The ratio of labor to material component of
construction will remain constant.

On the left-hand side of Chart 9.2, the major
exogenous variables are enumerated. Public consumption appears as an exogenous value, derived from the
macro-model and converted into a vector by the public-
expenditure submodel before being fed into the
principal model (box P). Skilled manpower supply
is again exogenous to the model for the first years,
and then becomes endogenous. In fact, at every
period of the time phase, it enters as a lagged
endogenous variable. This also holds for the capital
stock and net investment. Export enters into the
principal model as an exogenous variable, determined
within the export submodel. Imports are endogenous
to the principal model, whereas the import propensities
are determined by the import submodel.

Aid enters into box P as an exogenous variable
determined by the level and pattern of foreign aid
received. Further, the total level and composition

of the terminal capital stock enters into the principal
model as a policy variable. Indeed, the vector of
capital stock at the terminal period presents the
solution value of the steady-state model. Thus, it
is regarded as the linking factor in this dual scheme
of planning. The objective function, covering the
whole intervening period, enters the main box from
the top side of the chart.

Finally, the solution values of the transient-
state model are shown in the right-hand corner boxes
in the chart as estimates of consumption, investment,
and output. The rate of growth of output, together
with the capital coefficient matrix, determines the
net investment needed for the next period, and feeds
back into the box. Imports are again determined in
the main box. National income is estimated from
gross domestic output and shown under the domestic-
output box. This national income is then passed
through the income/consumption submodel in order to
derive the demand for private consumption. The
supply of private-consumption goods is given by the
principal model and placed at the right-hand side
of the box. At this level the demand/supply balance
in the private consumer's market is assured via the
tax/subsidy submodel.

The transient-state model has a theoretical
and a computational presentation. In its computational
aspect, it has again three major formulations and
thirteen alternative runs. In its theoretical
presentation, it includes manpower planning within
its principal model, whilst in its computational
form it treats manpower in a separate submodel.
Again, the computational formulations are divided
into three parts:

(i)   with level and intertemporal phasing of aid
        given exogenously;

(ii)   with level of aid given exogenously while
        the phasing of aid is determined endogenously;

(iii)   with the assumption of a perfect substitua-
        bility of capital stocks between activity
        sectors.

CHART 9.2
Flow Chart of the Transient State

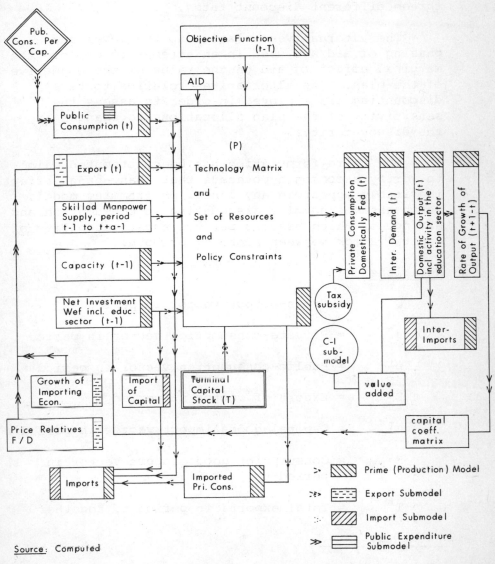

Source: Computed

149

The first formulation has, in turn, been tried with seven alternatives. Each alternative assumes a different aid condition and a different rate of time discount used in the evaluation of its objective. Chart 9.1 gives all these alternatives based on threee different discount rates.

The alternatives relative to the level and phasing of aid are used in an attempt to explore the marginal effect of aid on the value of the objective of the plan. The alternatives relative to time discounting are employed in order to assess the sensitivity of the plan allocations to changes in the discount rates.

The third formulation has been attempted mainly to verify a common hypothesis that "bang-bang" effects inevitably appear in any linear programming model, which assumes no time discounting in consumption and saving, or which assumes perfect substitutability of capital stock between sectors, or both.

Notations*

Q^t = Gross-output vector in period t

e^t = Private-consumption vector in period t

p^t = Public-consumption vector in period t

E^t = Export of vector in period t

m^t = Capital-goods import vector in period t

M^t = Consumption-goods import vector in period t

T^t = Total exports in period t, together

———————————

*Any notation with "underlying" denotes a six-sector classification of the theoretical model. Otherwise all notations refer to four-sector class-ifications.

TABLE 9.1

ALTERNATIVES IN THE TRANSIENT-STATE MODEL

Type of aid phasing	Rate of time discounting (percent)	Total aid (Rs. million)	Order
I Present model	10	43.6	196.144
II " " "	20	"	"
III " " "	30	"	"
IV " " "	10	87	"
V Perspective Plan-ning Division	10	49.2	"
VI " " "	20	"	"
VII " " "	30	"	"
VIII Optimum	10	"	197.154
IX " "	20	"	"
X " "	30	"	"
XI Present model, with perfect substituta-bility between capita-	0	43.6	148.144
XII " " "	10	"	"
XIII " " "	20	"	"

                    = with aid, <u>less</u> total noncompetitive
                      intermediate imports

Q^T = Terminal-period-output vector, derived
                     from the steady-state model

$[a_{ij}]$ = Current flow coefficient matrix

$[R_{ij}]$ = Replacement-investment matrix, (4 x 4)

$[K_{ij}]$ = Fixed (extension) capital flow matrix
                     (K_{ij}^*) + inventory-holding matrix (S_{ij})

r = Rate of growth of population

i'_j = The coefficient of imports of non-
                     competitive goods to gross output in
                     the form of a row vector

A_i = The constant of the linear equation
                     relating the net fixed-capital forma-
                     tion in a period and the total import
                     of capital goods, and time

b_i = Regression coefficient relating linearly
                     capital-goods imports and total net
                     fixed-capital formation, with time as
                     the second variable

A_j = Vector of constants of the linear
                     regression equation relating consump-
                     tion-goods imports and total export
                     earnings available for consumption-
                     goods imports

b_j = The vector of regression coefficient
                     of the above equation

$\hat{\alpha}$ = Diagonal matrix, each element of the
                     diagonal equal to (1 + the ratio of
                     idle capacity to total capacity in
                     the corresponding sector of the base)

c_i = Regression coefficient relating linearly
the import of capital goods to a time
trend

Exogenous Variables

A = current flow and replacement flow coefficient
matrix

K = Capital flow and inventory flow coefficient
matrix

Q^O (Base-period output vector)

I^O (Base-period extension investment vector)

E^t t from 1 to 10

P^t public-consumption vector, t from 1 to 10

e^O base-period consumption

A^t t from 1 to 10

Q^T T = 11

Parameters

1. $[a_{ij}]$ $\left.\begin{array}{l}\text{(i)} \ [a_{ij}] + [R_{ij}] = [A_{ij}] = A \\ \text{(ii)} \ [K^*_{ij}] + [S_{ij}] = K_{ij} = K\end{array}\right\}$

2. $[K^*_{ij}]$

3. $[S_{ij}]$

4. $[R_{ij}]$

5. $\hat{\alpha}$ = diagonal matrix

6. r = rate of growth of population

7. i_j

8. A_i

9. A_j

10. b_i

11. b_j

12. c_i

The Model Equations

The first set of equations in all these transient
models represents the constraints imposed by the
supply-demand relations of current transactions in
terms of commodities and services. It shows that
supply can exceed demand, but the reverse is an
impossibility in real terms (i.e., in any model
running at constant price). The excess supply denotes
stock building or sometimes (as will be discussed in
detail later on) building of idle capacity. In the
case of labor service, it may mean either unemployment or underemployment.

The second set of equations originates from the
need to guarantee that current output will not exceed
the existing capacity of the economy at any time.
In the manpower sector, it means that the demand for
skilled manpower cannot exceed the existing stock,
taking into consideration the new entrants and netting
the loss from retirements and deaths. The problem
of immigration and emigration is omitted from the
model. In brief, it states that the capital stock
available for production at any point of time must
be equal to the capital stock of the earlier period
corrected for its optimum utilization, together with
any investment made in that period to add to the
capital stock. Of course, this is true only in a
scheme of investment with an eighteen-month gestation
lag, as has been assumed in the producing sector of
the present model. For the manpower sector, for
scientists and engineers, gestation lags of three
and five years are assumed. Gestation lag in this
context means the time gap between enrollment and
final qualification in any training scheme. Therefore, the manpower stock available in any period is
constrained by the stock of the earlier period plus
whatever investments have been made three and five
years ago in terms of enrollments.

The third set of equations guarantees a minimum floor for per capita consumption in any period, together with a monotonicity in its movement. Thus, whilst the first two set of equations can be identified with technological constraints, the third falls in the category of political constraints.

The fourth, fifth, and sixth set of constraints refer to foreign trade. The fourth is a mixture of policy and technology. For example, aid is the outcome of international negotiations and good will. In the second formulation, it is made partly a matter of domestic-policy decisions: The country concerned can manipulate the time phasing of aid, given the global constraint of total aid over the whole plan period. The fifth set presents a few technological facts derived from econometric exercises conducted in two separate submodels, the export and the import submodels. The time trend in import substitution conceals, of course, some policy elements. The sixth set brings out some behavioral relations of consumers, and is again derived from an econometric submodel.

The seventh set of equations refers to one of the objectives of the plan, formulated as a constraint. It ensures reaching a 'target-production' level in the light of a desired terminal and post-terminal standard of living.

The eight and ninth sets of equations can be classed as "artifact" constraints. They are there primarily to guard against the familiar "bang-bang" or "flip-flop" typically associated with linear-programming planning models. To give economic inter-pretations, they help to avoid the problems of substitutability of capital stocks and the humping of consumption at the tail-end of the plan. It is indeed extremely difficult to decide the extent of substitution possible between capital stock or different sectors unless the capital data is very detailed and the information regarding technology is exhaustive. On the other hand, once we assume the monotonicity of output changes in the model, as in the eighth set, the need for substitution is ruled out. Also, this assumption of monotonicity of output changes is fairly realistic at the level of aggregation on which the model operates.

Algebraic Formulation
(in matrix notation)

Theoretical Model (Six Sectors)

$\underline{\text{Set I}} \quad Q^t \ \geq \ \underline{A} \ Q^t + \underline{K} \ \overset{k-1}{\Delta} \ \underline{Q} + e^t + p^t + E^t - m^t - M^t$

when   A   .   O
                    .
                    .
$\underline{A}=$ . . . .   j = 1 to 4
        a_{ij} .   O   for i as 5 and 6.
                    .
                    .

K=

$$K \quad . \quad \begin{array}{cccccccc} K^1_{15} & K^2_{15} & K^3_{15} & K^1_{16} & K^2_{16} & K^3_{16} & K^4_{16} & K^5_{16} \\[4pt] K^1_{25} & K^2_{25} & K^3_{25} & K^1_{26} & K^2_{26} & K^3_{26} & K^4_{26} & K^5_{26} \\[4pt] K^1_{35} & K^2_{35} & K^3_{35} & K^1_{36} & K^2_{36} & K^3_{36} & K^4_{36} & K^5_{36} \\[4pt] K^1_{45} & K^2_{45} & K^3_{45} & K^1_{46} & K^2_{46} & K^3_{46} & K^4_{46} & K^5_{46} \\[4pt] \cdots \\[4pt] K^1_{55} & K^2_{55} & K^3_{55} & K^1_{56} & K^2_{56} & K^3_{56} & K^4_{56} & K^5_{56} \\[4pt] K^1_{65} & K^2_{65} & K^3_{65} & K^1_{66} & K^2_{66} & K^3_{66} & K^4_{66} & K^5_{66} \end{array}$$

k_{ij}

j = 1 to 4
for i = 5 and 6.

when K is the old matrix. K_{mn}^t is the input coefficient of the manpower sector, comprising scientists and engineers.

t refers to the input at the tth period for a unit enrollment, at the end of the gestation period of investment. t equals 3 for scientists and 5 for engineers. K_{mn} refers to input from mth source to nth destination, m ranging from 1 to 6 and n referring to sectors 5 and 6.

ΔQ^{k-1}; when K= t+4, t+3, t+2, t+6, t+5, t+4, t+3,
and   t+2.   and t+2.
and ℓ= t+3, t+2, t+1, t+5, t+4, t+3, t+2, t+1.
and $\underline{Q}$ refers to sectors 3 and 5

Set II

$$\underline{K}\Delta Q^1 \leq \underline{K} \overset{\wedge}{\underset{\alpha}{}} \underline{Q}^O + \underline{Io}$$

when $\underline{Io} = Io + I_s^{-3} + I_e^{-5}$ I_s^{-3} = Total investment in education three years earlier for producing scientists.

I_e^{-5} = Total investment in education four years earlier for producing engineers.

Set III

$$e^t \geq {}_e t-1 \ (1+r) \quad \text{where} \quad t = 1 \text{ to } 10$$

Set IV

$$T^t = i' \ E^t - i'_j \ Q^t + A^t; \ t = 1 \text{ to } 10$$

Set V

$$i'm^t = A_i + b_i \ i'[K^* \ (Q_{t+1} - Q_t)] + c_i^t$$

Set VI

$$M^t = Aj + bj \ (T^t - i'm^t); \ t = 1 \text{ to } 10 \text{ i } bj = 1$$

Set VII

$$\underline{K} \overset{\wedge}{\propto} \underline{Q_o} + I_o + \sum_{t=1}^{10} I^* \geq \underline{K} \, \underline{Q}^T$$

Set VIII

$$\underline{Q}^t > \underline{Q}^{t-1}, \text{ t from 1 to 11}$$

Set IX

$$\underline{Q}^t \leq \underline{Q}^T. \quad (t=11) \quad (\text{when } \underline{Q}^t = \text{Target outputs}).$$

_____

*When investment vector (commodity-wise) for scientists will cumulate from minus three to seventh year and for engineers from minus five to fifth year.

Set	Description	Number of Equations
I.	$Q^t \geq A Q^t + K (Q^{t+1} - Q^t) + e^t + p^t + E^t - m^t - M^t$ ($t = 1$ to 10)	(40)
II.	$KQ^1 \leq \hat{K} \propto Q_o + I_o$	(4)
III.	$e^t \geq e^{t-1} (1 + r)$ where $t = 1$ to 10	(40)
IV.	$T^t = i' E^t - i'_j Q^t + A^t$; $t = 1$ to 10	(10)
V.	$i'm^t = A_i + b_i\, i'\, [K^* (Q_{t+1} - Q_t)] + C_i\, t$, $t = 1$ tc 10.	(10)
VI.	$M^t = A_j + b_j (T^t - i'm^t)$, $t = 1$ to 10, $i'b_j = 1$	(40)
VII.	$\hat{K} \propto Q_o + I_o + K(Q^{11} - Q^1) \geq KQ^T$	(4)
VIII.	$Q^t > Q^{t-1}$, t from 1 to 11	(44)
IX.	$Q^t \leq Q^{T*}$, $(t = 11)$	(4)
	Total	196

$A = (A_{ij})$; $K = (K_{ij})$; $K^* = (K^*_{ij})$.

159

Computable Model

Formulation 2 (Alternatives 8 to 10)

1. The number of structural equations = 197

2. The number of structural endogenous variables = 154

3. Constraints:

Set	Description	Number of Equations
I.	$Q^t \geq A Q^t + K (Q^{t+1} - Q^t) + e^t + p^t + E^t$ $-m^t - M^t$ (t = 1 to 10)	(40)
II.	$KQ^1 \leq K \hat{\alpha} Q_o + I_o$	(4)
III.	$e^t \geq e^{t-1} (1 + r)$ where t = 1 to 10	(40)
IV.	$T^t = i'E^t - i'_j Q^t + \lambda_i \sum\limits_{t=1}^{10} A^t;$ (i = 1 to 10) (t = 1 to 10)	(10)
V.	$i'm^t = A_i + b_i i'[K* (Q^t)] + C_i t;$ t = 1 to 10	(10)
VI.	$M^t = A_j + b_j (T^t - i'm^t);$ t = 1 to 10, i'bj = 1	(40)
VII.	$K \hat{\alpha} Q_o + I_o + K (Q^{11} - Q^1) \geq KQ^T$	(4)
VIII.	$Q^t > Q^{t-1};$ t from 1 to 11	(44)
IX.	$Q^t \leq Q^{T*}$ (t = 11)	(4)
X.	$\sum\limits_{i=1}^{10} \lambda_i = 1$	(1)
	TOTAL	197

Formulation 3 (Alternatives 11 to 13)

1. The number of structural equations = 148

2. The number of structural endogenous variables = 144

3. Constraints:

Set	Description	Number of Equations
I.	$Q^t \geq A Q^t + K (Q^{t+1} - Q^t) + e^t + p^t + E^t$ $- m^t - M^t$ (t = 1 to 10).	(40)
II.	$KQ^1 \leq K \hat{\alpha} Q_o + I_o$	(4)
III.	$e^t \geq e^{t-1} (1+r)$ where t = 1 to 10	(40)
IV.	$T^t = iE'^t - i_j' Q^t + A^t;$ t = 1 to 10	(10)
V.	$i'm^t = A_i + b_i i' [K* (Q_{t+1} - Q_t)] + C_i t;$ t = 1 to 10	(10)
VI.	$M^t = A_j + b'_j (T^t - i'm^t);$ t = 1 to 10, i'bj = 1	(40)
VII.	$K \hat{\alpha} Q_o + I_o + K (Q^{11} - Q^1) \geq KQ^T$	(4)
	TOTAL	148

NOTES

1. R.S. Eckaus and K.S. Parikh, Planning for
Growth: Multisectoral Intertemporal Models Applied
to India, (The M.I.T. Press, 1968); Alan S. Manne
and Thomas E. Weisskopf, "A Dynamic Multisectoral
Model for India, 1967-75," in A.P. Carter and A.
Brody, eds., Applications of Input-Output Analysis,
(Amsterdam: North Holland Publishing Co., 1970).

2. Rosenstein-Rodan, P.N. Capital Formation
and Economic Development, (London: George Allen and
Unwin, 1964).

3. Central Statistical Organisation, National
Income Statistics, (Delhi: Government of India Press).

10

The parameters to be estimated for the model can be divided into two groups: those for the principal steady-state and transient-state models and those for the different submodels. The methods of estimation differ accordingly. The principal models use linear relations derived from point observations, without any stochastic terms. They are closest to the Leontief system. The estimations of the parameters in the sub-models in general contain stochastic terms, derived either from cross-section or from time-series data. To introduce some comparability, an attempt is made to derive some measurement of stability of the parameters estimated from a single point of observation in the principal model.

The parameters of the principal models refer mainly to the coefficients of production functions in comparatively disaggregated form. They are con-fined to estimating (a) the current flow coefficient matrix (known as A matrix), (b) the capital flow coefficient matrix (known as K matrix), (c) the inventory flow coefficient matrix (known as S matrix), and (d) the replacement flow coefficient matrix (known as R matrix). Originally, they are all derived in 22-sector classification. Subsequently they are abridged into 4-sector classification, before being fed into the transient-state model. Chapters 10 to 17 discuss the detailed methods of computation of these parameters, together with the relevant light

they throw on the structure of the economy. Chapter
18 deals with the problems of estimation of the export
and import submodels, and Chapter 19 with the consumption income submodel. The macro-economic model
is a slightly revised version of the official model.
An attempt is finally made to show how data are pro-
cessed before being fed into the steady-state and
transient-state models.

11

CLASSIFICATIONS AND CONCEPTS

In the current flow transaction matrix for 1959, prepared by the Inter-industry Study Group (ISG) of the Indian Planning Commission, the following considerations were kept in view in deciding its industrial classifications (i.e., activity sectors):

1. Homogeneity of outputs and inputs.

2. Availability of data.

3. Third Plan target specifications.

4. The CSO national-income classifications, together with the international standard industrial classifications.*

It should be emphasized at this point that the classification finally adopted in the matrix is not strictly on an activity or product basis, but primarily on an establishment (i.e., a plant) basis.

_____

*The author was officer in this group, in charge of the preparation and consolidation of this matrix.

167

Theoretically, this is inferior to the activity basis in the context of inter-industry analysis, where emphasis is to be placed on the homogeneity of inputs and outputs. The sector classifications based on the establishment criterion may not satisfy the above conditions, since they may include many multiproduct firms. In spite of this, the establishment (i.e., the principal product) criterion is adopted because it is found practically impossible to allocate the inputs shown against an establishment between the different types of products produced by that firm.

In the course of this work, it is further realized that the detailed classification adopted by the ISG unit (Table 11.2) can be built up with available data for the agriculture and organized-manufacturing sectors, although it will not be possible to work in such depth with some of the other sectors, such as small-scale industries, transport, services, and professions, mainly because of the scarcity of data in these sectors. For example, the most recent data on small-scale industry (National Sample Survey Round 14, 1958) are available for 1958 only on the basis of cruder groupings, and do not permit a fuller break-down comparable to that of the organized sector of the Annual Survey of Industries (ASI), which runs into a five-digit classification. Similarly, for this year, no information is available in ready-made reliable form on the material-input structure for such sectors as construction, public administration, banking, insurance, and other services. Accordingly, these sectors were completely omitted from the acti-vity classifications adopted in the above-mentioned matrix.

However, since the final-demand vector of the matrix is computed by a residual flow method, the material-input components of construction activities are consequently added to the gross capital-formation vector. Similarly, the material-input components of public administration are added to the public-expendi-ture vector, and those of banking, etc., to the private-consumption vector, all lying in the final-demand quadrant of the table.

The value-added components of these sectors are computed on the basis of the CSO National Income Statistics, and are placed under the respective column heads. (See Table 11.1 in pocket at back of book.)

This rather unconventional approach does not affect the estimates of value added in the economy, although it understates the estimates of gross national output.* Fortunately, the material-input components of these sectors are rather low, thus causing the bias in gross-output estimates to be sufficiently low.

Further, it was felt that if the inter-industry study was to be useful for the Fourth Plan projections, it should be made readily available within a short time. Accordingly, it was decided to abridge the detailed sector classifications, from 93 initially suggested sectors to 29; 6 for agriculture, 3 for mining, 17 for industries, 1 for trade and services, and 2 for transport.

CONCEPTUAL FRAMEWORK OF THE 29 x 29 MATRIX

The columns in the matrix present the input structure of the respective sectors, whereas the rows trace the pattern of absorption or use of the output of each respective industry-sector by the other sectors of the economy. As it is a current-flow matrix, it refers to current inputs and outputs, i.e., all inputs that are consumed and all outputs that are produced in the current period, only covering twelve months and normally one calendar year. There are some sectors where a deviation from the calendar year is necessary because of the nature of the data (e.g., agriculture refers to the harvest year). The whole table can be divided into four major quadrants:

(i) The inner matrix (presenting the flow of materials and services between activity sectors, i.e., production sectors)

_____

*When the absorption of the services of these sectors was very low in the inner matrix.

(ii)   Below the <u>inner matrix</u> (presenting the absorption of the primary factors in sectors--primary factors being defined as sectors whose supply is not a function of the level of activities in the different sectors of the economy over the relevant period)

(iii)   Final demand, domestic and exports net of imports

(iv)   Below the final-demand sector (presenting the direct absorption of services by final consumers, where no activity is presumed to be involved--in the form of intermediate processing--in the act of rendering the services to the absorbing units).   In a conventional presentation this quadrant shows a zero value.

The whole of the matrix can be presented in rows and columns by the following two indentities: first, total intermediate demand for a commodity plus demand by the final consumers (i.e., private consumption, public consumption, and capital formation), added to the demand by the overseas market (i.e., exports) will equal total domestic output plus imports; and second, the payments for total inputs of materials and services plus wage payments (i.e., for labor services, which is a primary factor) plus non-wage payments (payments to factors such as land, capital, and organi-zation, including provisions for depreciation on an accounting basis) will equal the total value of gross output.

These two identities can be developed both at purchasers' price and producers' price.   In the present exercise, the choice is made in favor of producers' price.   The primary reason is that the input/output coefficients, which translate the technical relation-ship of an activity into value terms, are normally liable to the vitiated if direct taxation and distribu-tive margins are grafted to these ratios and if taxes and distributive margins are regarded as purely exo-genous factors from the point view of technological and technical relationships.   In contrast, the ISI table for 1955/6 presents the current flows at market prices (the 1955/6 table is in fact an updating

of another ISI table of 1953/4), i.e., including indirect taxation.

The present table treats imports differently
than the ISI table. Total imports are divided into
intermediate, noncompetitive imports, and others.
The concept of noncompetitiveness is computed with
reference to 1970, in consultation with the technical
branch of the Industry Division of the Indian Planning
Commission. The elements of the inner matrix, i.e.,
absorptions of current inputs by different sectors,
are made net of noncompetitive imports. The rest of
the imports by sectors are subtracted in the conventional way from the "row-wise commodity flows" of
each sector, in the final-demand part of the table.
In this revised context, total domestic supply + competitive imports = total intermediate demand, domest-
ically fed, + final demand (domestic) + exports.
Regarding the method of computation, the matrix is
generally computed in columns, although there are
few sectors where "row" figures are utilized. Initially, the matrix was not square. The output data
were available in detailed commodities (which numbered
nearly 350 in the field of manufacturing and nearly
35 in other fields) whereas the input data were available in crude groupings and could be allocated to far
fewer sectors (e.g., only to 60 industries in the
field of manufacturing). Besides, for many small-
scale industry sectors, separate input columns, differentiated from the large-scale organized sectors, could
be indentified, but their absorption in rows could
not be differentiated from that of the corresponding
large-scale sectors. This resulted in a rectangular
matrix with the number of rows less than the number
of columns. However, as has already been mentioned,
the matrix was subsequently abridged into 29 x 29 in
the final ISG table, and further into 22 x 22 sectors
in the present computable model structure.

THE CONCEPT OF HOME FINAL DEMAND

Whatever is produced in the domestic economy,
net of domestically-produced intermediate consumption
and exports, and inclusive of consumption-goods and

capital-goods imports, is available for consumption
by the final consumers and can be referred to as
"home final demand." Capital goods which are absorbed
by the activity sectors are placed in this category
because they cannot be considered as inputs currently
consumed over the year by the activity sectors. In
national income terminology, the home final demand,
as defined above, can be termed as gross domestic
expenditure. In the present exercise, gross domestic
expenditure is further subdivided into (i) private
consumption, (ii) public consumption, and (iii) capital
formation (gross). As a preliminary, the aggregate
estimate of final demand is subdivided into 29 broad
sectors, similar to the matrix classification. This,
again, is done by calculating the elements of the
final-demand vector on a residual-flow basis, i.e.,
it is calculated as the difference between the domestic
output of individual sectors inclusive of net imports
(import-export) and the intermediate consumption of
that sector's output.

In order to further disaggregate the sector-wise
estimates of final demand thus computed in sectors
between consumption and fixed-capital formation, an
attempt is made to locate those specific production
sectors that contribute either wholly to intermediate
inputs and to capital formation, or wholly to intermediate inputs and to consumption. Subsequently, in
the first set of industries, commodity balances in
the form of the first identity are formulated, in
order to derive capital-formation estimates (constituted in terms of these commodities), by a residual
flow method, i.e., by the difference between their
outputs and intermediate consumptions adjusted for
imports and export. In other words, it is assumed
that these commodities do not contribute to consumption

Similarly, the commodity flows that will contribute exclusively to consumption and to intermediate
uses are located, and, again by the difference method,
the estimates of their final consumption are calculated. It should be emphasized here that the commodity flows for consumption and capital-formation
items can be strictly separated in these cases and,
therefore, the adoption of the residual method in

both cases should not sound anomalous. In very few
cases is the same commodity absorbed both as a consumption and as an investment item. Specific treat-
ments in these cases are made in consultation with
relevant divisions of the Planning Commission.

Public-consumption figures are computed independently and are derived from national and state
budgets, and from the norms derived from random samples
drawn on the bills of purchases of a large number of
central-government administrative units. The private-
consumption figures are again estimated by the difference method between total consumption and public consumption.

When the above methods of estimation are adopted,
inventory changes are likely to be concealed either
in the capital-formation figures or in the private-
consumption figures, according to the nature of the
commodity composition of the inventories.

Exports are calculated at ex-factory prices, i.e.,
at "source" prices. This makes it necessary to reduce
the f.o.b. export values by the trade and transport
margin of the respective exportable commodities.
Imports are shown at c.i.f. prices and are divided
into noncompetitive intermediate imports, capital-
goods imports, and others.

The calculation of noncompetitive imports and
the rest will be dealt with in detail in later chapters.
The estimates of exports and imports are derived
directly from customs data and information from the
Ministry of International Trade.

INDIVIDUAL SECTORS

Manufacturing broadly constitutes the processing
part of the output derived from agriculture and
mining. Conceptually, the output of the agricultural
and mining sectors should be almost wholly absorbed
as inputs in the manufacturing sector. There will
be a few exceptions, such as certain raw vegetables,
coal, etc., that may go directly to final consumers
in significant quantities.

The manufacturing sector is subdivided into 60 subgroups in the detailed industry classification and 17 subgroups in the present abridged matrix. For the detailed matrix, no estimate for the small-scale sector is available. The estimates for the manufacturing sectors consist of three components:

(i) Contributions from the large-scale manufacturing sectors, i.e., establishments employing 50 or more with power and 100 or more without power.

(ii) Contributions from the medium-scale units, employing 10-49 with power and 20-99 without power.

(iii) Contributions from all other very small units, mostly on a household basis and not covered by the Factories Act.

Large-Scale Sector

·Detailed data on inputs and outputs and capital structure in the large-scale manufacturing sectors are available in the Annual Survey of Industries (ASI), commencing in 1959. Prior to this, there are the Census of Manufacturers (CMI) reports, supplemented by the reports on the Sample Survey of Manufacturing Industries (SSMI), which were discontinued from 1958. The sector classifications adopted in the ASI reports are more detailed, running into five digits. There are approximately 200 sectors. These 200 industry sectors are aggregated into 60 broad subgroups, primarily in the light of the specifications used in setting the plan targets. Although tea and coffee manufacturing are covered in the manufacturing part of the ASI reports, both are treated in this study outside the manufacturing sector, and are included in the agriculture sector. As it is very difficult to differentiate the agricultural and the processing activities in the case of tea and coffee, since they usually take place under the same administrative unit, it has been decided to amalgamate tea and coffee manufacturing in the agricultural sector. Again, the ASI reports do not cover some public undertakings, the most important of which is a reply to a questionnaire, sent to Hindustan Steel Ltd., for the present purpose, has been utilized in formulating the relevant information in the matrix.

As the matrix is formulated basically in columns, ASI tables presenting the consumption of fuel and other materials and services are relevant for the present purpose. The material-input figures are given commodity-wise and at purchasers' price, i.e., end-point price. Industrial outputs are also given by commodity, but at ex-factory price. For the sake of expediency, an individual industry in the detailed classification (five-digit classification of ASI sectors) is assumed to produce a single product. Thus, no major errors are introduced, since the ASI classification is sufficiently exhaustive. As a second stage, each commodity input of the ASI industries is allocated to the source of its origin, in terms of the industry classification.

In almost all industries, however, the ASI reports group together several unspecified input items under a single head, classified as "others;" as a result, the origin of these inputs cannot be allocated to any single industry. The percentage of these unclassified heads relative to the total value of material input of any industry varies from 5 percent to 33 percent of the total. In order to disaggregate them, a 10 percent sample is taken of the actual establishment returns representing all the individual industries (approximately 8,500 schedules). The principle of selection for this purpose was decided in consulation with the CSO, primarily on the basis of the following considerations:

(i) Details of the input and output data reported

(ii) location (to give appropriate geographical representation to the sample)

(iii) size (to take note of the scale of production)

(iv) product mix (to select only those

establishments whose principal product is identified
with the main product of the industry sector to which
they belong).

The commodity contents of the unclassified heads
are estimated from input contents in the corresponding
individual establishment returns. Thus, the percentage
relation of a commodity input to the total inputs,
or outputs, in a sample establishment is assumed to
hold good for the industry as a whole.

However, this method of disaggregation will
create problems (i) when the percentage composition
of a commodity to total output will vary widely from
establishment to establishment within the same industry sample and (ii) when the aggregate of the
individual commodity estimates will not match with
the total value given under the the head "unclassified
others" in the report.

The first problem can be solved by taking the
average of the percentage composition obtained from
different establishment returns, and the second by
writing up or writing down the individual estimates
of commodity inputs combined under the head "others"
in the report. This is done so that the total of the
estimated value of component inputs equals the reported
value of the unclassified head, "others."

The individual establishment report includes
another heading, "consumer stores," which does not
comprise more than 10 percent of the total value of
input in any single case. The constituents of these
composite heads are regarded as identical with the
rest of inputs in the schedule, and are accordingly
disaggregated.

Subsequently, the input structure of the detailed
industrial classification as given in the ASI is
aggregated into an industrial classification of 60
manufacturing sectors, adopted by the Inter-industry
Group, and into 29 abridged sectors which were ultimately used for projection purposes in the official
Draft Fourth Plan (see Table 11.2).

Medium-Scale Sector

The medium-scale sector comprises factories
employing 10 to 49 men with power and 20 to 99 men
without power. Data regarding this sector are available in the sample part of the ASI report. This survey was conducted on a "three-digit basis-of-industry
classification" and, therefore, was cruder in detail
than the data available for the large-scale sector.
To enable comparison with the large-scale sector and
to build up the input structure of the medium-scale
sector so as to match it with the inter-industry
classification, it is assumed that the structure of
an individual industry in the large-scale sector
shown against a three-digit classification will hold
good for the medium-scale sector, from the point of
view of their inputs.

The volume of stocks of finished products in the
medium-scale sector is estimated on the assumption
that the stock/output ratio is the same as in the
large-scale sector.

The ASI report gives no depreciation figures,
so these have been estimated for the medium-scale
sector by assuming that the relations between the
values of fixed capital and depreciation in the large-
scale industry sector in 1959 will also hold good
for the medium-scale sector. Accordingly, a flow
matrix for the medium-scale sector, with input
structure at purchasers' price, is computed for the
60 x 60-order matrix.

Small-Scale Sector

Small-scale industries are defined as those
smaller than registered factories, i.e., those employing less than ten persons with power or less than
twenty persons without power. They are normally
referred to as household enterprises. The ASI report
does not cover them, and the most recent data on this
sector come from the fourteenth round of the National

TABLE 11.2

Abridged 29-Sector Classifications
of Industry*

1.	Food grains	Paddy (1) Wheat (2)
2.	Cotton	Cotton (8)
3.	Jute	Jute and other fibres (9)
4.	Oil seeds	Groundnut (6) Other oil seeds (7)
5.	Plantations	Tea and coffee (including manufacturing) (14) Other plantation crops (rubber) (15)
6.	Other agriculture, etc.	Other cereals (3) Pulses (4) Sugar cane (5) Tobacco (10) Fruit and vegetables (11) Spices (12) Other agricultural products (13) Lac, gums, and resins (16) Other forest products (17) Animal husbandry, etc. (18) Fisheries (19)
7.	Coal	Coal (21)
8.	Iron ore	Iron ore mining (22)
9.	Other mining	Nonferrous metal mining (23) Crude petroleum and natural gas (24)

---

*Adopted in the Planning Commission's interindustry table. Numbers in brackets denote the sector number in the detailed classification of industry.

TABLE 11.2 (CONTINUED)

		Other mining (25)
10.	Iron and steel	Ferro alloys and alloy steels (26)
		Other iron and steel (27)
11.	Aluminum and other nonferrous metals	Aluminum and other nonferrous metals (28)
12.	Nonelectrical equipment	Heavy ferrous products (30)
		Light ferrous products (31)
		Nonelectrical equipment (32)
		Construction, mining equipment (33)
		Machine tools (34)
		Textile machinery (35)
		High precision products (51)
		Special industry machinery (36)
13.	Electrical equipment	Heavy electrical equipment (37)
		Other electrical equipment (38)
		Cables and wires (39)
		Other electrical equipment (40)
14.	Transport equipment	Automobile industries and trucks and buses (41 & 42)
		Tractors and bulldozers (43)
		Repair of motor vehicles (44)
		Scooters, etc. (45)
		Railway locomotives (47)
		Railway rooling stock (48)
		Shipbuilding, etc. (49)
		Other transport equipment (50)

TABLE 11.2 (CONTINUED)

15.	Chemicals and allied	Coke and gas making (53)
		Heavy inorganic (55)
		Heavy organic (56)
		Synthetic fibres (57)
		Dyestuffs (58)
		Drugs, etc. (59)
		Soap (60)
		All other chemicals (62)
16.	Petroleum and coke by-products	Petroleum and coke by-products (61)
17.	Fertilizers	Fertilizers (54)
18.	Cement	Cement (63)
19.	Glass, wood and non-metallic industries	Glass (64)
		Structual clay products (65)
		Other nonmetallic mineral products (66)
		Wood (67)
20.	Food, beverages, and tobacco	Food-grain processing (68)
		Sugar manufacture (69)
		Beverages (70)
		Tobacco (71)
		Oil and fats (72)
		Preservation and canning of fruits (73)
		Other food products (74)
21.	Textiles	Cotton spinning, processing (75)
		Cotton spinning and weaving (76-77)
		Other textile spinning (80)
		Manufacture of textiles n.e.s.
22.	Jute and coir	Jute processing (78)
		Jute and other coarse fibres (79)
		Spinning and weaving (80)
		Coir manufacture (81)
23.	Rubber and leather	Rubber tubes, tires, etc. (83)

TABLE 11.2 (CONTINUED)

		Preparation of hide and skin, etc. (84)
		Leather products (85)
24.	Paper and paper products	Pulp paper and paper products (86)
		Printing and publishing (87)
25.	Generation and transmission of thermo electric power irrigation and hydroelectric	mission of thermo-electric power (88)
		Irrigation and hydroelectric (89)
26.	Other industries	Other industries (90)
27.	Railway transport	Railway transport (91)
28.	Other transport	Other transport (92)
29.	Trade margin and indirect taxation	Trade and Indirect taxation (93)

ABRIDGED 22-SECTOR CLASSIFICATIONS*

22-Sector Classifications		Corresponding 29-Sector Classifications
1.	Cement	Sector (18)
2.	Glass, wood, nonmetallic	(19)
3.	Rubber and leather	(23)
4.	Paper and paper products	(24)
5.	Food, beverages, and tobacco	(20)
6.	Textiles	(21)
7.	Jute and coir	(22)
8.	Cotton	(2)
9.	Food grains	(1)
10.	Jute	(3)
11.	Oil seeds	(4)
12.	Plantations	(5)
13.	Fertilizer	(17)
14.	Other agriculture, including Fisheries, forestry and animal husbandry	(6)
15.	Iron ore	(8)
16.	Transport equipment and	

181

TABLE 11.2 (CONTINUED)

14. Other agriculture, including
     Fisheries, forestry and
     animal husbandry   (6)
15. Iron ore   (8)
16. Transport equipment and
     allied equipments   (14)
17. Electrical equipment   (13)
18. Aluminum and nonferrous metals   (11)
19. Other mining   (7), (9)
20. Iron and steel   (10)
21. Nonelectrical equipment and
     fabricated ferrous and non-
     ferrous products   (12)
22. Chemicals, power, transport,   (15), (16)
     services, and miscellaneous   (25), (26)
     industries.   (27), (28)
                                          and (29).

Sample Survey (No. 68) for the period July 1958-June
1959. The present exercise covers January 1959-Decem-
ber 1959; the difference in time coverage, which we
have decided to overlook, is only six months.

     The ASI report published information on outputs,
inputs (fuel and material), repairs and maintenance,
and wages and salaries in sample households. By using
relevant sampling factors, the aggregate values of
outputs and inputs are calculated for the population
from the samples.

     The industry sector in this report is subdivided
into 15 broad groups. These are more or less comparable with the abridged industry classification used
in our 29 x 29 matrix. The small-scale sector cannot,
therefore, be further subdivided into a more detailed
classification.

     The input estimates in the report are available
in broad groups, such as raw materials, fuel and
lubricant, and small machinery. The detailed input
structure is built under these global figures by

using the norms from the ISI 1955-6 table. As technological changes are slow in the household sector,
the use of norms from a past flow matrix can be reasonably justified.

There is a large proportion of self-employed
labor in the small-scale sector. This is converted
into its wage component by using the number of "self-
employeds" and their earning rates, as obtained from
the same report.

In 1959, the contribution of the small-scale
sector to total manufacturing was nearly 26 percent,
while that of the medium-scale sector was only 5 percent. Total gross output in the manufacturing sector,
and the corresponding contribution of the small-scale
sector in 1959 are given in Table 11.3.

The flow matrices of the 17 abridged sectors for
large, medium-scale, and small-scale industries are
superimposed on one another in order to produce the
flow matrix for 1959 for the whole of the manufacturing
sector. At this stage the matrix is derived at purchaser's price.

In the inter-industry classification adopted by
the ISA, there are five sectors in mining. In the
29 x 29 matrix they are reduced to three. In our
attempt to build up an abridged matrix in connection
with our work with the United Nations Coal Transport
Team, the mining sector was further reduced to two
major groups - "coal" and "other mining."* Later on,
it was realized that for the purpose of export study,
and also for a study of transport problems, it was
necessary to deal with iron ore separately.

The three-sector matrix for mining is computed
primarily from the data obtained in the "Indian Minerals Year Book", published by the Indian Bureau

---

*I was in the team in my capacity as a member
of the research staff of the Indian Planning Commission.

TABLE 11.3

OUTPUT OF TOTAL MANUFACTURING AND SMALL-
SCALE SECTORS, 1959 (Rs. million)

Industry Sector	Manufactures		Percent of Small-scale to Aggregate Manufacturing
	Aggregate	Small-Scale	
Iron and Steel	2,366	-	-
Aluminum and other nonferrous	186	-	-
Nonelectrical equipment	3,189	994	31.2
Electrical equipment	1,018	-	-
Transport equipment and allied industries	2,379	126	5.3
Chemicals	2,120	195	9.2
Petroleum and by-products	720	-	-
Fertilizer	256	-	-
Cement	444	-	-
Glass, wood, and non-metallic mineral products	1,889	976	51.7
Food, beverages, tobacco	14,512	6,374	43.9
Textiles	8,526	1,570	18.4
Jute and coir	1,617	158	9.8
Rubber and leather	1,536	526	34.2
Paper and paper products	1,303	7	0.5
Electricity generation and transmission	1,246	46	3.7
Other industries	1,007	473	47.0
	44,314	11,445	25.8

of Mines.   Besides this the "Monthly Coal Bulletin,"
issued by the Chief Inspector of Mines, was also consulted.

   To reach the input structure for coal and other
mining, the norms from the ISI inter-industry table
for 1955/6 were consulted and compared. The rows of
the mining sector are primarily formulated from the
input structure of the manufacturing sector, because
in the case of mining, the manufacturing sector will
be the sole consumer and the likely level of self-
absorption in this sector tends to be very low. Later
on, the above flows are converted into producer's
price by making the estimates net of trade and transport margins.

   Five sectors are allocated to transport in
the detailed industry classification; in the abridged
industry classification, they are reduced to two:
rail transport and other transport. It should be
noted at this point that the 29 x 29 matrix in our
exercise does not include shipping and air transport.
As a result, the output estimates derived from the
above matrix are under estimated. But in percentage
terms, the difference is found to be insignificant.

   The column and row for railway transport are
computed from the report of the Railway Board, Volume
II (Statistics) published annually by the Ministry
of Railways, Government of India. Table 29 of the
report shows the principal commodities carried by
government railways and the earnings therefrom in
1958/9 and 1959/60. In order to get the figures for
the calendar year 1959, an arithmetical mean is computed from the average of the data pertaining to the
two financial years. The earnings of government railways derived from the movement of goods are spread
over, between different sectors, as the "transport"
component in the respective sectors, by the pattern
of consumption of those commodities by the different
sectors. That part of transport earning derived from
the trans-shipment of a commodity from its place of
origin to the port is placed under the export vector
in the matrix, and against the row vector for rail
transport. The earnings from passenger transport are

placed under the final-demand vector of the matrix
and are allocated to the specific type of final demand
by methods that will be discussed in detail in subsequent paragraphs. The column of the rail-transport
sector has two major components, consumption of fuel
and consumption of other materials. The fuel-con-
sumption data are derived from Table 27 of the Railways Board report, and are available in great detail.
The consumption of other materials is computed from
Table 38, "Statement of Value of Stores purchased by
the Government Railways." Consumption or purchases
of materials by the railway workshops have been removed from this table, since these consumptions are
to be regarded as capital items, and do not strictly
fall under current inputs.

The estimates of wages and salaries are computed
from Statement 40 of the same report. Care is taken
to exclude workers employed in different railway
workshops or in different capital formation projects.

The "other transport" sector includes primarily
mechanized road transport (both in the public and private sectors) and bullock cart transport. For mechanized transport, reliable data on its input structure
is available in the report of the Public Transport
Undertakings; norms derived from this report are used
with the necessary adjustments for the private-sector
undertakings. Also, specific data and information
obtained from the Transport Division of the Planning
Commission, from the Transport Committee and from the
Research Cell of the Transport Ministry are taken into
consideration in the computation of the rows and columns of this sector. But the computation of the row
vector for the "other transport" sector raises some
difficulties. The estimates of total earnings for
"other transport" are taken from the CSO publication,
"Basic Statistics relating to Indian Economy." The
row of this sector is computed primarily from the norms
of the ISI table for 1955/6. (See Table 11.4 in pocket
at back of book). No data on the absorption pattern
of "other transport" services by detailed activity are
otherwise available, except for some nominal information regarding a few stray sectors that can be used
to cross-check in specific cases. The earnings from

passenger traffic are also calculated on the basis
of data obtained from the Transport Division of the
Planning Commission and are utilized in building the
row vector of the matrix against the final-demand
quadrant of the table.

Any estimate of the input structure for agriculture in India would be extremely difficult, especially one that attempts to disaggregate it into as
many as six subsectors. The estimates of output, however, are comparatively reliable and are derived from
information in the publications of the Ministry of
Agriculture and the CSO. The information relating
to the sum total use of inorganic fertilizer is also
reliable, although less so in its allocation between
different agricultrual sectors.

It is relatively easy to obtain the former from
production statistics, since the number of production
units is small and all of them are in the public sector. It is also possible to obtain information on
the distribution of fertilizer, but with less reliability. The input structure of different agricultural
crops in terms of other major inputs like organic
fertilizer, basic implements, minor irrigation, soil,
etc., is computed from the farm-management survey
which was conducted under the auspices of the Ministry
of Agriculture. These sample surveys are not random,
however, nor are they taken at the same period of
time, so that the estimates thus derived cannot be
considered very reliable. To give an example, the
estimate of total fertilizer consumed, calculated by
blowing up the norms derived from the farm-management
studies at one stage of our work, significantly
exceeded the supply of chemical fertilizer for 1959.
This happened even when allowance was made for any
contribution to/from inventory holdings.

The services and indirect taxes sector is built
up by a broad residual flow method. So far, all the
rows and columns of the inner matrix are built at the
purchasers' price, i.e., end-point price. Totals of
trade margins and transport payments made by any
industry or establishment are defined as the difference between the estimates of inputs valued at the

purchasers' price and <u>valued at</u> the ex-factory price.
The ex-factory price for the product of any industry
sector can be calculated from the quantum and value
figures given in the ASI report on the manufacturing
sector. The ex-factory prices for mining and for
agriculture are obtained from the "Mineral Year Book"
and from the estimates given by the National Income
Division of the CSO, respectively. The purchasers'
price for the same commodity in different sectors
will differ, depending on the transport (largely
guided by location) and distributive elements of the
respective sectors. But for the purpose of the present
exercise, an average purchase price is computed for
every commodity.

It should be noted in this context that these
price data can in no way be regarded as exhaustive,
and alternative sources are tapped in order to build
up the price information needed for the matrix.

The difference between the average purchasers'
price and the average producers' price gives the
total of transport and trade margins together with
the indirect taxation on intermediate inputs. These
estimates were kept in a single row in an earlier
table which was computed in connection with the U.N.
Coal Transport Team's investigations. In the present
exercise, the transport elements, calculated independently from other sources, are deducted from the
above estimates in order to build up the row for trade
and indirect taxation separately in the inner matrix
of the table.

Finally, the output of the <u>trade and services</u>
sector is calculated, not directly from any independent source, but indirectly, by aggregating the
absorption of trade and services as inputs in all
the sectors of the economy (i.e., a demand approach).
This is the single exception in the whole exercise,
where output is not estimated by the supply approach.

As has been explained, sectors such as agriculture
and manufacturing are initially presented at purchasers' price. But when the sectors on trade and
services and indirect taxation are added (the method of

computation has already been explained), it is
necessary to reduce the other sectors of the matrix
to producers' price. This avoids doublecounting of
the values of trade and services and indirect
taxation in the intermediate sector. Thus, all the
elements in the matrix are written by the ratio of
producers' to purchasers' price in the respective
sectors (in certain sectors, such as mining, the
figures were originally at ex-factory price, and
no adjustments are therefore needed).

SPECIAL CASES

In some manufacturing industries, electricity is
generated within the factory for internal consumption,
while a good deal of electricity is wasted on trans-
mission. The ASI report does not contain such information, so to make the necessary adjustments, the
report of the energy study team of the World Bank was
consulted.[1]

In the ASI report, it was found that petroleum
refineries were not properly represented. Information
in this sector was therefore supplemented from the
Indian Petroleum Handbook.[2]

FINAL-DEMAND VECTOR

The final-demand vector consists of (i) public
consumption, (ii) private consumption, (iii) capital
formation, (iv) exports, and (v) imports. The public-
consumption vector is estimated from the report of
the Directorate of Supply and Disposals, and the CSO
White Paper entitled The National Income and Expenditure.[3] The defense-expenditure estimates are highly
approximative.

The estimates of the private-consumption vector
are calculated by the residual flow method and are
valued at ex-factory prices. Hence, the derived
private-consumption vector is at ex-factory or producers' prices. The estimates for trade and services
together with indirect taxation are computed by

aggregating in every column the trade and transport
margin on each element of the consumption vector (by
calculating the retail-trade margin for the respective
market). At this point, it should be noted that our
29 x 29 abridged matrix does not include professional
services, banking, insurance, and catering services
in the list of activity sectors presented in the
matrix. The paucity of data for these sectors does
not permit the building of the input structure in the
present matrix with sufficient reliability. Therefore, it was decided to merge the inputs of these
sectors into the estimates of the private-consumption
vector. The value-added components of the above sectors are computed from the CSO National Income Statistics.

Capital formation in the economy is divided into
two major groups: (i) plant and machinery, and (ii)
construction. The pure machinery component is calculated by the industry of origin (i.e., sector-wise
from supply considerations) by the residual flow
method.

The treatment of the construction sector is somewhat unorthodox in this exercise. Lack of data made
it difficult to compute separately the input structure
for construction. Therefore, construction activity
is divided into two broad components in the present
matrix, namely, the absorption of building materials,
including iron and steel and the labor component.
Estimates of the former are made by the same residual
flow method (detailed commodity-wise) whereas the
estimate of the labor component is derived from the
CSO capital-formation estimates.

Data on exports and imports (at f.o.b. and c.i.f.
prices) are available in the Monthly Statistics of
the Foreign Trade of India. This commodity-wise
data is aggregated first into the detailed industrial
classification, and subsequently into the 29 broad
subgroups for the abridged matrix. The c.i.f. prices
for imports are identified with the ex-factory prices
used in this exercise. F.o.b. prices for exports
are converted into ex-factory prices by subtracting
from the value of exports at f.o.b. prices the cost

of transport from the source to the port and the
trade margin.

The total import bill is subdivided into three
broad categories: intermediate imports, capital-
goods imports, and all other imports. The intermediate
imports are further subdivided into competing part
and noncompeting part. As we already explained, the
concept of noncompetitiveness is given a time dimension. For the purpose of this exercise, a period of
ten years is taken as the time horizon. Accordingly,
those commodity items of total intermediate imports
that are not likely to be substituted in their use
nor likely to be significantly supplemented in their
supply from domestic sources, even ten years hence,
are located and separated. In the second stage, an
input matrix, in which the point of destination of
the intermediate imports within the country is
located, is built in a rough-and-ready manner. In
the third stage, a certain degree of substitution is
assumed over the time horizon, and the absorption of
these imported elements in different industries is
accordingly reduced. In the fourth stage, the sums
of the noncompeting imports for each industry, in columns, are placed below the matrix, signifying the total
amount of noncompetitive imports in each industry.
The estimates of other imports in this exercise are
computed by deducting capital-goods imports (which
in this exercise are exclusively confined to machinery and equipment) and noncompetitive intermediate
imports from total imports. The heading "other
imports" thus consists of all consumption imports
together with all types of competitive intermediate
imports. The degree of substitution assumed in the
case of intermediate imports in this matrix equals
approximately 27 percent of the 1959 level.

NON-WAGE INCOME

The estimates of non-wage income are computed on
a residual basis. This is expressed as the difference between the total gross output at ex-factory
prices and the total expenditure on material services
and labor, for each sector. As the inner matrix does

not provide any row for the sectors, professional
services and banking and insurance, the values of material and service inputs in each industry are reduced
accordingly, and the figures on non-wage income are
inflated. Further, in certain sectors like agriculture and small-scale industry, where a large number
of people are self-employed estimates on wages and
salaries are undervalued, and accordingly the non-
wage income again suffers from corresponding over-
estimation. Conceptually, non-wage income refers to
the payments made to such factors as land, capital,
and organization. In the present estimates, non-
wage income is regarded gross of depreciation. The
concept of depreciation in this matrix is not very
consistent. For the agricultural sector, the economic
concept is used, whereas for the manufacturing sector
an accounting concept is used.* For the trade and
"other transports" sectors, depreciation figures are
impossible due to the paucity of data.

The row on wages and salaries in the present
matrix includes money payments, together with the value
of other facilities offered to employees. In other
words, it refers to the money value of the real wages
of employees.

A MEASUREMENT OF STRUCTURAL CHANGES

In this section, an attempt is made to assess
the degree of stability of the input coefficients
derived from the current flow matrix. Three major
factors can affect the stability of these coefficients:

(1). Changes in relative prices

(2). Changes in technology (defined as changes
in the material-input components of outputs)

_____

*The economic concept is derived from the farm-
management norms collected by the Indian Ministry of
Agriculture.

   3. Changes in the composition of the intrasec-
toral outputs or inputs (i.e., product mix or input
mix)

   With regard to any changes due to a variation
in the price relatives, the findings of Chapter 10
convince one that the scope for such a possible
change in India is not very great. As for technological changes, the popular contention is that their
effect is more conspicuous in the use of labor and
capital than of material inputs. As for the third
type of charge, an attempt is made to arrange sectors
(within the limitations of data) in such a way as to
make them as homogeneous as possible, either from
the point of view of inputs or outputs.

   In the present model, the base period coefficient
matrix is used for the purposes of projection. It
contains no significant adjustments for any likely
changes in these coefficients due to a change in
price relatives. However, with a few adjustments
where the directional changes due to technical progress are too obvious (as, for example, the switchover
from coal to electricity or oil), it is interesting to
compare the input coefficients of 1955/6 and 1959, as
obtained from the two respective matrices, to discover
whether the result would lend support to the above
approach.

   Comparisons were, however, difficult, first
because the former table had a 36-sector classification, whereas the latter had a 29-sector classification, and second, because the former had the intermediate input coefficients, gross of the imported
elements while the latter had the same coefficients
net of the imported elements of noncompeting type.

   For the sake of compatibility, therefore, it
was decided to aggregate both the tables into a
14-sector classification, as follows:

   1. Cement

   2. Glass and wood

3. Leather and rubber

4. Paper and paper products

5. Food, beverages and tobacco

6. Cotton and other textiles

7. Jute and coir

8. Plantations

9. Other agriculture

10. Nonferrous metals

11. Other mining

12. Iron and steel

13. Engineering, and

14. Power, transport, trade, chemicals, and miscellaneous.

The 1959 inter-industry matrix was converted into a "gross of import" concept.

The changes in the input coefficients of the two years were compared in two different ways:

(a) $(a_{ij})^C = \dfrac{(aij)^{59} - (aij)^{55}}{\dfrac{(aij)^{59} + (aij)^{55}}{2}}$ (59 referred to 1959) (55 referred to 1955/6)

when aij referred to input coefficients of jth sector drawn from ith industry.
(b) By comparing the gross output for both years, computed on the assumption of 1959 final-demand vector holding good for 1955/6 and 1959 and using the 1955/6 and 1959 coefficients as parameters alternately.

GRAPH 11.1

Frequency distribution of the
changes in the sectoral input
coefficients of the Indian
economy between 1955/56 and 1959

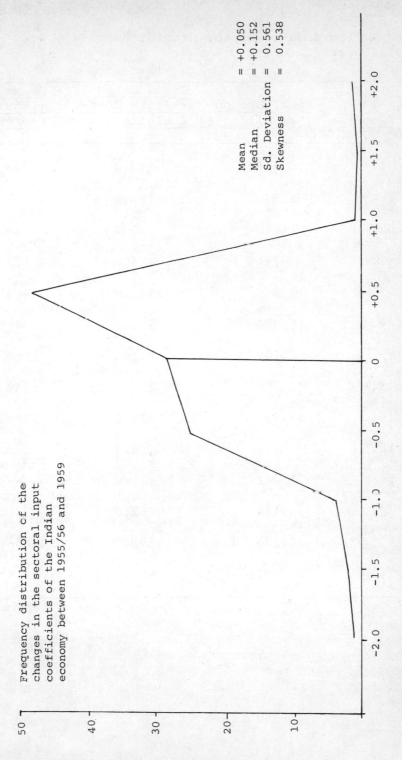

Mean   = +0.050
Median   = +0.152
Sd. Deviation = 0.561
Skewness   = 0.538

Source: Present model.

The results of the second exercise are as follows:

Sectors	Final Demand (Rs. million)	Gross Output (1955/6 Coefficients)	Gross output (1959 Coefficients)
1.	418	42.4	43.8
2.	1,376	189.0	191.1
3.	1,002	127.2	153.2
4.	744	124.0	132.5
5.	11,887	1521.8	1454.0
6.	6,900	951.3	845.3
7.	1,149	171.1	160.0
8.	1,504	204.3	240.4
9.	54,457	7811.1	8581.8
10.	-174	8.2	8.2
11.	282	111.6	85.3
12.	1,444	382.0	230.8
13.	4,524	591.5	656.0
14.	22,703	4068.1	3975.1

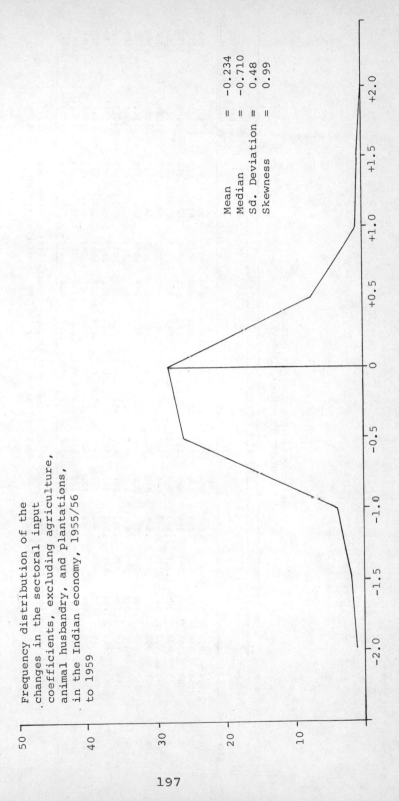

GRAPH 11.2

Frequency distribution of the
changes in the sectoral input
coefficients, excluding agriculture,
animal husbandry, and plantations,
in the Indian economy, 1955/56
to 1959

Mean   = -0.234
Median   = -0.710
Sd. Deviation = 0.48
Skewness   = 0.99

TABLE 11.5

INPUT/OUTPUT MATRIX AND GROSS OUTPUTS
WITH "MIXED" TECHNOLOGY, 1955-59

Sectors producing	Sectors Absorbing*														Final demand net of imports (Rs. Million)	Gross output (Rs. Million)
	1	2	3	4	5	6	7	8	9	10	11	12	13	14		
1	1.008	.010	0	0	0	0	.001	0	0	0	0	0	0	0	418	433
2	.024	1.056	.007	.012	.009	.006	.003	.003	.003	.004	.008	.005	.012	.006	1376	2416
3	.004	.004	1.105	.004	.002	.005	.004	.001	0	.003	.001	.005	.012	.010	1002	1470
4	.005	.003	.005	1.188	.003	.012	.001	.002	0	.003	.001	.005	.013	.008	749	1265
5	.003	.003	.010	.010	1.111	.004	.007	.004	.012	.002	.001	.002	.003	.007	11887	17096
6	.001	.002	.031	.040	.001	1.215	.003	0	0	.001	0	.001	.003	.003	6900	8546
7	.210	.006	.019	.004	.005	.010	1.229	.002	0	.003	.009	.004	.003	.004	1144	1773
8	0	0	.044	0	0	0	0	1.000	0	0	0	.001	.003	.004	1504	1563
9	.098	.119	.149	.121	.412	.336	.506	.052	1.201	.023	.010	.025	.052	.052	54457	75173
10	.001	.002	.001	.008	.004	.001	.001	.001	0	1.211	.001	.022	.027	.003	174	79
11	.032	.065	.004	.008	.008	.003	.001	.028	0	.228	1.048	.067	.023	.005	282	838
12	.001	.005	.006	.013	.002	.002	.002	.001	.004	.010	.003	1.149	.114	.003	1494	2286
13	.014	.010	.025	.013	.021	.020	.025	.003	0	.036	.034	.236	1.158	.023	4504	6284
14	.414	.281	.302	.305	.241	.283	.197	.107	.039	.394	.128	.472	.357	1.152	22703	31875

*Sectors defined in the text; Input + output (1955/6 technology) = 33.7; input + output (1959 technology) = 35.3
Input + output (1955 Agricultural technology and 1959 industrial technology) = 29.2

The first is a more rigorous test than the second, because in the second case we cannot compare the input coefficients for each type and each sector separately. But taking into consideration the source, the coverage, and the methods of computation of the two matrices which are so widely different, one would be reluctant to adhere to a very rigorous test for comparing the two sets of coefficients.

The changes in the coefficients, calculated according to the first formula, are arranged by proper weighting in the form of a frequency distribution. (The weights are equal to the average of the first and second years' value of the input items corresponding to the particular index (aij).) The skewness of the distribution gives an indication as to the direction of the changes, and the mean value and standard deviation gives an indication as to the extent of dispersion of the changes. With a low standard deviation and a near-normal distribution, the changes observed would be assumed to be very low, and random on the average.

The comparisons between the input coefficients of the two years according to this method gives a negatively skewed distribution (of the difference in the percentage input component) between the two years (see Graph 1). As is evident from the diagram, the distribution of changes in coefficient is highly negatively skewed (-.536), and the mean of the changes is 5 percent in favor of higher material input content, with the standard deviation of .56.

As is obvious from the following table, the percentage differences in the aggregate predicted gross outputs are very low, although there are a few specific sectors where the differences are rather high. As has already been discussed, with observations at only two points of time, any rigorous statistical-significance test would not be possible. However, it is interesting to note that whichever method one adopts, (a) or (b), one arrives at more or less similar conclusions. To give an example, if one associates technical progress with the economization of material inputs, then both results would suggest that in the

aggregate, the Indian economy had not achieved any
technical progress defined in the above way. A result
of this nature would be hard to accept, and it is
indeed contrary to any popular view.

But if one separates the sectors of agriculture,
fisheries, forestry, and plantations from the rest
of the economy, then, according to both methods,
substantial technical progress has been achieved in
the rest of the economy (which would be in conformity
with popular expectation). Graph 11.2 gives the frequency distribution of "changes of input coefficients"
in the economy, excluding agriculture, plantations,
and fisheries, computed by the first method. The
distribution is in this case positively skewed. The
mean is -.235 and the standard deviation + 48. The
skewness is +.099.

A similar result is obtained when the gross output requirements are computed against the 1959 final-
demand vector, assuming a mixed technology, i.e.,
agriculture having 1955/6 coefficients while industry
has the 1959 input coefficients (see Table 11.5).

In the aggregate the input-output ratio comes to
33.7 percent with 1955/6 technology, 35.3 percent with
1959 technology, and 29.2 percent with the mixed technology.

This chapter has shown that input coefficients
in India changed over this period, but not too drasti-
cally, at the level of disaggregation at which the
present model would work. Perhaps it should be reit-
erated that the data on which this inference is based
should be viewed with caution, and any plan or projection based on these inputs coefficients as parameters should be interpreted with proper care.

Therefore, in the ensuing model, independent
adjustments are always made when these coefficients
are used and the situation warrants such adjustments.

It is a pity that, due to the absence of a comparable capital-flow matrix in the planning literature
of India, an onalogous check on the capital coefficients used in this model is not possible.

NOTES

1. Report of the Energy Study Team of the World
Bank, submitted to the Indian Planning Commission.
1963 [unpublished].

2. Ministry of Petroleum and Chemicals, <u>Indian
Petroleum Handbook</u>, (Delhi: Government of India
Press).

In this chapter an attempt is made to test the
hypothesis that there is a block triangular structure
in the production complex of the Indian economy.
Table 11.4 presented the inter-industry current flow
matrix of India (1955/6) prepared by the Indian Statistical Institute, whereas Table 11.1 represented the
official table, again prepared in India, for 1959.

In parallel studies in other countries, any
coefficient which is less than $1/n$, n being the number
of sectors, is neglected in order to derive the basic
block structure of their economy. The present analysis tries to make this condition more rigorous by
extending the value of n to the number of sectors
present in the original table and not in the condensed
table (which has a 22-sector classification). The
rationale of the attempt with the condensed matrix
stems from the fact that any inference drawn from
this chapter is meant ultimately to have a bearing
on the computable 22-sector planning model developed
in Part II of this study.

To start with, all possible alternative permuta-
tions of the arrangements of the industry sectors
are attempted in order to bring out the best possible
block character of the whole matrix, shown in Table
12.1 and 12.2, referring to the years 1955/6 and 1959.
(Table 12.2 can be found in the pocket at the back of
the book.)

According to these two tables, the Indian economy seems to show three major blocks, block 1 referring to agriculture and that part of manufacturing which is based on the agricultural complex, block 2 to the metal complex, i.e., drawing their inputs primarily from the mining and metal industries, and block 3 to power, transport, services, and the chemical group of industries, often known as universal intermediates. The last block thus has a property of contributing (in the form of supply of inputs) to all the remaining sectors of the economy, whilst almost exclusively drawing its own inputs from within its own sector.

If one were to delve further, one would notice that for the year 1955/6, block 1 had self-consumption of material inputs as high as 79.7 percent consumption of inputs from the metal block of only 1.5 percent and the rest of consumption from the third block of industries, normally referred to as the infrastructure. Block 2 had self-consumption as high as 51 percent, consumption from the agricultural complex of 3.7 percent and from the universal block of nearly 46 percent. All the above transactions were calculated at current prices. If one were to make a similar study with respect to the table prepared by the Indian Planning Commission, one would notice that the first block again had self-consumption of 66.2 percent, consumption from the second block of 3.3 percent and from the third block of 31 percent. With regard to the metal-based industries, again self-consumption was very high (50 percent), whereas its dependence on block 1 was nearly 7 percent and on the rest approximately 44 percent.

Thus, a comparison of the structure of the economy over the two years, as revealed from the two tables, would suggest that the interdependence between the almost independent blocks has increased over time. Agriculture has become increasingly dependent on engineering sectors and sectors supplying chemicals and power. This change is a common experience in the process of any economic development; but should not read anything more into them than this, since the two tables are not strictly very comparable.

TABLE 12.1

TRIANGULATION OF THE CURRENT FLOW COEFFICIENT MATRIX, 1955/6

Industry	1	2	3	4	5	6	7	8	9	10	11	12	13	14	15
1. cement	1.1	0					1.1				0.1		0.1		0
2. other building material and glass	0.4	0.2	0.1	0.4	0.3	0.2	0.2	0.2	0.2	0.1	0	1.0	0.2	0.1	0.5
3. leather and rubber	0.5	0.1	5.0	0	0	0.1	0.1	0						0.4	0.4
4. paper and paper products	1.0	0.7	0.3	15.7	0.3	0.3	0	0.1	0.1		0.3	0	0.1	0.3	0.5
5. food		0	0.3	0.3	11.8	1	0.7	0.2	0.3	2.3				0	2.0
6. cotton and other textiles		0	6.8	1.0	0	25.2	2.2				0.1			0.1	0.2
7. jute and coir	9.3	0.3	1.9	0.2	0.7	0.6	12.0	0	0.1	0	0.1	1.0	0.5	0	0.3
8. agriculture		0.3	0	0	24.9	15.7	28.5	5.2		38.5					1.4
9. plantation			6.2		3.4										
10. animal husbandry, etc.	0	6.8	8.3	3.8	13.8	1.7	0	17.0	3.6	0	0.2	0	0.4		4.3
11. nonferrous metals		0.1		0	0						23.3		9.6	8.4	0.1
12. other mining	8.1	3.1	0.3	0.8	0.4	0.5	2.1	1.1	2.6	0	10.0	3.0	6.3	0.6	1.2
13. iron and steel	0.9	0.6	0			0	0				8.3	0.3	21.4	20.0	0.4
14. engineering and metals	2.1	0.3	0.5	3.1	0.4	0.6	1.0	0.3	0.1	0.1	4.2	1.5	5.9	6.1	1.8
15. power, chemicals, transport and services (incl. docks)	34.1	22.0	32.9	39.0	15.8	21.2	26.8	2.2	8.9	3.3	33.8	42.1	30.3	25.2	15.3

Source: Indian Statistical Institute.

205

Another feature which results from these exercises, and which I feel is of major economic significance, is the dependence of block 2 on block 1,
much more than the dependence of block 1 on block 2.
The sectors that joined the two blocks are "other
agriculture," and glass, wood, and nonmetallic industries. But the second sector is, to a large extent,
a case of misspecification, because conceptually the
glass and nonmetallic industries should not have been
placed within the first block of industries but should
have been placed in the metal group of industries
(sacrificing, of course, the cause of triangulation
of the matrix).

It is well known that the block triangular
character of the structure of any economy has very
important developmental implications. In brief, all
industries which are placed above a specific one in
the given order of industry-arrangements in the matrix
are the principal consumers of the product of this
specific industry; whereas all industries below the
industry of reference are the principal suppliers of
inputs of the same industry. (We confine ourselves
in this respect only to the supply of materials in
a current flow sense.) The above ranking of industries according to their mutal interdependence would
give us a rough clue as to the scale of priorities
to be recommended in the context of development planning, especially when the economy would be regarded
as near-closed.

However, in the process of triangulation of the
matrix, it was necessary to neglect very small coefficients. It was interesting to investigate the degree
of error that may have been introduced in this process.
In order to calculate it, three alternative vectors
of gross output were computed with an unadjusted
matrix, a matrix adjusted in the form of a triangular
shape, but not ignoring the coefficients more than
$\left(\frac{1}{n}\right)$* lying <u>outside</u> the triangle, and a matrix assuming

---

*n = the number of sectors in the matrix.

a strict triangularity, all being estimated against
the final 1959 bill of goods.

When the vector of output in the second exercise
was compared with that of the first, an error of 4.7
percent was introduced in the aggregate. This seemed
at first sight very gratifying, but in specific sectors
the divergence was found to be significantly large.
In the third exercise, the aggregate percentage error
as against the first was as high as 12 percent; and
worst of all, in a few specific sectors, the targets
were completely off the mark. It is very interesting
to note that in an attempt to locate the error in
the estimates of the sectoral output measured as the
difference in the estimates between the original and
the triangular matrix for the year 1959, it was discovered that in 64 percent of all cases the error
was less than 15 percent, but in the rest it was
very large. The errors in the estimates for cement,
food, beverages, textiles, food grains, jute, oil
seeds, plantations, transport equipment, electrical
equipment, iron and steel, chemicals, and power were
within reasonable margins, whereas in such sectors
as nonelectrical equipment, aluminum, and fertilizers,
they were very large. This suggests that any programming attempt that deals with the economy in separate
subsectors (as recommended by Alan Manne in the Fourth
Input/Output Conference in Geneva) must be discouraged.[1]
In general, all the output targets in the above second
and third exercises suffered from a consistent significant downward bias. This is yet another reason
that lends support to the belief that any material-
balance approach (which has an implicit assumption
of more or less triangular intersectoral relations
and which was very popular with the Perspective Planning Division of the Indian Planning Commission)
must be supplemented by rigorous input/output exercises in the plan formulation.

Referring to Tsukuy and Simpson's article, it
is most interesting to note that the industrial
structure (as exhibited in the block character of
economic activities) of the five countries developed
by the authors exactly resembled that of India, with

a threefold "block"* composition of the economy,
notwithstanding all the differences in statistical
presentation and their stages of development.[2] I am
therefore inclined to agree with these authors that
there is most probably a fundamental structure of
production in almost all modern economic societies.

THE INTERDEPENDENCE OF THE INDIAN ECONOMY

    An attempt has been made to bring out the inter-
dependent nature of the Indian economy by developing
a block character of the production matrix. An alternative approach will now be suggested.[3] This will
take into account both the direct and indirect interdependence between the different activity sectors
and will assign values or weights to measure the
degree of interdependence in terms of first round,
second round, or subsequent rounds of inter-relatedness. To give an example, the first round inter-relations between agriculture and iron and steel might
be nil, but the second round of interdependence could
be traced via the equipment sector producing implements for agriculture.

    According to the above definition, total inter-
relatedness would be equal to diversification (i.e.,
first-round inter-relations) plus indirect inter-
relations derived from subsequent rounds.

The basic materials for studying the interdependence
between the different sectors of any economy will be
supplied by its inter-industry current flow transaction matrix, say of the Leontief type. The matrix
as such cannot exhibit total interdependence since
it presents only the interdependence of the first
degree (i.e., first-round, as already defined).

    To calculate the coefficient of interdependence,
it is necessary to calculate the different powers of

_____

*Although not completely independent.

the matrix. The formula for interdependence is given
by the reciprocal of the harmonic mean of the submatrix
B, provided all the elements of the original matrix
are non-negative; B matrix is defined as the order
matrix, each element representing the stage (referring
to the power of "A") where a positive value will
appear. If after n operations* some of the elements
still continue to be zero, then one can interpret
the order of the elements of the matrix as infinity.
Hence, the degree of inter-relatedness is equal to

$$\frac{1}{n.n} \sum_{i=1}^{n} \sum_{j=1}^{n} \left(\frac{1}{x}\right)^{ij}$$

where x is equal to the number of rounds after which
aij becomes positive for the first time, x varying
from 1 to infinity and n representing the order of
the matrix.

If the original matrix has all positive elements,
it suggests that the economy has the highest inter-
relatedness. On the other hand, if all the elements
in the matrix are zero it suggests that there is no
relationship between the different sectors. Hence,
it is obvious that the coefficient of inter-relatedness
will always lie between zero and +1. The extent of
the direct relationships and the indirect relationships existing between different sectors can be measured by dividing the above formula into two parts,
as follows:

$$\frac{1}{n.n} \sum_{i=1}^{n} \sum_{j=1}^{n} \left(\frac{1}{x}\right)_{ij} = \frac{1}{n.n} \sum \left(\frac{1}{x}\right)_{ij} + \frac{1}{n.n} \sum \left(\frac{1}{x}\right)_{ij}$$

when x=1   when x ≠ 1
i.e. 2 to n - 1,...∞

when the first component gives the degree of diversification and the second component the degree of inter-
relatedness.

This method of sectoral interdependence can be
computed for the economy as a whole and also for
each different sector. If one calculates the coefficient of inter-relatedness in rows, the extent to

_____

*n = order of the matrix.

which the particular industry is related with non-
zero activities to the other sectors of the economy
is explained. (See Table 12.3.)

The index of diversification for the year 1959
is calculated as .35 and indirect inter-relatedness
as .29, giving the total inter-relatedness as .64.
If one were to delve further, one would notice that
sectors such as chemicals, power, transport, and
services, together with other agriculture, including
forestry and animal husbandry, have the highest inter-
relatedness whereas sectors like transport equipment,

TABLE 12.3

INTER-RELATEDNESS OF THE INDIAN ECONOMY, 1959
(with a 22-sector classification)

(a)	Index of diversification = .35		
(b)	Index of indirect inter-relatedness = .29		
(c)	Index of inter-relatedness = .64		
Index of inter-relatedness in separate sectors:			
1	.50	12	.54
2	.77	13	.63
3	.70	14	.89
4	.70	15	.38
5	.68	16	.05
6	.58	17	.61
7	.79	18	.68
8	.51	19	.82
9	.51	20	.66
10	.48	21	.84
11	.42	22	1.00

iron ore, jute, cotton, and food grains have the
lowest economic inter-relatedness. A similar attempt
is made, with the inter-industry table of 1955/6
prepared by the Indian Statistical Institute, to
calculate the inter-relatedness of the Indian economy
in that year.   (See table 12.4.)

TABLE 12.4

INTER-RELATEDNESS OF THE INDIAN ECONOMY, 1955/56
(with a 15-sector classification)

(a)   Index of diversification = .61
(b)   Index of indirect inter-relatedness = .18
(c)   Index of inter-relatedness = .79
Index of inter-relatedness in separate sectors:

1	.50	9	.53
2	.97	10	.83
3	.73	11	.67
4	.85	12	.97
5	.80	13	.73
6	.73	14	1.00
7	.90	15	1.00
8	.73		

Note:

1. Cement
2. Other building materials
   and glass
3. Leather and rubber
4. Paper and paper
   products
5. Food, beverages, and
   tobacco
6. Cotton and other
   textiles
7. Jute and other fibres

8. Agriculture
9. Plantations
10. Animal husbandry
11. Nonferrous metals
12. Other mining
13. Iron and steel
14. Engineering and
    metals
15. Power, chemicals,
    transport, and
    services.

As is obvious from the table 12.2, industries
like power, chemicals, transport, services, and
engineering have the highest inter-relatedness similar
to the earlier findings, whereas industries like
cement, plantations, and nonferrous metals have the
lowest coefficient of interdependence.

In any attempt to compare the two coefficients
of inter-relatedness between the two years, one would
face difficulties, as the industry heads in the two
tables are not strictly comparable.

For the sake of better comparisons the current
flow matrices of the Indian economy for the above
two years are aggregated into 14 sectors, in order
to ensure a maximum possible comparability between
the two.

COMPARISONS OF THE "INTER-RELATEDNESS" OF THE
ECONOMY BETWEEN 1955/6 AND 1959

| Sectors | Coefficient of inter-relatedness | |
	1955/6[a]	1959[b]
1	.54	.54
2	.96	.86
3	.71	.75
4	.89	.79
5	.79	.71
6	.75	.75
7	.93	.89
8	.54	.58
9	1.00	.89
10	.68	.75
11	.96	.89
12	.79	.71
13	.96	.93
14	1.00	1.00

[a]Based on ISI table
[b]Based on PC table

The comparison between 1955/6 and 1959 reveals
that over the four-year period, the coefficient of
diversification fell, whereas the coefficient of
indirect inter-relatedness rose and the overall inter-
relatedness of the economy remained stable. The
differences in the coefficient of interdependence
within the agricultural complex, the metal-industry
complex, and the rest of the economy were then studied
separately; again, all the coefficients in both years
thus calculated are almost identical. These findings
should serve as a guide to planning. It is believed
in contemporary development literature that the progress in a sector can spread its maximum impact on
the economy provided the technological convergence
of the sector is very high. By technological convergence, some authors imply a sector having a very
high inter-related coefficient. In this context,
the tables show that such sectors as transport, power,
and chemicals have very high inter-related coefficients.
Indeed all development literature recommends the
development of these very sectors as an infrastructure
to any growth process.

Further, an attempt is made to compare the rank-
ings of the industries in the two years according to
their inter-related coefficients. The value of the
rank correlation is as high as 0.94, which again
suggests that whether one bases plan strategies on
the 1955/6 or on the 1959 table, one may expect the
same broad directions.

PRICE ASSUMPTIONS IN THE
INTER-INDUSTRY MODELS

The current flow coefficient matrix, to be used
in the present model for estimating the consistent
set of output targets for the terminal year of the
plan, conceptually needs revision at every period of
time to adjust for change in the price relatives and/
or change in product mix and/or change in technology.
The likely changes that could arise out of the problems of product mix are taken care of by assuming
that all the sectors represent approximately homogeneous activities or maintain an unchanged output

structure within themselves. To accommodate changes
due to price effect or technology effect, one should
ideally undertake the following matrix operations,
as R. Stone did in his computable planning model for
the United Kingdom.[4]

$$_{01}A = r \hat{p} _0A \hat{p}^{-1}s \qquad \text{when}$$

A represents the current flow transaction matrix, O
represents the base year, l represents the given year
(i.e., $_{01}$ A represents A matrix after price and technology corrections), p represents the price index in
the given year in relation to the base year expressed
in the form of a diagonal matrix, r represents technical change as affecting uniformly all the inputs
of a sector, and S represents technical change, again
uniformly affecting the same inputs in all the sectors.

    We shall start with the problem of price adjust-
ments. For India it is extremely difficult to build
up price indices for all the different sectors of the
matrix in a completely comparable form. The extent
of error likely to be introduced in the model if no
corresponding price adjustments are made must be
assessed.

    Price adjustments are not needed when price
relatives remain unchanged in all the sectors of the
economy; when the production matrix has a block
diagonal shape, and the price movements within each
block are more or less the same, although the inter-
block price movements may be significantly different;
or when the value added per unit of output remains
unchanged.*

    The first condition is very unrealistic and is
definitely not applicable in the case of India over
the period 1959 to 1965/6.**

_____

    *In this case the price vector will remain
unchanged, in the projected period.

    **1959 refers to the reference year of the
input/output table and 1965/6 the base year of the
model.

The third condition could reasonably be assumed
to be satisfied for projection in a model like the
present one (and unlike Stone's computable model),
where Leontief's fixed coefficient assumptions are
maintained even in the case of primary inputs. However, a few ad hoc adjustments are made in later
chapters, in specific sectors, to take care of obvious
technological changes. Above all, the need for the
second condition to be satisfied will arise because
of our usage of the 1959 coefficient matrix for the
year 1964/5 (as the base year of this model) and at
the same time because prices have changed significantly in the meantime.

It is necessary, therefore, to explore whether
the third condition is valid over this period in the
Indian economy.

By suitable rearrangement of the sector classifications (22 sectors) of the Indian economy for 1959,
a strong block character of the matrix was located
(excluding sector 22, which could be referred to as
"universal intermediates"). Thus, excluding sector
22, the economy could be divided into three compari-
tively independent activity blocks, the first representing cash crops and industries fed by cash crops
as inputs, the second representing food crops and
industries based on food crops, and the last representing industries based on mining. The details of
the industry heads are given in the inter-industry
matrix converted into a block structure in Table 12.5.
In Table 12.6 an attempt is made to bring out the
extent of the block independence of the four groups.
Cash crops and industries based on cash crops had a
high degree of self-consumption (82.9 percent).
Similarly, the food-crop industry had 92.1 percent
self-consumption, the mining industry 71.6 percent
and the service industries 91 percent. Once it was
proved that the Indian economy had a block diagonal
character over this period, it was possible to explore
by the analysis-of-variance approach whether the
price relatives over the sample period within each
of the blocks changed less, compared to their changes
between the blocks.

TABLE 12.5

INTER-INDUSTRY TABLE 1959 CONVERTED INTO A BLOCK STRUCTURE (4 blocks)

		3	4	6	7	8	10	2	5	9	11	12	13	14	1	15	16	17	18	19	20	21	22
Rubber and leather	3	9.3	0.1	0.2	0.2			0.1	0.1								1.8	0.3				0.1	0.8
Paper and paper products	4	0.2	15.7	0.7				0.1					5.0					1.8				1.0	0.6
Textiles	6	2.3	2.8	17.1	0.2			0.1										0.7					
Jute and Coir	7	0.1	0.2	0.6	8.7			0.2	0.3				1.2		17.0		0.1	0.4		0.8			0.3
Cotton	8	.		21.6	2.2																		
Jute	10				33.3		4.1																
Glass, wood	2	0.7	0.9	0.3	0.1			5.0	0.6						2.0	2.9	0.3	2.7		0.3		0.6	0.5
Food, beverages and tobacco	5	0.6	0.6		0.1				9.6				0.8	2.7				0.2					0.5
Food grains	9								11.0	4.5													
Oil seeds	11									6.2	13.0												
Plantation (a separate block)	12	4.0										34.1						0.7				0.2	
Fertilizer	13					0.2	0.5			9.3	0.5	0.4	30.8	0.4									
Other agriculture	14	9.0	6.8	0.8	1.0	9.1	6.9	8.4	12.3	13.8	10.0	2.2		14.5			6.8	0.7	0.5			0.1	3.3
Cement	1							0.9													2.1		
Iron ore	15																2.1				2.1		
Transport equipment	16																14.3		17.4				
Electric equipment	17				0.1												0.5	6.0	17.8				
Aluminum and nonferrous metals	18	0.1	0.5					0.1							1.8	12.9	2.1	3.9		3.5	1.2	2.4	0.2
Other mining	19	0.1	0.4	0.1				5.7	0.5				3.5				2.1	1.1	3.5	2.1	3.0	3.0	0.3
Iron and steel	20	0.3	0.1					0.3									7.5	5.0	0.5	2.1	11.3	11.6	31.0
Nonelectrical equipment and fabricated ferrous and nonferrous products	21	1.4	0.5	10.1	1.5			0.2							0.2	7.1	0.7	7.2	1.6	2.1	11.6	6.4	1.5
Chemicals, power, transport, services, and misc. industries	22	22.0	21.2	11.6	12.6	2.2	1.2	22.0	17.6	2.9	1.7	9.2	16.9	7.1	32.4	11.4	21.4	21.3	26.3	9.5	31.0	23.3	11.2

TABLE 12.6

"BLOCK" NATURE OF THE CURRENT FLOW INTER-INDUSTRY MATRIX, INDIA 1959
(current input flows: percent)

Sectors or Blocks	Transaction within the block, including labor and capital (percent)	Material only (percent)	Transaction outside the block (percent)	Transaction outside the block but excluding trade, transport, power, chemicals, etc. (percent)
I. Cash crops and industries based on cash crops	82.9	28.6	17.1	5.5
II. Food crops and industries based on foods crops	92.1	29.7	7.9	0.8
III. Mining and mining-based industries	71.6	22.5	28.4	4.4
IV. Service-based industries and universal inter-mediates	91.8	17.2	8.2	8.2

TABLE 12.7

PRICE MOVEMENTS WITHIN AND BETWEEN BLOCKS

Source of variation	1958	1959	1960	1961	1962	1963	1964
Mean sum of squares between blocks	1823.5	172.6	808.7	948.2	1084.2	989.1	6150.2
Mean sum of squares within blocks	92.6	176.7	229.3	322.0	401.5	789.0	905.6
F* ratio (calcu-lated) 4.37	19.68	0.98	3.53	2.94	2.70	1.25	6.79

*The value of F4.37 was tested at 5 percent level of significance (single-tailed) where subscripts refer to degrees of freedom.

Block I.   Cash crops and cash-crop-based industries.
Block II.   Food crops and food-crop-based industries.
Block III. Plantations.
Block IV.   Mining and mining-based industries.
Block V.   Power and chemicals.

For this purpose, 42 wholesale price indices
were used, spreading over 1957 to 1964; the sum of
squares between and within the blocks were then calculated. Relying on the calculations given in Table
12.7, and using the "F" test, it appeared that our
hypothesis was valid at the .05 level of significance
in all but two years. The limitation of this type
of statistical test is apparent when the price series
are few and unweighted. However, in the light of
the above findings, by making no price corrections
on the 1959 matrix to be used for the year 1964/5,
no significant error may have been introduced in the
estimates. As for other likely errors originating
from a change in the input coefficients consequent
on technological improvements, they have already
been discussed under the heading of structural changes.
Here again, I am convinced that the margin of error
in such cases is likely to be small.

NOTES

1. Allan S. Manne and Thomas E. Weisskopf,
Dynamic Multisectoral Model for India, 1967-75.
Memorandum No. 57, December, 1967.

2. David Simpson and J. Tsukuy, "The Fundamental
Structure of Input-Output Tables, an International
Comparison," Review of Economics and Statistics, Vol.
XLVII (1965).

3. Borrowed from Chiou-Shuang and Edward Ames,
"Economic Inter-relatedness," Review of Economic
Studies, 1965.

4. R. Stone, A Programme for Growth, Series 3.
(Published for the Dept. of Applied Economics, Cambridge, by Chapman and Hall, 1963).

13

COMPUTATION
OF FIXED
CAPITAL/CAPACITY
MATRIX

An attempt will now be made to compute a 22 x 22 matrix of fixed-capital coefficients at purchasers' and producers' prices for 1961. For this purpose, the sectors selected are similar to those used for the computation of current flow matrix for 1959.

The computation involves four major stages of calculation: calculation of the commodity component of fixed capital stock; the relation between capacities and the capital stock associated in any sector; the assumption of gestation period for investment; and the adjustments for underutilization of capital.

All these four stages are computed for each of the 22 sectors of the economy, comprising manu-facturing, agriculture, mining, and trade, transport, and distribution.

COMMODITY COMPONENTS OF NET
FIXED-CAPITAL FORMATION

The parameters in the manufacturing sector are estimated primarily from the ASI survey of India for 1960/1. It should be borne in mind at this stage that this survey covers only the large-scale or-ganized sector of manufacturing activities. Since 1959, the ASI survey has replaced both the Census of Manufacturing Industries and the Sample Survey of

Manufacturing Industries, which were conducted regularly on an annual basis. The coverage of the survey includes the entire factory sector, excluding only the sectors under the control of the Defence Ministry, oil-storage depots, and technical-training institutions. All factories employing 50 or more workers with the aid of power or 100 or more workers without the aid of power are included. The remaining factories, namely, those employing 10 to 40 workers with the aid of power or 20 to 99 workers without the aid of power, are covered on the basis of random samples.

Appropriate adjustments for the sector excluded from the above census (i.e., small-scale manufacturing) are made and are described in subsequent sections of this chapter.

The ASI presents the book value of capital stocks under four headings: construction, plant and machinery, transport equipment, and other assets, for every calendar year. It is universally recognized that the book values of capital assets carry very little economic meaning as inputs to production, because book-value estimates of different parts of capital stocks carry price valuations (and are depreciated accordingly) which are relevant to different periods of time within their life span. However, a difference between the book values of productive capital existing at the end of 1960 and 1961 would unequivocally represent the addition to capital stock (in an accounting sense) at current prices (to be more precise, also at purchasers' prices). In a more disaggregated form, as in this case, this incremental capital stock could then be recorded in the four broad commodity compositions derived at their 1961 prices. A further breakdown of the above four parts into 22-sector classification is carried out as follows:

Construction components are broken down into iron and steel, cement, building materials, wood, nonelectrical and electrical equipment, chemicals, labor components, etc. These are derived from the construction component given in Table 2.6 of "Estimates of Gross Capital Formation in India" 1948/49 to 1960/61 by CSO, and confined only to the construction part

relevant to the urban sector. The plant and machinery
component is divided into electrical equipments and
nonelectrical equipments. These are primarily guided
by the nature of activities (i.e., type of production)
under the 400-industry classifications, and by other
available specific engineering information.

Information on transport equipment is available
separately in the CSO report. The items under "other
fixed assets" are classified under sector 22.

There are some sectors where the above marginal
approach gives economically meaningless results.*
For example, in a few cases, the incremental fixed-
capital stocks are seen to be associated with a
corresponding negative increase in some of its commodity components. In these rather odd cases, the
average relations (of commodity components) are taken
in the final estimates.

Sector 22 warrants a special treatment. It is
divided into two parts: Part I, comprising material
components such as chemicals, other manufacturing,
and electric power generation; and Part II, comprising
service components such as trade, transport, and other
professional services. The treatment of Part I is
similar to that described above, whereas Part II is
treated differently, as will be explained later.

All the above estimates cover only the factory
sector. An attempt is made in subsequent discussions
to extend the coverage by using the proportion of the
weightage of the organized sector given in the 1959
census together with that given in the sample part
of the ASI report, to the weightage of the household
establishments covered in the SSMI reports (for details, see Chapter 11), and by allowing for any
differential rates of growth of the organized and
unorganized sectors between 1959 and 1961. This

_____

*Not exactly meaningless, as it might suggest
"substitution" effect.

approach implicitly assumes that the commodity component of incremental capital stock will be alike in
both the large-scale and small-scale sectors. This
might not be regarded as a very realistic assumption,
but any aspirations toward further sophistication
with the existing data seem a waste of effort.

     The estimates of net investment (in the form
of physical capital) in the agricultural sector for
1961 are conducted in three stages: by recording
the "actuals" of the public-investment outlay in
agriculture for 1961/2 from the Third Plan Mid-Term
Appraisal;[1] by estimating private-sector investment
in agriculture in 1961/2 (assuming the proportion
of private-sector investment in agriculture in 1961/2
to have remained the same as in the five-year total);
and by assuming that the labor component (as percentage) of total agriculture investment will be the
same as the labor component of rural constructions
for the whole economy, for the year 1961/2. Finally,
the above estimates are written down roughly to
arrive at the investment figures for 1961 in a rough-
and-ready manner.

     The construction component of total net in-
vestment in the agricultural sector is derived by
substracting the estimates of total agricultural
machinery produced and imported in India in the same
year from the aggregate net investment estimates in
agriculture, excluding labor component (i.e., a
residual approach). The estimates of domestically-
produced agricultural machinery plus imports are
derived from a Planning Commission Papers, "Notes
on Perspectives of Development, India, 1960/1 to
1971/6," (1964). All agricultural machinery is
regarded as belonging to the nonelectrical-machinery
group in the present classification.

     The above residue is branded as the pure con-
struction element of fixed investment and is
disaggregated into commodity components, borrowing
the national coefficients for construction vector
derived from CSO estimates.

     Lastly, the commodity compositions of agricultural

net investment (fixed) in all its subgroups, i.e.,
crop-wise, are regarded as the same; this assumption
is a rather heroic one, but is unavoidable because
of paucity of data.

In the mining sector, the total value of incremental fixed-capital stock is derived indirectly.
The net output figures (value added) for the year
1960/1 for this sector, divided into five groups,
are derived from Reddaway's estimates.[2] The capital/
gross output ratios for these sectors are derived
from Alan Manne's estimates and are combined with
Reddaway's estimates of sectoral income as weights
to derive the aggregate capital/output ratio
(extension) for the mining sector as a whole.[3]

The incremental income between the years 1961/2
and 1962/3 is derived from the Indian Government
publication "National Income and Expenditure." The
incremental gross-output estimates have been derived
from the income figures by assuming the same gross/net
output ratios in the year 1962/3 as were prevalent
in 1959. The incremental gross-output estimate
multiplied by the incremental capital/output ratio
gives us the requirement of the total fixed capital
(extension) in the mining sector for 1961, (assuming
a gestation lag of more than one and a half years).

The commodity components of the total fixed
capital are calculated by borrowing Alan Manne's
norms on "construction" and "machinery."[4] The construction part of this sector is further subdivided
into the present 22-sector classification. This is
done by assuming the commodity and labor component
of this sector to be similar to that of the national
aggregate.

Trade, transport and distribution are treated
on a residual flow basis in the form of equating
total demand and total supply of individual capital
goods prevalent in 1961, adjusted for replacement
investments.

The commodity components of aggregate fixed
capital, including replacement investment at

purchasers' price, are broken down into two broad categories constituting construction and machinery. These are presented for 1960/1 in the CSO report, "Estimates of Capital Formation in India for 1948/9 to 1960/1."

The total construction activity is then converted into a net concept by excluding the replacement investment. For this it is assumed that the ratio of replacement to total gross fixed investment in 1960/1 given in the CSO estimates will hold good for the construction part. The construction element of net fixed-capital formation is further netted from labor components by assuming the labor component of gross construction activity to be applicable for the "net" concept.

The commodity component of construction is derived by adopting the CSO's pattern of commodity elements of total construction in the year 1960/1. The CSO estimates are derived by a residual flow method, i.e., domestic production of these commodities, net of any intermediate consumption, augmented by any import, reduced by any export, and laslty adjusted for stock changes. Evidently, the exercise will give the construction vector at purchasers' price for the year 1960/1.

Similarly, total supply of machines is estimated by the Central Statistical Organisation by residual flow method for the year 1960/1.

A disaggregation of the total machinery estimates between electrical equipment, nonelectrical equipment, and transport equipment is computed as follows:

1. Estimates of total production (domestic) of the three types of equipment

2. Total imports less exports of these items

3. Percentage contribution of the total supply of these items to intermediate and final consumption, assuming the corresponding coefficients derived from the 1959 table are valid for the year 1960/1

4.   Adjustments to stock positions

1 + 2 - 3 - 4 gives the proportions of three commodity components of the CSO estimates of machinery gross of replacement. This composition of commodity content of gross fixed-capital formation is used to break up the net capital-formation figure for machinery for the same year, assuming the net/gross ratios for the aggregate capital formation and for the machines to be the same.

The commodity composition of the fixed-capital formation (extension) for the sectors of trade, transport, and services are, therefore, the residual element; this residual element is calculated as the difference between the total capital-formation vector (extension type) derived from the CSO estimates (adjusted to the 1961 basis) and the total for the rest of the economy, comprising manufacturing, agriculture, and mining, all of which are estimated separately.

CAPITAL/CAPACITY RATIOS AND THE UTILIZATION OF CAPITAL IN THE ECONOMY

For the purpose of planning and estimation of the fixed investment requirements for a specified rate of growth in an economy, one would strictly be interested in fixed capital/capacity ratios in a technical sense for all the disaggregated sectors of the economy, and their changes over time. This is developed by dividing the present section into three parts: adjustments for the degree of utilization of capacity, adjustments for gestation lags, and the likely trend in the capital/capacity ratios. The concept of capacity is difficult to measure. Output may fall short of or may surpass capacity. The definition of capacity indeed is partly technical and partly behavioral. In any planning process when a capital/output ratio (derived from a single observation point) is to be used for the purpose of estimating the investment requirements, it assumes implicitly that the degree of utilization of the capital stock will not change over the plan

period. This is a very irrational assumption in the
present case, especially when a considerable amount
of idle capacity is found to have existed at the base
year of the plan. The problem becomes still worse
if one tries to measure capital/output ratios in an
incremental form, because in the relevant period the
whole or part of the incremental output may come in
the form of a better utilization of the existing
capital stock, and not from an increment in the physical level of capital stock at all.

The present study makes adjustments for capacity
utilization as follows:

Installed capacity in the Indian context is defined as the optimum output obtainable on purely
engineering considerations when the capital is
associated with 2½ shifts of labor (each of eight hours
duration) a day. This standard definition of capacity
is adjusted for different industries, depending on
their seasonal aspect or special production characteristics. The estimates of installed capacity, both in
1961/2 and in 1960/1, are obtained from the industrial
development program and the Third Plan mid-term
appraisal of the Government of India.[5]

The estimates for installed capacity are given
in the above reports under the heading,"commodity
classifications," in great detail. They are then
matched with the 400-sector classification of the ASI
report for 1962 on an industry basis, defined on a
principal-product criterion and subsequently grouped
into 22 sectors.

The incremental capacity thereby obtained for
1962, corresponding to incremental fixed capital over
1961, is regarded as a purely technical concept.* It
was discovered from the experience of many specific
industries that in the actual production process, full
utilization of capacity may not always be possible.

———————————

*Assuming the proportion of idle capacity to
remain the same in 1962 as in 1961/62.

In the plan estimates for the year 1965/6, some
underutilization of capacity is assumed on the basis
of expected maximum efficiency of the productive units,
and making full allowance for the existence of
structural idle capacity due to long gestation of
investment.*   Therefore, our above incremental
capacity is again written down by the coefficient of
planned idle capacity as obtained from the Program
of Industrial Development, and is calculated on the
basis of the planned provisions made in the official
plan for the year 1965/6.   In fact, structural idle
capacity depends on (a) gestation of investment,
(b) rate of growth of the sector concerned, and (c)
life of the capital asset.

Say:

  m = average life of capital

  r = the compound rate of growth of gross invest-
      ment

  I = index of gross annual investment

  K = index of gross capital stock

  x = the period after completion of the investment
      outlay and before the plant is in full pro-
      duction, so that n, m, and K^1 is the gross
      capital stock index embracing only those
      investments in full operation.

Then the position is:

$$I = e^{rt} \qquad \qquad (1)$$

$$K = \int_{t-m}^{t-x} I\,dt = \frac{e^{rt}\,(1 - e^{-rm})}{r} \qquad (2)$$

$$K^1 = \int_{t-m}^{t-x} I\,dt = \frac{e^{rt}\,(e^{-rx} - e^{-rm})}{r} \qquad (3)$$

[index of
gross
annual
invest-
ment rate
at year t]

*Eighteen-month production lag, after making
price corrections to capacity figures for 1962.

TABLE 13.1

FIXED CAPITAL/OUTPUT RELATIONS

1	2	3	4	5	6	7	8	9	10	11	12	13	14
	Average Capital Capacity (1961)	Average Capital Planned Capacity (1961)	Average Capital Output (1961)	Marginal Capital Capacity (1961)	Marginal Capital Planned Capacity (1961)	Marginal Capital Output (1961)	Marginal Capital Output; Regression Coefficient (Time Series) 1948-58	Bharadwaj Capital Coefficient[g]	Vinod Prakash's Capital Coefficient[h]	Sandee's Capital Coefficient	Ahuja's Capital/ Net Output Coefficient[i]	Reddaway's Capital /Net Output.[j] 1960/1	Capital Coefficient implicit in PPD estimates (1965-71)
1. Cement	.655	.677	.762	b	b	x	1.460	.402	2.300				
2. Glass, Wood, Nonmetallic Minerals	.217	.304	.369	.137	.192	.234	.547	.591	.650		4.810		
3. Rubber, Leather	.114	.133	.134	.120	.148	.294	.069	.182	.450				
4. Paper	.275	.343	.543	.089	.073	.238	.710				4.420		
5. Food, Beverages	.142	.147	.161	1.006	.320	.112	.123	.267	.380	.700[a]	2.430		.492
6. Textiles	.233	.239	.248	.235	.240	.242	.373	.447	.730				
7. Jute and Coir	.172	.159	.197	.041	.037	.035			.630		3.910		
8-12. Agriculture										2.000			
13. Fertilizer	1.035	1.294	1.722	1.589	1.985	3.203			1.500				2.047
14-15. Other Agriculture and Mining.													
16. Transport Equipments	.306	.312	.344	.208	.213	.221			.700				.729
17. Electrical Equipments	.259	.288	.274	.449	.682	.249	.322	.710	.650				.747

228

18.	Aluminum	.436	.436	.283	.305	2.345	.155	.962	3.000			3.340
19.	Other Mining											
20.	Iron and Steel	.544	.545	.801	.339	.337	.440	1.137	2.350	3.100	2.770	3.570
21.	Nonelectrical	.242	.250	.347	.281	.301	.382	.352	1.000	3.500	3.680	1.160
22.	Chemicals, power, and other industries	.241	.251	.402	526	.336	.676	.461	.738	1.040	4.210	1.251

Manufacturing Total	.270	.286	.334	358	.331	.319
Small-Scale	c	c	c	c	c	c

Com-bined Av. Manuf = .4 Approximate
.900 1.800

	.480	2.600^d 1.000

Agriculture .900
Mining d

Trade and Transport Services	2.006		6.5)^f
Labor Component of construction	0.429		2.0

Economy (Aggregate) 1.490   2.00   2.2(net) 1.700

a Output has different connotation and capital refers to extension investment only

b Not economically meaningful

c Small-scale included in the large-scale sector

d Includes mining but excludes small-scale manufacturing

f Transport and communication = 6.5
  and other services = 2.0

g Structural Basis of India's Foreign Trade. Bombay University, 1962.

h "Fixed Capital Coefficients and Replacements Requirements," Report no. 2, Studies in the Structure of the Indian Economy.

i "The Capital Output Ratio in Indian Economy." The Indian Economic Journal, 1961.

$$K^1/K = \frac{e^{-rn} - e^{-rm}}{1 - e^{-rm}} \quad (4)$$

with $n < m$ and $r < o$, $e^{-rn} < 1$, that is, equation (4) is less than one. This ratio will further diminish t with an increase in the rate of growth of investment (r) and the gestation period (n). If the gestation of investment is three years, the life of capital thirty years, and the rate of growth 10 percent, then the structural idle capacity comes to nearly 27 percent whereas if the gestation is six months, the life of the asset ten years and the rate of growth 3 percent, then structural idle capacity comes to 5 percent.

By the above adjustments we arrive at four sets of estimates: average capital/output ratios, marginal capital/output ratios, marginal capital/capacity ratios, and planned marginal capital/capacity ratios (See Table 13.1).

For the purpose of this model, the marginal concept is preferred to the average concept for two major reasons, conceptual and statistical. Conceptually, we have no reason to assume that the incremental capital/capacity ratio is equal to the average capital/capacity ratio in a dynamic society when new production units adapt modern techniques. Besides, the model is mainly concerned with the estimates of requirements for the extension investment for incremental capacity. Replacement investment for the existing capital stock is treated separately in later sections. Statistically, valuation of capital stock is a large problem, especially when one has to deal with the capital-stock estimates obtained as book values. Normally, by convention, book values of capital represent the purchase price of the capital equipment at the time of purchase after adjustment for depreciation. However, it was discovered that in certain cases revaluations of the capital stock in the light of price changes had already taken place. This problem of valuation is largely avoided when incremental capital stocks are calculated, since they represent additions at the current price. (In these exercises we have used the relations between capacity and material

component of capital stock, instead of those between
the total of capital stock and capital stock at the
current price).

The incremental capital/capacity ratios (in terms
of the extension investment of fixed capital structure)
for total manufacturing and its disaggregated sectors
are thus calculated. Exceptions are made for three
different industries: cement, jute, and aluminum.
In these cases, the incremental capital/capacity ratios
give rather erratic results. Accordingly, attempts
are made to estimate the marginal capital/output ratios
from time-series data, on the assumption of a linear
relation between capital stock and output for these
three separate industries. The price corrections for
capital stock over the time series are carried out in
a very rough-and-ready manner.

The estimates for the sectors of agriculture,
mining, and trade, transport, and services are confined
initially to the concept of incremental capital/output
ratios for 1961, because it was felt at the time that
the measurement of capacity would be rather difficult
in these sectors. In the case of agriculture, a
further adjustment is made in the incremental capital/
output ratio, calculated on the basis of a single year
of observation, 1962, because this year is not regarded
as a typical year (it was an unusually bad harvest
year for India). An alternative calculation of capacity utilization in agriculture, mining, and trade,
subsequently made in the later sections, is used in
our model.

For agriculture, the very concept of capacity
is difficult to calculate in the Indian context,
because any statistics of shift work among the agricultural labor force, in the context of disguised
unemployment, are difficult to formulate. It was
therefore decided for the first stage to switch over
to the concept of gross output. But gross output in
Indian agriculture is in its turn found to have a low
degree of sensitivity to changes in labor or capital
inputs at any given time. This is due to the fact
that in Indian agriculture, capital input is too low,
with varying degrees of over-utilization, labor input

is very high with a high degree of under-utilization
(which is almost unquantifiable), and the most important variable--weather--is normally ignored. In
fact, the most important explanatory variable in
Indian agriculture in the short run is weather; it
is followed by inputs like fertilizers and irrigation.
Success or failure of the monsoon in Indian has been
observed to have a cyclical pattern. Hence, it was
decided not to derive the estimates of incremental
capital/output ratio from any particular year (say,
1961), but from an average of the incrementals
spread over a few years. The logic of this approach
is that the abnormalities of the weather and many
short-term factors are likely to be cancelled out
and a stable relation between capital and output is
likely to emerge.

For this purpose, the incremental net output in
agriculture during the Fourth Plan is estimated by
applying the proportion of agriculture* to the total
incremental national income, over the same period.
The total incremental national income is given by the
Perspective Planning Division of the Indian Planning
Commission, all valued at 1960/1 prices.

Similarly, incremental fixed investment** in the
agricultural sector, including irrigation, forestry,
and fisheries, is estimated from the Fourth Plan
estimates (between 1964/5 and 1969/70) revalued at
1960/1 prices from the original valuation at 1965/6
prices. The estimates of the incremental capital
stock/net output ratios thus derived are computed
(gross) from the net/gross output ratios obtained from
the current flow transaction table for India 1959.***

----

*Derived from the White Paper as an average of
the years 1960-66.

**Excluding labor component.

***The logic of the approach is to work out the
implicit capital/output ratio used in the Fourth Plan
projections by the official planning body in India.

The estimate of incremental capital/gross output (.9)
thus computed is higher than Reddaway's estimate of
.6 (gross) and .9 (net) and lower than Alan Manne's
figure of 1.5 gross and 1.1 net.

The capital/output ratios for all the six subgroups belonging to the agricultural sector are estimated by assuming the same comparative differences in
the capital/output ratios between all the sectors as
are observed in Alan Manne's work in Sankhya, 1965.
The capital/output ratio derived from the total value
of fixed investment allocated to agriculture in our
flow matrix to the incremental net output in 1962 is
2.0, which is slightly higher than expected, as 1962
was not regarded as a very good year. This again
supports the view that the point estimate of capital/
output ratios in agriculture is a poor tool for planning purposes.

The estimates of capital/output ratios presented
in Alan Manne's study for the five detailed subgroups
of the mining sector are combined as weights with the
gross output of these sectors in 1961 at 1960/1 price,
in order to derive the aggregate incremental capital/
output ratios for mining as a whole.

The incremental gross outputs in trade, transport,
and services between 1961/2 and 1962/3 are derived
from the estimates of incremental national income (by
origin) over the period, as given in the CSO national
income estimates, after being adjusted to a gross
concept by being written up with factors derived from
the 1959 current flow transaction table. The net
capital formation for 1961 divided by the incremental
gross output for 1962/3* gives the corresponding
capital/output ratio in this sector. Subsequently,
the incremental capital/gross output ratios are derived for sector 22 (in our standard sector classification) by combining the capital/capacity ratios of
chemicals, manufacturing, power, trade, and transport

---

*Strictly, it should be 1962, allowing for an
eighteen-month production lag.

with the corresponding incremental gross outputs
(1962) as weights.

ADJUSTMENTS FOR GESTATION LAGS

The incremental capital/capacity ratios, as
estimated above, assume a gestation lag of roughly
one and a half years. In reality, however, there
are sectors where the lags are found to be <u>more</u> or
<u>less</u> than the assumed eighteen-month gestation.
By gestation lag in investment, we mean the total
time interval that normally occurs between the decision
to invest, recorded in the statistics of investment
outlay of a year, and the outputs arising from those
investment activities. In reality, the investment
expenditures and the output flows will both be spread
over a period of time. However, for the present
purpose, a "fixed gap" concept is assumed, and on a
priori information, provisions are made for the gestation lags to differ between sectors while the value
of capital/capacity ratios are adjusted accordingly.

Lastly, the incremental capital flow coefficient
matrix is formulated (for material component only)
for 1961 at purchase price. Each element of the
22 x 22 matrix, along any column, shows the "industry"
component of capital stock needed for producing 100
additional units of new planned capacity in the
respective industries.

The table of capital coefficients at producer's
price is similarly computed from the above fixed
investment (net) flow matrix at purchaser's prices,
by using the distributive margin for each industry
separately (see Table 13.2).

The estimates of distributive margins are
borrowed from the current flow transaction matrix
(1959), and are based on different official publications, including the Annual Survey of Industries.

TABLE 13.2

CAPITAL FLOW COEFFICIENT MATRIX (INCREMENTAL) 1961 (EXTENSION INVESTMENT)
(at producers' prices)

	1	2	3	4	5	6	7	8	9	10	11	12	13	14	15	16	17	18	19	20	21	22
1. Cement	2.6	0.4	0.4	1.1	0.6	0.3	0.2	3.9	3.9	3.9	3.9	3.8	2.6	7.6	5.9	0.4	1.2	0.3	5.9	2.1	0.6	7.2
2. Glass, wood, nonmetallic	6.9	1.0	0.9	3.0	1.6	0.8	0.7	10.0	10.0	10.0	10.0	9.8	6.7	15.6	15.8	1.0	3.1	0.8	15.8	5.5	1.5	18.9
3. Rubber and leather																						
4. Paper and paper products																						
5. Food, beverages, and tobacco																						
6. Textiles																						
7. Jute and coir																						
8. Cotton																						
9. Food grains																						
10. Jute																						
11. Oil seeds																						
12. Plantations																						
13. Fertilizers																						
14. Other agriculture, inc. forestry and animal husbandry	6.4	1.0	0.9	2.8	1.5	0.8	0.7	13.8	13.8	13.8	13.8	13.5	6.4	27.0	14.8	0.9	2.9	0.8	14.8	5.2	1.4	14.6
15. Iron ore																						
16. Transport equipment	3.1	0.7	0.4	0.7	0.7	0.3							0.2			0.2	2.0	0.1		1.7	0.5	
17. Electrical equipment	2.3	2.2	0.3	1.0	0.5	0.3	0.2						2.2		5.0	2.4	13.6	5.6	5.0	0.1	0.5	21.1
18. Aluminum and nonferrous metals																						
19. Other mining																						
20. Iron and steel	8.3	1.2	1.2	3.7	2.0	1.0	0.8	12.3	12.3	12.3	12.3	12.0	8.3	24.0	19.3	1.2	3.8	0.9	19.3	6.7	1.8	22.9
21. Nonelectrical equipment and ferrous and non-ferrous products	71.0	6.5	5.8	35.3	14.6	12.9	9.0	5.3	5.3	5.3	5.3	5.2	107.0	10.3	67.3	8.7	19.2	12.8	67.3	2.3	12.4	16.2
22. Chemical, power, other industries, trade and services	45.4	6.3	4.9	23.2	10.4	7.7	5.5	61.1	16.1	16.1	16.1	51.8	64.1	31.6	52.0	6.6	22.3	9.3	52.0	10.0	11.4	59.0

NOTES

1. Planning Commission, Third Plan Mid-Term Appraisal, (Delhi: Government of India Press, 1963).

2. W. B. Reddaway, The Development of the Indian Economy, (London: George Allen and Unwin 1964).

3. Alan Manne, A Consistency Model of India's Fourth Plan. Studies on the Structure on the Indian Economy. Report No. 1, M.I.T. Center for International Studies, Cambridge, July, 1964.

4. A. S. Manne and A. Rudra, "A Consistency Model of India's Fourth Plan," Sankhya, Series B, Vol. 27, Parts I and II, September,1965.

5. Planning Commission, Program of Industrial Development, 1961/66, (New Delhi, Government of India Press, 1962) and The Third Plan: Mid-Term Appraisal, (Delhi: Government of India Press, 1963).

14

MARGINAL STOCK/OUTPUT FLOW COEFFICIENT MATRIX

The working capital requirements of an economy can be divided into three parts: the work in progress, the stock of finished goods, and the stock of raw materials, including spare parts and stores.

The size of work in progress per unit of output depends on the cost of recurring inputs (i.e., wages, raw materials) per unit of output and on the time lag between the application of recurring inputs and the arrival of outputs.

The stock-holding of finished goods can be motivated by transaction needs, speculative needs, and precautionary needs.

Similarly, the stock-holding of raw materials may be undertaken for transactions (to maintain normal convenience of production), or may be used for speculation, or as a precaution, or all three together. These three motivations are not always well demarcated.

Besides the above three types of inventories, there is a fourth one, stock-holding by consumers. For the purpose of the present planning model, it is of interest to have an estimate of stock coefficients that would be functionally related to the level of production, and not subject to speculative fluctuations or random disturbance. Hence the lack of

interest in stock-holding by consumers, which is in
a sense not functionally related to the level of
productive activity of an economy (and hence needs
a completely different treatment in a planning model).

There are different kinds of simple and comparatively complicated mathematical models for inventory
holdings, depending on the optimization principle
adopted in a programming framework. Under certain
simplified assumptions, these optimization criteria
lead to the proportionality condition between the
increase in the level of inventory holding and the
square root of the volume of sales of an industry.

Any econometric fit of the functional relations
between the inventory holdings and the level of gross
output over a time series is expected to cancel the
random and speculative movements in the stock-holding
of a business enterprise, and could therefore be regarded as giving an estimate of the planned inventory-
holding of a productive activity. In the present
section I have tried to derive a statistical fit,
assuming both linearity and log linearity, to formulate a functional relation between inventory holding
and output.

The estimation is carried out in two major stages,
commodity or industry composition of stocks, and the
planned level of stock-holding, expressed as a function
of the volume of sales (for the purpose of this present
exercise, gross outputs and sales volume are used
synonymously). Assuming a linear relation in the
second stage, one arrives at a satisfactory stable
relationship between inventory holdings and gross
value of output by a single-stage least-square approach. The marginal coefficients which result from
these fits are identified as incremental inventory/
output ratios for the purpose of the model.

However, this treatment of the stock/output ratio
is possible only in manufacturing. In other sectors,
paucity of data prevents a similar treatment. In
these sectors, the incremental stock/output ratios
recorded for 1961/2 are regarded as applicable in
general for this model.

Manufacturing

The statistics on total inventory-holding for raw materials, finished goods and semifinished goods are collected for 1960 and 1961 from Annual Survey of Industries reports, consisting of 400 separate individual industries' returns. These are subsequently converted into our adopted industrial groupings. The stocks of any year are assumed to have been revalued conventionally at the ruling price prevailing in that year. Therefore, the stock differences between 1960 and 1961 can be assumed to be incremental stock-holdings in 1961 at 1961 prices, plus the valuation of the earlier period stocks by price differences between 1960 and 1961. (Price changes between 1960 and 1961 were very small.) Of the three major commodity components of stock holdings, the items under finished and semifinished goods are assigned to the industry represented by the column (i.e., diagonal elements in the matrix). On the other hand, the raw-material components of the stock-holding are distributed along the columns, according to the current input structure of the industry revealed from the 1959 current flow transaction matrix. This finally produces the commodity composition (in terms of industry of origin) of a given inventory-holding, in all the manufacturing sectors covered in the ASI reports.

At this stage, a rather heroic assumption is adopted, namely, that the composition of stocks in the large-scale sector will remain valid in the small-scale sector of manufacturing. The next important stage in the present exercise is to work out the so-called normal relations between output and stocks for the different manufacturing sectors. To compute these parameters, regression equations of working capital are fitted on gross output for twelve industries from the CMI data.

Extremely good fits are obtained in almost all cases, (See Table 14.1). At this stage, however, it should be borne in mind that the CMI covered 20 or more with power, and hence these parameters were not strictly comparable with the earlier part where

the current and capital flow matrix have been computed
based on the ASI report.

When the marginal coefficients derived from the
time-series analysis and adjusted for "coverage" and
"mix" differences, are compared with the marginal
coefficients for the year 1961, derived from the
Annual Survey of Industries report, they match very
well* and in most cases lie within reasonable ranges
of error. In those cases where marginal coefficients
could not be calculated from time-series data or are
not available, we adopt average or marginal coefficients estimated from one-year data obtained from
the 1961 ASI report.

The estimates of stock changes in food grains
for the year 1960/1 are derived from publications
of the Central Statistical Organization, Government
of India. The gross output of food grains in the
year 1959** is derived from the current flow transaction table, 1959. The Annual Abstract of Statistics
shows that the rate of growth of output for food grains
between the two years was 6 percent. The increase
in the price of food grains over the same period was
calculated at 1.7 percent. From this the gross output
of food grains for the year 1960/1 at current prices
is estimated and, subsequently, the incremental gross
output between 1959/60 and 1960/1 at 1961 prices is
derived. The corresponding incremental stock/output
ratio in agricultural sector is accordingly calculated
at .202. Similarly the stock/output ratio for the
sector other agriculture is estimated at .056.

For cotton plantation and oil seeds, no estimates
of stock changes are available in the CSO estimates.
As a result, it is necessary to borrow stock figures
calculated for the three sectors taken together from
Reddaway's book. The ratio of incremental stock to
incremental output is estimated for these three sectors taken together and is assumed to hold good for

---

*Log-linear and linear relations gave equally
good results.

**In fact, it referred to harvest year, 1959/60.

TABLE 14.1

TEST OF "FIT" OF THE INVENTORY EQUATIONS

Industries	Coeff. of determination.	Von Neumann Ratios	T-Values
1. Food and beverages	.800	2.418	5.750
2. Chemicals	.990	2.940	2.889
3. Tannings	.851	2.201	6.836
4. Cement	.911	1.042	9.119
5. Wood and glass	.940	1.882	11.367
6. Paper and matches	.889	1.551	8.078
7. Textiles	.633	1.556	3.848
8. Jute textiles	.602	2.316	3.617
9. Aluminum, copper and brass	.668	1.753	4.133
10. Iron and steel	.824	2.734	6.208
11. Bicycles	.976	2.304	18.234
12. Electrical and Mechanical Eng.	.987	1.324	24.556

Source: Census of Manufactures in India, (Delhi: Government of India Press, 1949-58).

TABLE 14.2

ESTIMATES OF STOCK/OUTPUT RATIOS IN INDIAN MANUFACTURING

Industries	Stock as percentage of average output	Stock as percentage of marginal output	Stock as percentage of marginal output* (time-series regression)
1. Cement	29.4	30.9	41.2
2. Glass, wood and non-metallic products	32.0	41.6	33.8
3. Rubber and leather	24.5	35.4	29.7
4. Paper and paper products	26.5	19.3	33.3
5. Food, beverages, and tobacco	35.9	67.9	25.8
6. Textiles	29.2	31.0	38.2
7. Jute and coir industries	25.0	24.8	...
8. Fertilizers	40.7	...	...
9. Transport equipment	38.7	34.7	...
10. Electrical equipment	41.5	39.1	...
11. Aluminum and non-ferrous	63.9	...	...
12. Iron and steel	32.8	24.5	39.8
13. Nonelectrical equipment	43.8	38.2	...
14. Chemicals, power, and other manufacturing	31.5	31.0	16.8

*Adjusted for coverage and mix differences.

Source: CMI and present model.

each of them individually. For the "jute" sector,
the average stock/output ratio is accepted, since
this sector had practically a negative output change
and no changes in the level of stock of inventories,
during 1960/1. Lastly, these coefficients are assumed
to hold good for the year 1961.

Mining

The total stock changes in the year 1960/1 in
iron ore are estimated as Rs.4.0 million in Alan
Manne's study,[1] whereas the total incremental output
in 1960/1 is estimated (at current price) at Rs.16.9
million by observing a 15.2 percent rate of growth
of output of iron ore during 1959/60 and price index
between the two years standing at 108.7. The incremental stock/gross output ratio is consequently calculated at .237. There is another alternative approach that could have been attempted. This is based
on the following information obtained from the Reserve
Bank of India's surveys on the finances of joint stock
companies in India. Since the number of observations
are very small, a sophisticated test for statistical
fit is impossible. However, assuming that the speculative and other random changes in stock-holding cancel
out during the period, the aggregate stock/output
ratio comes to .197. Again, it is gratifying to note
that it is very near to our other alternative estimate.

MINING (1955-59)
(Rs. one million)

Years	1955	1956	1957	1958	1959	Total
Net Value Added	241.1	267.9	328.2	346.6	341.0	1524.8
Gross output to Net value ratio	-	-	-	-	1.22*	
Working capital	57.3	61.4	70.9	81.5	88.0	359.1

*Inter-industry Table, ISG (PC), 1959.

Source: Reserve Bank of India, Bulletin, September 1957 and
September 1961.

TABLE 14.3

STOCK/OUTPUT (INCREMENTAL) FLOW MATRIX, 1961
(at producers' prices, in percentages)

Supply		Absorption																				
	1	2	3	4	5	6	7	8	9	10	11	12	13	14	15	16	17	18	19	20	21	22
1 Cement	3.9																					0.1
2 Glass, wood, non-metallic		11.4	0.3	0.2		0.2										0.1	0.1				0.3	0.6
3 Rubber & leather	1.3		12.8			0.1										1.0	0.1					0.4
4 Paper and paper products	0.1	0.2	0.2	22.4		0.4							3.0				0.7				0.5	1.0
5 Food, beverages, & tobacco			0.2	0.1	17.1								0.5				0.1					0.1
6 Textiles		0.1	0.7	0.6		14.5											0.3					0.2
7 Jute & coir	10.7	0.1				0.3	18.6						0.7				0.2					0.9
8 Cotton						11.3		39.6														
9 Food grains					0.6				20.2													
10 Jute							2.4			39.6												
11 Oil seeds			1.4		0.3						39.6						0.3				0.1	
12 Plantations												39.6										
13 Fertilizers													24.4									
14 Other agriculture		4.3	2.7	1.5	0.6	0.4								5.6		3.7	0.3	0.4				0.8
15 Iron ore															23.7					0.6		
16 Transport equip.																8.8						
17 Electrical equip.																0.3	14.4				0.8	
18 Aluminum & non-ferrous metals				0.1												1.1	1.6	18.0	23.7	0.3	1.3	0.2
19 Other mining	1.2	2.9		0.1									2.1				0.4	16.8		0.7	3.4	
20 Iron & steel		0.2	1.1													4.1	2.0	0.4		18.4	5.5	0.3
21 Nonelectrical equip.	0.1	0.1	0.5	0.1	0.1	0.5	0.1									0.4	2.9	1.5		2.9	12.2	1.9
22 Chemical, transport, trade, other industries, power	23.9	14.1	9.5	8.2	6.9	10.4	3.7						10.1			15.2	14.8	27.4	16.9	16.9	17.5	6.9
Δ stock/Δ output	.112	.337	.297	.333	.256	.378	.248	.396	.202	.396	.396	.396	.408	.036	.237	.347	.392	.637	.237	.398	.382	.168

244

Trade, Transport, and Services

The incremental output in this sector is estimated
by combining the estimates of chemicals, other manufacturing, and power derived from the Annual Survey
of Industries report, with those for trade, transport,
and services, derived from the national income and
expenditure statistics adjusted for gross-net relations. For the sector "trade" an alternative estimate
is obtained from Sen.[2] Aggregate incremental stock
ratios are obtained by the weighted average of stock/
output changes in all the above sectors.

Finally, the stock flow coefficient matrix for
1961 is computed by recording the amount of stock
changes needed for a change of 100 units of output
in all the sectors of the economy and are represented
by the columns of the table. Adjustments are made
for transferring the estimates from purchasers' to
producers' prices (see Table 14.3).

NOTES

1. Alan S. Manne and A. Rudra, "A Consistency
Model of India's Fourth Plan" Sankhya, Series B. Vo.
27, Parts I and II, (September, 1965).

2. A.K. Sen. "Estimates of Working Capital in
India," in P.N. Rosenstein-Rodan, ed. Pricing and
Fiscal Policies, (London: George Allen and Unwin, 1964).

15

The concept of replacement investment has no
standard connotation in economic literature. Replacements might suggest substitution of old worn-out capital by an exact replica, or value for value, or capacity for capacity. The third concept is more relevant
for economic analysis. But statistical information
on a new investment replacing worn-out capital by an
exact capacity at a given time is extremely difficult
to obtain. On the other hand, by taking the second
concept, one may be replacing worn-out capital by the
original cost price of the replaced capital revalued
at current price, but thereby may be increasing the
productivity of the replaced stock of capital in terms
of capacity of production. The first concept is ruled
out as completely unrealistic. Hence, on balance, the
second concept is, despite its limitations, easier
to conceive empirically and is adopted in this study.

The second difficulty in estimating replacements
arises from the lack of unanimity regarding the different notions of the lifetime of an asset after
which it needs replacement. The problem arises,
first, because an asset is a composite concept, whose
parts have varying life spans, and little detailed
information. Second, the concept of "a fixed lifetime" is very unreal, and a probability distribution
of lifetime of assets sounds closer to reality, although it would be difficult to estimate. Lastly,

the technical lifetime of an asset, which is comparatively easier to estimate, may be different from its
economic lifetime, which in its turn depends on many
other economic and noneconomic factors distinct from
the technical workability of capital. However, as
an easy compromise, in most literature on "replacement
investment," a fixed lifetime of an asset is assumed
as a convenient working hypothesis (perpetual inventor
theory). This approach is also difficult to formulate
empirically in the developing countries, as it require
data on capital investment for the previous 30 to 50
years and a reliable price index of capital goods.
It was found, for instance, that this approach would
be unworkable in the case of India because reliable
statistics on capital-formation estimates were available for only a few years, and that too in a highly
aggregated form.

As an alternative, it was necessary to adopt an
accounting concept of replacement investment. According to this concept, the replacement of a capital
asset begins at the moment it is born and is completed
throughout its lifetime. The problem is simplified
in the present case by assuming a conventional straigh
line depreciation method, a fixed lifetime of asset,
and a fixed capital/stock gross output ratio over time
in all of the sectors of the economy.

On this basis, the ratio of depreciation provisio
to total gross output of an activity sector can be
regarded as replacement coefficient (assuming accounting life is equal to economic life of a capital) and
can be used as a parameter in this model.

The next major task in building the replacement
investment matrix is the disaggregation of the replacement estimates into their respective commodity
components.

Returning to the specific problem of estimation
in India, it was noticed that no information on replacement investment was available for the year 1960/1
except an aggregate figure of Rs.9,120 million for
the fixed capital stock part of the whole economy.

TABLE 15.1

REPLACEMENT INVESTMENT/GROSS OUTPUT MATRIX 1961
(Producers' price: in percentages)

	1	2	3	4	5	6	7	8	9	10	11	12	13	14	15	16	17	18	19	20	21	22
1. Cement	2.1	0.3	0.1	0.2	0.2	0.1	0.1	0.1				0	3.0	0.6	0.4	0.1	0.1	1.4	0.5	1.4	0.5	0.6
2. Glass, wood, nonmetallic	3.4	0.4	0.3	0.3	0.3	0.2	0.1					0.1	4.9	1.0	0.6	0.3	0.2	2.3	0.8	2.3	0.8	1.0
3. Rubber and leather																						
4. Paper and paper products																						
5. Food, beverages, and tobacco																						
6. Textiles																						
7. Jute and coir																						
8. Cotton																						
9. Food grains																						
10. Jute																						
11. Oil seeds																						
12. Plantations																						
13. Fertilizers																						
14. Other agriculture, inc. forestry and animal husbandry	2.8	0.4	0.1	0.2	0.2	0.1	0.1					0.1	4.2	0.8	0.5	0.2	0.2	2.0	0.6	1.9	0.7	0.8
15. Iron ore																						
16. Transport equipment																						3.9
17. Electrical equipment	1.5	0.4	0.3	0.2	0.2	0.2	0.2					0.1	3.0	0.5	0.6	0.3	0.2	2.0	0.6	1.8	0.7	0.5
18. Aluminum and nonferrous metals																						
19. Other mining																						
20. Iron and steel	4.9	0.7	0.4	0.4	0.4	0.2	0.2					0.1	7.2	1.5	0.8	0.4	0.3	3.4	1.2	3.3	1.3	1.4
21. Nonelectrical equipment and ferrous and non-ferrous products	22.4	4.1	2.4	2.3	2.3	3.1	1.5					1.0	19.3	2.2	5.6	2.1	0.9	17.7	4.7	15.9	6.3	2.5
22. Chemical, Power, other industries, tradeds industries and services																						
Replacement/output	.370	.063	.035	.036	.026	.039	.021					.010	.414	.066	.034	.034	.020	.084	.226	.103	.107	5.2% aggregate

Mostly replacements are of current input types

Alan Manne gives an estimate of the total replacement investment needed between 1960/1 and 1970/1,
at 1960/1 prices, and their composition in major groups
such as construction, general equipment, and transport
equipment.[1] Assuming that the distribution of the
replacement investment over the 22 sectors of the
present industrial classification covering the decade
1960/1 to 1970/1 would hold good in the year 1960/1
under the global constraint of Rs.9,120 million, we
estimated the whole replacement-investment vector
for 1960/1. The replacement investment/output ratios
for each sector were then derived by estimating the
ratio of replacement to gross output for each sector
individually.

The detailed commodity breakdown of replacement
investment in each sector is computed from the commodity composition exhibited in the capital (extension) output matrix applicable to the smaller subgroups
under construction, general equipment, and transport
equipment (See Table 15.1).

NOTE

1. Alan s. Manne, A Consistency Model of India's
Fourth Plan. Studies on the Structure of the Indian
Economy. Report No. 1, MIT Center for International
Studies, Cambridge, July, 1964.

FIXED CAPITAL COEFFICIENTS

There are three major classes of capital/output ratio in the present estimates:

(a) Fixed capital/output ratios (extension).

(b) Inventory-holding/output ratios.

(c) Replacement of fixed capital/output ratios.

Group (a) is further subdivided into seven subgroups-- each dealing with different concepts of fixed capital/ output ratios, net of replacement. From the point of view of estimations procedure, the first six refer to a point estimate, exclusively confined to the year 1961, and the seventh is an estimate derived from time-series data.

Table 13.1 presented the seven alternative estimates for all the 14 manufacturing-industry sectors. As is evident, all the estimates are different, and a choice is necessary, bearing in mind the purpose of the exercise. In the context of the present investigation I preferred the incremental fixed capital (net) to planned capacity relations.

Descending to details, for the manufacturing sector in India three exceptions are made to the above rule. For cement and paper, the incremental

capital/output ratios derived from the time-series
data are adopted, as the information on capacity
utilization in these two sectors is not very reliable.
For jute and coir, the average capital/capacity ratios
are adopted, as incremental ratios in these cases
have little meaning when the absolute levels of output are on the decline.

Between the different estimates based on average
and marginal concepts or between output and capacity
concepts, the marginal ones are higher than the
average ones in the majority of cases, although for
a few individual sectors the bias goes the other way.
The estimates in terms of capacity and in terms of
output similarly show differences in specific sectors,
although in the aggregate they are fairly near to
each other (the capital/capacity ratios being slightly
lower than the capital/output ratios). The incrementa
capital/capacity ratio in manufacturing as a whole
stands at .40 in the aggregate. (It is slightly
underestimated as the labor component of capital stock
is excluded. After necessary adjustment it comes to
.57.)

A further attempt was made in Table 13.1 to
compare these estimates with the estimates of a few
other authors in comparable sectors. In this connection, however, it should be mentioned that so far
no capital flow matrix, like that in the present
exercise, has been computed for India.[1]

Columns 8, 9, 10, 11, 12 and 13 present the
nearest comparable estimates from some alternative
sources. Of these Ahujaya's and Reddaway's estimates
are on a net output basis (i.e, value added) and
none of them have subscribed to the concept of capacities. One thing is obvious from these comparative
sutdies--the capital/output ratios in almost all the
estimates have an upward bias compared to the present
one. One likely reason is the choice of the concept
of gross output against that of capacity, in all
these studies. Another is the exclusion of labor
components from the capital-stock estimates in the
present study. A third reason may be that all the
alternate estimates are based on some sort of sample

data, and mostly from either big, well-organized
establishments or public-sector programs, where
the ratios may have every reason to be on the high
side. The Perspective Planning Division's estimate
of 3.6 and Sandee's of 3.2 both seem definitely to
be on the high side.

But it is interesting to note that the present
estimates of capital output ratios for the manufacturing sectors, together with mining and adjusted for
netting, compare extremely well with Reddaway's
estimates for the manufacturing, mining and small-scale
sectors taken together.

The capital/output ratio for agriculture in the
present estimate is higher than that of Reddaway
when transferred from the gross to the net concept.
The estimate made in the Perspective Planning Division
exercise is as high as 1.4, and so seems very much
on the high side.

The capital/output ratios for power in the present
estimate compare very well with the Perspective
Planning Division's estimate of 2.27. This again
substantiates one of our basic hypotheses, that the
estimates given by the Perspective Planning Division
differ significantly from those in this study only
when a sector contains a sizeable contribution from
a comparatively large number of medium or small-scale
unorganized establishments.

For the sector, trade, transport, and services,
the capital/output ratio in the present estimate is
2.34 and is much higher than that of Reddaway which,
translated into gross terms, would approximate to
1.8. Reddaway himself, of course, admits that his
estimate is very shaky in this field. The aggregate
capital/capacity ratio for the whole economy in the
present estimate stands at 1.49 and is much lower
than the capital/net output ratio of Reddaway's
exercise. Converted to the gross concept, Reddaway's
estimate would boil down to approximately 1.8. But
again, when adjustments are made for the labor component in the aggregate capital/output ratio of our
estimate, the two show a closer matching.

I should like to warn against the practice of using the estimates of capital coefficients of other countries in the planning model of any country. This practice was adopted in India's Second Plan, and it may also have been implicitly adopted in the subsequent plans. This study has already demonstrated the great divergences that the capital-coefficient estimates of a country might exhibit, with only very small changes in the concepts and definitions, even within the same country.

ALTERNATIVE ESTIMATES OF INVENTORY HOLDINGS

The nature of the relation between planned inventory-holding and total volume of output may be linear, exponential, or nonlinear. It is popularly assumed that the inventory holding should increase only in proportion to the square root of sales. In the present exercise, I tested all the hypotheses and finally accepted the linear one. Table 14.2, column 4, presents the marginal inventory/output ratio (based on time series) in the 14 manufacturing sectors. The same table shows the two other alternative estimates of inventory holdings in the manufacturing sector. Table 14.1 presents the coefficient of determination, the values, and the Von Neumann ratios for the 14 industry groups available in the CMI reports for India. As is evident, the fits were satisfactory in almost all the cases.

The only exceptions to the above time-series approach are fertilizers, aluminum, and nonferrous metals. Time-series data in these industries are unavailable in the census report. Hence, it was decided to adopt an average concept in these cases. If these industries are of very recent origin (which they are), our assumption of an average ratio may not be very objectionable. For industries with asterisks in this table, point estimates (i.e., relating to the year 1961) of the marginal ratios were preferred since the CMI classification for these industries does not match satisfactorily with the sector classifications of the present exercise.

TABLE 16.1

STOCK/OUTPUT ESTIMATES FOR AGRICULTURE,
Mining, Trade, and Services

Items	Coefficient	Aggregate Coefficient
1. Food	0.202	
2. Cotton, jute, oil seeds, and plantations	0.396	
3. Other agriculture, including forestry, fisheries, and animal husbandry.	0.056	0.16-0.17
4. Iron ore and other mining.	0.237	
5. Trade, transport and services	0.112	

It is evident from the findings that the stock/
output ratios in the different branches of manufacturing vary over a very narrow range and in general
are higher in the capital-goods industries than in
the consumer-goods industries. Food and jute industries rank as the two lowest, whereas aluminum and
nonelectrical industries rank as the two highest,
in the order of magnitude of the stock/output ratios.

The Table 16.1 presents the incremental stock/
output ratios for the year 1960/1 for agriculture
and for mining, trade, transport, and services. In
the agricultural sector, the highest level of stock-
holding is observed in the cash-crop and plantation
sectors. In other agriculture, it is very low since
it combines sectors like fisheries and forestry,
where the stock accumulation needed may be pretty
low. Trade, transport etc., again show a low stock/
output ratio. But the estimate of this sector should
be taken with a pinch of salt, since this sector is
essentially a residual one.

ESTIMATES OF REPLACEMENT INVESTMENT

The replacement investment/gross output ratio
is more an accounting than an economic concept in
this work. The percentage of replacement to gross
output seems to be 6 percent* in the aggregate of
the economy, with very little dispersion in individual
sectors, except in the case of cement, fertilizer,
aluminum, iron and steel, nonelectrical equipment,
chemicals and power, all of which have a higher estimate of replacement investment as a percentage of
output. This is presumably due either to the
capital-intensive nature of these sectors, or the
higher rate of technical progress in these sectors,
where obsolescences are likely to be very fast, or
to both. A careful scrutiny of the replacement-investment matrix (see Table 15.1) convinces one that

---

*8.6 percent including the labor component of
construction

the building component of total replacement investment
is always lower, and the machine component higher,
when compared to the commodity composition of total
net new investments in the economy.

NOTE

1.   See P. N. Mathur and R. Bhardwaj, eds.,
Economic Analysis in Input-Output Framework,
(Bombay: Vora and Co., 1965).

Idle capacity is defined as unrealized output expressed as a percentage of full-capacity production. Full-capacity production is again defined as output generated from a capital stock when associated with a normal (technically optimum) shift work of labor. The detailed problems regarding the measurement of capacity have been discussed in earlier chapters.

Idle Capacity in the Indian Economy

Idle-capacity estimates for 1961 and 1962 in the manufacturing sector are presented in Table 17.1, and show a decline from 1961 to 1962. But the high percentage of idle capacity prevailing in the manufacturing industry even in 1962 can not be regarded as a healthy sign for the Indian economy, especially since it is admitted that capital as a productive resource has acted as a constraint in the growth of this economy and has agravated the very grave foreign-exchange situation. Viewed from the disaggregated level, the degree of idle capacity observed is very high in capital-goods industries as opposed to consumer-goods industries. Indeed, idle capacities as high as 25 percent in fertilizer, 32 percent in iron and steel, 37 percent in chemical and power, and 37 percent in paper and paper products, are very difficult to justify from any economic logic, especially when all these industries are suffering from excess

TABLE 17.1

IDLE CAPACITY IN INDIAN MANUFACTURING 1961/2
(Percent)

Sectors	1962		1961	
	Actual	Planned	Actual	Planned
1. Cement	14.1	0.9	13.8	0.5
2. Glass, wood, and non-metallic products	41.2	17.8	41.2	17.8
3. Rubber and leather	15.0	-4.9	7.5	-14.1
4. Paper and paper products	49.4	36.9	47.1	27.2
5. Food, beverages, and tobacco	12.2	8.8	15.0	19.2
6. Textiles	6.0	3.8	6.5	4.3
7. Jute and coir products	12.5	19.2	14.8	21.3
8. Fertilizers	39.9	24.9	35.6	19.5
9. Transport equipment	11.0	9.3	11.9	10.4
10. Electrical equipment	5.6	-5.0	17.7	11.7
11. Aluminum and nonferrous	28.4	20.3	-	-
12. Iron and steel	32.0	31.7	32.8	32.6
13. Nonelectrical equipment	30.3	25.2	31.2	26.2
14. Chemicals, power, and other industries	40.4	37.4	43.5	32.8
	19.7	14.7	23.2	17.2

demand, measured by their increasing profit margins.
One likely explanation may lie in the shortage of
imported material inputs acting as constraints, while
another may be the large gestation lags in these
heavy capital projects.

The concept of idle capacity is rather ambiguous
in agriculture and is difficult to calculate. The
major reason for the difficulty is the lack of data,
since agriculture in India is highly unorganized,
with a large number of smallholdings. Besides, the
concept of capacity which is associated with the
existence of unused capital stock is not very relevant
in the case of agriculture in India, since the capital
component in relation to output is very low. It is
not related to output with reasonable sensitivity
over the time-series data, and is to some extent
always overused. Therefore an alternative concept
of idle capacity in the agricultural sector is used
here. It is a concept based on utilization of land,
instead of capital. In fact, this is a concept which
is used in official plan projections in India. To
be more specific, we confine ourselves to a concept
of "norm," as normal utilization of land, which is
defined as yield per acre per crop observed over a
long time-period, adjusted for any trend in productivity. Therefore, according to this method, the
idle capacity in sector x in the period t is equal
to the area under cultivation of the relevant crop,
multiplied by the productivity at period t, corrected
for any trend, less observed production at the same
period and divided by the output with normal utilization of land.

The trend in crop productivity is calculated by
making productivity a linear function of time by
ordinary least-square methods. In cases where no
trend in productivity in linear form is observed,
log-linear relations are attempted. In a few cases,
no significant changes in productivity are observed.
In these cases production is made a linear function
of area under cultivation. The regression results
are shown in Table 17.2.

From the regression analysis, conducted for six

TABLE 17.2

RELATION BETWEEN PRODUCTIVITY, OUTPUT, AREA,
AND TIME IN AGRICULTURE
(1948/9 TO 1962/3)

Item:		
Food Grains		
(1) py = .495 + .014t	R^2 = .760	VNR = 2.1
(.019) (.002)		
Sugar		
(1) PY = 29.645 + .718t	R^2 = .557	VNR = 1.62
(1.512) (.166)		
Cotton		
(1) Log PY = -.882 + .144 Log t	R^2 = .541	VNR = 2.96
(.069) (.034)		
Plantations		
Log PY = -.441 + .042 Log t	R^2 = .442	VNR = 2.08
(.026) (.013)		
Oil Seeds		
Prod. = -407.386 + .520 Area	R^2 = .771	VNR = 1.84
(921.8) (.075)		
Jute		
Prod. = -274.1 + 6.641 Area	R^2 = .771	VNR = 1.45
(3793) (.561)		

PY = Productivity; Prod. = Production; t = time

Source: Ministry of Food and Agriculture, Community Development
and Cooperation, Area, Production and Yield of Principal Crops in
India, 1949-50 to 1965-6. November, 1966.

major groups, it can be seen that the highest productivity changes per unit area have taken place in
sugar, whereas practically no productivity changes
have taken place in the jute industry.

In the light of the above results, idle capacity
in 1961/2* in the six sectors is as follows:

TABLE 17.3

IDLE CAPACITY IN AGRICULTURE

Crop	Idle Capacity (Percent)	Excess Capacity (Percent)
Food Grains		1.1
Sugar		4.7
Cotton	3.5	
Plantation	3.8	
Oil Seeds	0.4	
Jute		8.4

In general, in 1961, India was very near full-
capacity production in some sectors of agriculture,
and much below capacity production in manufacturing.
In other sectors like transport and services, capacity
calculations are difficult. It is assumed in the
analysis that transport is working at full capacity
and that services are moving with an average spare
capacity equal to that of the rest of the economy.
The above results regarding agriculture and manufacturing have, in my opinion, important economic
implications. The results undoubtedly point to the
need for reallocating labor and other current inputs

_____

*1961/2 harvest year is identified with 1961
calender year.

in favor of manufacturing and redeploying capital
assets in favor of agriculture, where the major scope
of increasing production is limited by an improvement
in productivity arising from more capital inputs
together with water and fertilizer.

Second, the comparatively higher spare capacity
in manufacturing suggests the usefulness of expanding
the export of metal-based industries where spare
capacity is highest and whose bases are not in agriculture, especially when agriculture is acting as a
constrained sector with a very high-capacity utilization.

When the details of the changes in land productivity were examined, it was noticed that commercial
crops like sugar had the highest growth, whereas crops
like jute, with a stagnant or ever-dwindling world
market, had the lowest. But in the context of the
need for rapid economic growth, and of the general
shortage of capital, the presence of high spare
capacities in power, iron, and steel are very dis-
turbing and need special investigation.

18

The export projections are exogenous to the prime (transient-state) model, and also to the steady-state one, and are estimated by a separate econometric model of the export sector. First, this model is wholly demand-oriented. The logic of this demand approach is that, in the Indian context, the top planning priority should be export, and it is domestic demand that should be made to bear the main burden of a demand/supply equilibrium, through the instruments of price changes of fiscal operation.

Second, the model is based on a disaggregated sector classification, because it was felt that projections made from any aggregated export relationship are bound to be biased when the mix, comprising the aforesaid aggregative sector, is changing very fast, as in India, and further when the sectors with faster rates of growth are consistently associated with income and price elasticity either above or below the average.

There is another type of problem--specification error--in using aggregated export function. Sometimes one may note a significantly high income and price elasticity in the aggregate export function. But at the same time, one may find very low price elasticity in any one or more of the subsectors. In

this case, the aggregative approach will impute,
price sensitivity to a sector when genuinely it is
not there.

In addition, since both the principal models
(steady-state and transient-state) in the present
study are in a disaggregated form, it is necessary
to develop a corresponding disaggregated export
sector.

Tables 18.1 and 18.2 give the regression values
both in log-linear and linear terms of the functional
relations in the export sector. Equations (2), (4),
(5), and (7) have been selected for this model.

India's export bills falls into four broad divisions:

1. Agriculture including forestry and animal
husbandry

2. Processing industries drawing their raw
materials from agriculture

3. Manfacturing industries drawing their raw
materials from mining and metal goods

4. Mining and mineral products

The export market of India is also divided into
two major submarkets: developed countries and
developing countries.

The prices of export goods in the two markets
and in the domestic market in the four broad classifications are estimated in comparable form from the
United Nations Year Book. It is further assumed
that the exports of agriculture and agriculture-based
industries are absorbed primarily by the developed
countries, whereas machinery and mining-based industries mainly cater for the developing countries.

With the basic assumption, as stated above,
regression equations are fitted to explain the volume
of exports of the four types of goods assuming a

TABLE 18.1

EXPORT FUNCTIONS (LOG-LINEAR TRANSFORMATION)
(Rs. '00,000)

1. Log (Export of agriculture) = 6.027 + .863 Log (GDP developed economy) R^{-2} = .713 VNR. = 2.7
   (.951) (.20-)

2. Log (Export of agriculture) = 8.923 + .879 Log (GDP developed economy) - .635 Log $\left(\frac{DP}{WP}\right)$ R^{-2} = .789 VNR = 2.18
   (1.820) (.173)   (.358)

3. Log (Export of agricultural-based industries) = 7.315 + .588 Log (GDP developed economy); R^{-2} = .260 VNR 2.06
   (1.499) (.316)

4. Log (Export of agricultural-based industries) = 10.807 + 1.282 Log (GDP developed economy) - 1.444 log $\frac{DP}{WP}$ R^{-2} = .627 VNR = 3.27
   (.170) (.346)   (.550)

5. Log (Export of mining-based industries) = -4.674 + 2.862 Log (GDP backward economy) R^{-2} = .797 VNR = 2.22
   (2.570) (.536)

6. Log (Export of mining-based industries) = -2.903 + 3.25 Log (GDP backward economy) - .769 Log $\frac{DP}{WP}$; R^{-2} = .768, VNR = 2.55
   (4.57) (.991)   (1.598)

7. Log (Mining Export) = 11.670 - .772 Log (GDP developed economy); R^{-2} = .679 V.N.R. = 1.58
   (2.888) (.611)

8. Log (Mining Export) = 23.603 - 1.511 Log (GDP developed economy) - 1.844 Log $\frac{DP}{WP}$ R^{-2} = .307 VNR = 2.51
   (7.358) (.681)   (1.300)

9. Log (Mining Export) = 11.996 - .843 Log (GDP backward economy) R^{-2} = .136 VNR 1.59
   (2.745) (.582)

10. Log (Mining Export) = 23.084 - 1.49 Log (GDP backward economy) - 1.75 Log $\frac{DP}{WP}$ R^{-2} = .366 VNR 2.44
    (6.646) (.614)   (.983)

11. Log (Total Export) = 7.429 + .765 Log world income R^{-2} = .617 VNR = 1.18
    (1.035) (.218)

12. Log (Total Export) = 13.527 + 1.005 Log world income - 1.554 Log $\frac{DP}{WP}$; R^{-2} = .843 VNR 2.46
    (2.075) (.160)   (.501)

Notes: Brackets denote standard errors.
DP = Relevant domestic prices.
WP = Relevant world prices.
Developed countries: North America, Europe and Oceania together with Japan and South Africa.
Backward economies: Latin America, East and South East Asia, Middle East, Africa (Algeria, Congo, Ghana, Kenya, Morocco, Nigeria, Malawi, Zambia, Rhodesia, Sudan, Tanganyika, Tunisia, Uganda, and Egypt).

267

TABLE 18.2

EXPORT FUNCTIONS, LINEAR RELATIONS
(Rs.'00,000)

Export of agriculture = 3478.9 + 185.96 Index of growth of developed countries
(4551.7) (39.8)
R^{-2} = .748 VNR = 2.72

Export of agriculture = 17808.3 + 186.6 Index of growth of developed countries - 134.8$\frac{DP}{WP}$

(74.3)

R^{-2} = .818 VNR = 2.18

Export of agricultural- = 9327.5 + 132.6 Index of growth of developed countries
based industries (7512.4) (65.7)

R^{-2} = .305 VNR = 2.10

Export of agricultural- = 27057.6 + 263.9 Index of growth of developed countries - 299.6 $\frac{DP}{WP}$
based industries (8825.6) (70.1) (117.6)

R^{-2} = .637 VNR = 3.4

Export of mining- + 15293.4 + 200.2 Index of growth of backward countries
based industries (4569.9) (40.4)

R^{-2} = .803 VNR = 1.67

Mining export = 5458.1 - 20.8 Index of growth of developed countries
(2047.8) (17.9)
R^{-2} = 0.048 VNR = 1.56

Mining export + 13475.3 - 40.6 Index of growth of developed countries - 59.2 $\frac{DP}{WP}$
(5791.6) (21.2) (40.5)
R^{-2} = .102 VNR = 1.57

Mining export = 5716.0 - 23.4 Index of growth of backward countries
(1972.0) (17.5)
R^{-2} = 102 VNR = 1.57

Mining export = 13271.8 - 41.3 Index of growth of backward countries - 56.9 $\frac{DP}{WP}$
(5276) (19.7) (37.4)
R^{-2} = .263 VNR = 2.28

Export (total) = 11419.3 + 453.5 World income
(13664.9) (117.5)
R^{-2} = .664 VNR = 1.16

Export (total)= 93500.0 + 570.0 World income - 909.2 $\frac{DP}{WP}$
(26872.9) (81.9) (107.2)
R^{-2} = .869 VNR 2.56

---

linear and log-linear trend. The main explanatory
variables for this purpose are the changes in the
income of the importing countries and the relative
price movements of those products within and outside
India.   Table 18.1 and Table 18.2 give the regression
equations of the export model, and the basic data
derived from 1956-65 world export prices. In the
log-linear model, the values of the income and price
elasticity of agricultural goods are estimated at
.879 and - .636 respectively. Both these results are
in conformity with general expectations and suggest
that the export possibility for India's agricultural
goods is not too promising and that the market is
rather stagnant (Equation 3).

     With regard to the income and price elasticity
of agricultural-based industries, they are quite
high for this sector (Equation 4). Similarly, the
metal-based industries have a high income elasticity
in the export market (developing countries) although
a comparatively low price elasticity. This result
is slightly difficult to explain because it suggests
that in the developing countries, Indian machines
are imported in response to the demand generated by
the development process and irrespective of the
relative prices of these goods. The one possible
explanation is that the sellers of machinery in this
part of the world may have been enjoying a sellers'
market rather than a buyers' market. However, this
hypothesis needs further exploration. Exports of
mineral goods, on the other hand, have a declining
market and a negative income elasticity but a negative
price elasticity. This means that to give further
impetus to exports of mineral goods, what is needed
is a reduction in mining prices in India.

     In general, the above pattern suggests that
any attempt to forecast the future prospects of
Indian exports in aggregate terms will be difficult.
It also suggests that the strategy of Indian exports
should be built up more in terms of machinery and
processing goods than in terms of conventional
primary goods. Having taken into account the aggregate
exports of India as an alternative approach, over
the plan period, the income elasticity of export is

unity and the price elasticity is -1.6. This again
suggested that if one wants to increase Indian exports
by more than the average rate of growth of world
income, which is not very high, the only solution is
to increase the efficiency of the exporting industries
and to reduce the price of Indian goods abroad. In
the steady state formulation, the sector classification
ran into 22 separate groups. Hence the estimates
of the above 4 aggregated groups are further subdivided
into 22 corresponding sectors to match with that
model, by assuming a linear relation between the
individual elements of the group and the group total.
Table 18.3 gives the regression equations for this
purpose. The fits of the equations for cotton textile
exports and exports of glass and wood are not very
satisfactory, but the rest are statistically acceptable. All export projections are given in 1959
prices, in conformity with the pricing convention
adopted in the present model. The sources of information for the present export study are the
Annual Statement of Foreign Trade, published by
the Government of India, together with the Annual
Abstract of Statistics and the United Nations Statistical Yearbook: The period covered is 1957-65.

For each year of the transient-state model,
the export projections are given initially in the
above four groups and are then expanded into a 22-
sector classification (as adopted in the steady-
state model). Finally they are again aggregated
into four groups, to adjust in the sector classification used in the transient-state model.

The Import Submodel

The coefficients relating to the import sector
of the model are estimated briefly as follows:

The imports are classified into three major
categories: (1) Intermediate imports, (noncompeting
imports contributing to the capital formation of
the country; and (3) consumer-goods imports going
to households, government, and corporate sectors as
direct consumption.

TABLE 18.3

SCALAR EXPORT CONVERTED TO VECTORS
(Rs'00,000)

I. Agriculture

1. Cotton export = 741.6 + .034 Ag. Exp. R^{-2} = .080 VNR = 2.22
     (1176.1) (.048)

2. Plantation export. = 6316.6 + .358 Ag. Exp. R^{-2} = .797 VNR = 2.48
     (1660.7) (.067)

3. Other agric. export = -7058.2 + .608 Ag. Exp. R^{-2} = .830 VNR = 2.30
     (2537.7)   (.010)

II. Agricultural-based Industries

1. Rubber and leather export = 925.7 + .064 Ag. Based Exp. R^{-2} = .385
     (677.1) (.028)   VNR= 3.20

2. Food and bev. export = 5752.0 + .334 Ag. Based Exp. R^{-2} - .477 VNR = 1.55
     (3017.0) (.123)   1.55

3. Textile export = 4826.3 + .602 Ag. Based Exp. R^{-2} = .791 VNR = 1.50
     (2816.0) (.115)

III. Mining and Metal-based Industries.

1. Glass and wood export = 1370.5 - 0.42 Mining-based exp. R^{-2} = .110 VNR = 2.27
     (237.0) (.031)

2. Transport equipment exp. = -189.2 + .043 M.B.Exp. R^{-2} = .947 VNR = 2.58
     (29.6)   (.004)

3. Electrical equipment exp. = -70.4 + .028 MB.Exp. R^{-2} = .748 VNR = 3.54
     (45.9)   (.006)

4. Aluminum export = -10.7 + .030 M.B. Exp. R^{-2} = .820 VNR = 2.20
     (40.5)   (.005)

5. Iron and steel exp. = -2305.1 + .797 M.B. Exp. R^{-2} = .977 VNR = 2.00
     (350.0)   (.046)

6. Nonelectrical equipment exp. = 22.2 + .053 M.B. Exp. R^{-2} = .796 VNR = 2.33
     (76.3)   (.010)

7. Chemical and misc. exp. = 1.1808 + .090 M.B. Exp. R^{-2} = .525 VNR = 1.74
     (234.1)   (.031)

TABLE 18.4

IMPORT FUNCTIONS
(Rs.'00',000)

Capital-Goods Industries

(1) $M = 126.2 + .294T - 23.085^t$; $\bar{R}^2 = .951$ VNR = 1.35
     (26.6) (.029)   (3.614)

(2) $m_1 = 8.4 + 158M$ $\bar{R}^2 = .867$ VNR = 1.21
     (3.9)   (.018)

(3) $m_2 = -16.7 + .625M$ $\bar{R}^2 = .632$ VNR = 1.40
     (10.7)   (.048)

(4) $m_3 = 8.4 + .216M$ $\bar{R}^2 = .635$ VNR = 1.99
     (10.3) (.046)

$M = m_1 + m_2 + m_3$

Consumption-Goods Industries

(5) Other agric. = 16.6 + .169 Cons.Imp. $\bar{R}^2 = .697$ VNR = 2.02
    imports   (2.8)   (.003)

(6) Chemical-goods
    imports   = 4.1 + .101 C.I. $\bar{R}^2 = .$ 245 VNR = 1,05
                  (4.0) (.005)

(7) Paper imports = 5.7 + .078 C.I. $\bar{R}^2 = .307$ VNR = 1.65
                   (2.8)   (.31)

(8) Nonelectrical = .457 + .055 CI
    equipment   (2.5) (.029) $\bar{R}^2 = .185$ VNR = .591

(9) Textile = -.810 + .037 C.I $\bar{R}^2 = .140$ VNR = .732
             (1.893) (.021)

(10) Other imports = -27.3 + .561 C.I. $\bar{R}^2 = .865$ VNR = 2.78
                    (5.6)   (.064)

(11) Food and beverage
     imports   = 1.3 - .001 C.I. Very bad fit
                    (1.0)   (.011)

Intermediate Imports

Sectors	Proportionality Coefficients
1	.068
2	.001
3	.027
4	.038
13	.066
17	.039
18	.027
21	.099
22	.044

Capital-Goods Industries (Log Transformation)

(i) $\text{Log } M = -7.1 + 1.769\ I - .375\ t, \quad \bar{R}^2 = .898 \quad \text{V.N.R.} = 1.41$
$\qquad\quad (1.4) \quad (.202) \quad\ (.074)$

(ii) $\text{Log } \frac{M}{I} = -1.86 - .125\ \text{Log } t \quad \bar{R}^2 = .270 \quad \text{V.N.R.} = 0.92$
$\qquad\qquad\ (.101)\ (.053) \qquad\qquad\qquad\quad (\text{bad fit})$

Notation: M = Total capital-goods imports

m_1, m_2 and m_3 = Electrical, nonelectrical, and transport
$\qquad\qquad\qquad$ equipment imports

I = Total gross fixed investment

C.i. = Consumption-goods imports

In the first category, a proportional relation is assumed between the output and import contents of a noncompeting type in all of the 22 sectors. Further, it is assumed to remain constant over the period of the plan. This is perhaps slightly heroic. Econometric (time-series) relations between the intermediate imports and the output of the different industries in India in 8 major groups were attempted, but the results were not very satisfactory (i.e., no statistically significant functional relations were observed).

The regression coefficient of capital-goods imports is estimated on the basis of a linear rela-tionship between total gross fixed investment and the total of capital goods imported, with time as a second explanatory variable (representing the likely trend of the rate of import substitution). (See Table 18.4.)

Equation (1) in Table 18.4 presents this func-tional relation and is regarded as statistically quite satisfactory. An alternative formulation is attempted when total gross capital formation is taken as the explanatory variable, but the result is not very staisfactory. Equation (1) also brings out clearly the attainment of a significant degree of import substitution in the capital-goods sector over this period (1948-64).

In this equation, the regression coefficients asoociated with time as an explanatory variable have a negative sign and differ significantly from zero. The elasticity associated with the time trend in the log-linear relation also suggest a strong import substition in this sector. In another alternative formulation, where the average ratio of machinery imports to total fixed-capital formation is expressed as a log-linear function of time, the regression coefficients again have a negative value, suggesting the occurrence of import substitution in this sector. (See Table 18.4.)

The seclar estimate of the total volume of capital-goods imports is converted into a vector by

assuming a linear relationship between the total
value of capital goods imported and the import of
the individual items of capital goods. In this
case, again satisfactory fits are obtained. (See
Table 18.4.)

The above functional relations are formulated
from time-series data covering a period from 1947/8
to 1963/4 and obtained from Bipin Behari, together
with the CSO estimates of gross fixed-capital formation in India.[1]

It is assumed that intermediate imports of
competing goods will fall to zero by 1975/6. For
the consumption-goods sector, no formal functional
relationship is used in the present model. First,
it does not seem possible to formulate any statistically significant functional relation between consumption-goods imports and other national-income
aggregates; and second, it is thought, for the
purpose of planning, that consumption-goods imports
can safely be treated as a residual, especially
when they do not contribute directly to any material
output growth in the economy. Beside, this approach
allows more maneuverability in the planning mechanism.

In the present model, therefore, imports of
consumption goods at any particular period are equal
to the excess of export earning and aid (net) over
the cost of import of intermediate (noncompeting)
and capital goods. The aid is taken in its net
concept after deducting servicing charges and in-
stalment payments on the earlier loans. All other
invisible items of imports and exports are neglected
on the assumption that they will balance with each
other.

NOTE

1. Bipin Behari, Imports in a Developing Economy, (Bombay: Vora & Co., 1965); Central Statistical
Organisation, Estimates of Gross Capital Formation
in India, 1948/9 to 1960/1, (1961).

In this model the consumption/income relation
is derived in aggregate terms. The scalar estimate
of total consumption expenditure is subsequently
translated into a vector by assuming a linear relation,
a log-linear relation, and a concentration-curve
approach between an individual item of consumption
and the total consumption expenditure.[1]

I will first develop the consumption-income
relation in aggregate terms and then the problem
of computation of the consumption vector against
a given consumption expenditure per capita as a
scalar value. Finally, we shall attempt to bring
out the role of these parameters in the proposed
programming model.

Private consumption (personal and corporate)
is made an endogenous variable in this model and
is regarded as functionally related to the private
disposable income at constant price. The econometric
relation between private consumption and private
disposable income at constant price is derived from
time-series analysis.

The data on private income are taken from
national income and expenditure statistics computed

by the CSO. They include gross national product
less government income together with transfer payments,
adjusted for earned income and private donations
from abroad.

Private consumption figures are not directly
available. Saving estimates at current and constant
prices are available both in the Reserve Bank of
India Report and in the report of the National Council
of Applied Economic Research (NCAER). (For both see
Table 19.1).[2] The concepts of saving in the two
reports are not strictly comparable, and the methods
of estimation are different. The NCAER further adopts
two different methods of estimating saving: direct
and indirect.

Private consumption at market prices is regarded
as the difference between private income net of direct
taxes (income tax, land revenues, and corporate taxes)
and private saving.

In this study, the private consumption estimates
given in the inter-industry presentation of commodity
flows are on a residual basis, and derived from
total domestic expenditure at market prices. That
the two estimates are conceptually identical is
demonstrated in Table 19.2 showing national-income
identities, where the equation under the first heading
presents the inter-industry commodity flows, while
the equation under the second heading presents the
time-series relations in terms of private consumption
and private income.

The inter-industry estimates are available at
only one point of time for the year 1959. Hence
this year is taken as a benchmark to compare the
estimates from the two different approaches. In
general, they show a good matching.

Private consumption at market prices calculated
from the time-series approach is equal to Rs.107,146
million. Private consumption at market price
calculated from the inter-industry flows is equal
to Rs.105,782 million (Table 19.3).

TABLE 19.1

ESTIMATES OF DOMESTIC SAVING
(Rs.million: 1948/49 prices)

Year	Reserve Bank				National Council of Applied Economic Research			
	Govern-ment	Cor-porate	House-hold	Total	Govern-ment	Cor-porate	House-hold	Total
1950/51	891	324	3817	5032	1114	309	6057	7479
1951/52	1707	581	2544	4832	1837	613	4449	6899
1952/53	989	10	2939	3933	903	238	7084	8225
1953/54	886	248	4275	5409	707	347	7183	8236
1954/55	999	538	6637	8174	992	454	8522	9997
1955/56	1178	631	8391	10192	1148	406	10546	12099
1956/57	1720	569	8183	10472	1550	619	8864	11028
1957/58	1498	171	5958	7627	1614	221	10611	12446
1958/59	1276	229	7036	8611	1323	364	8255	9941
1959/60	1857	528	7707	10092	1750	688	10357	12805
1960/61	2155	961	9236	12352	2053	1135	10946	14133
1961/62	3121	863	8138	12122	2111	1036	11124	14271
1962/63	3560	908	8539	13007	...	...	...	...

TABLE 19.2

NATIONAL INCOME IDENTITIES
IN THE PRESENT MODEL.
(At market prices).

a) C(pr)+C(pu)+I+(EX.-IM.)-I.T.-C.C.=N.P.(NET) at factor cost.................(1)

b) C(pr)=P.I.-(C.S.+H.S.) - D.T...(2)

c) P.I. = N.P.(Gross), at factor cost+T.P. - G.I. + Income (net) abroad........(3)

Equation (1) gives the inter-industry flows.

Equation (2) and (3) give the relations in terms of national-income aggregates.

   If equations (2) and (3) are put in equation (1), the two sides of this equation
would cancel. This would establish the exact matching of the two types of accounts.

NOTES

C(pr).= Private consumption at market prices.
C(pu).= Public   "   "   "
I.= Total Investment.
Ex.= Export, f.o.b.
Im.= Imports, c.i.f.
I.T.= Indirect taxes.
D.T.= Direct taxes.

P.I.= Private Income.
C.S.= Corporate Saving.
H.S.= Household Saving.
N.P.= National Product.
T.P.= Transfer payments.
G.I.= Govt. Income.
C.C.= Capital Consump-
      tion.

280

TABLE 19.3

COMPARATIVE ESTIMATES OF THE LEVEL OF CONSUMPTION, AND ITS SHARE OF NATIONAL INCOME, 1959/60

(Rs.million: at current prices)

Regression Model (NCAER)	Regression Model (RBI)	Inter-industry model, (Planning-Commission: Residual flow method).
1. Private consumption at 1948/9 prices = 105,854 (based on the equation: private consumption = 653.8 + .852 Disposal Income)	2. Private consumption at 1948/9 prices = 108,432 (Based on the equation Pr. Cons. = 865.0 + .856 Disposal Income)	
2. Indirect taxes at 1948/9 prices assigned to private consumption = 7,555 (N. Income Statistics - CSO)	2. Indirect taxes at 1948/9 prices assigned to private consumption = 7,555 (CSO).	
3. Private consumption at factor cost (1948/9 prices) = 98,299 (1 minus 2)	3. Private consumption at factor cost (1948/9 prices) = 100,877 (1 minus 2)	
4. Private consumption at factor cost (1959/60 prices) = 107,146	4. Private consumption at factor cost (1959/60 prices) = 109,956	105,782
5. As percent of N. I. = 77.4	5. As percent of N. I. = 79.4	78.2 percent*

*The estimate of national income in the inter-industry matrix (1959) was lower than the national-income statistics given by the CSO.

Source: Regression models based on NCAER data, Reserve Bank of India data, and a Planning Commission inter-industry table for the year 1959/60.

The private consumption estimate at market prices in the inter-industry table is comparatively lower than the one based on the time-series data, primarily because the estimate of gross domestic product in this table is slightly lower than the CSO estimate on which the time series is based. The relation between private income and private consumption at market prices is derived both in linear and log-linear terms.

With reference to Table 19.4, it is clear that the estimates of net investment (net investment = savings + net capital flow) in the NCAER report are higher than those available in the Reserve Bank of India report. In the same table, it is shown that the CSO estimates of investment are also higher than those of the Reserve Bank. The inter-industry estimates of 1959 net capital formation match well with the estimates given by the Reserve Bank.

The estimates of marginal propensity to consume relating to the private sector, derived from the NCAER and Reserve Bank of India data, match extremely well with each other. The propensity to consume in both cases is nearly 85 percent of private disposable income. However, preference is given to the estimates based on the Reserve Bank of India data because this is the official source.

From the point of view of goodness of fit of the above relations, there is very little to choose between the natural and log relations. (See Table 19.5.)

Apart from the aforesaid functional relations, it was necessary to derive one more functional relation based on the national income aggregates: the relation between indirect taxes and the gross national product (net). The importance of this relation will be obvious later.

The estimate of aggregate consumption expenditure is translated into a consumption vector by estimating relevant expenditure elasticities for different items of consumption. This, of course, entails a large

TABLE 19.4

ALTERNATIVE ESTIMATES OF NET CAPITAL
FORMATION, BETWEEN 1948/9 and 1960/1.*
(Rs. million)

	CSO	NCAER	RBI	Inter-industry
1948/49	4,690			
1949/50	4,810			
1950/51	4,800	7,770	5,340	
1951/52	7,910	9,170	7,530	
1952/53	4,430	8,140	3,913	
1953/54	7,610	8,460	5,615	
1954/55	7,790	9,620	8,107	
1955/56	9,860	12,010	10,337	
1956/57	16,620	14,870	14,543	
1957/58	12,670	19,550	12,869	
1958/59	16,800	14,250	13,307	
1959/60	16,630	16,180	13,603	1469.1
1960/61	19,590	20,290	18,692	

*In current prices, since the CSO estimates
were at current prices.

Sources: (i) CSO, National-income Statistics.
Estimates of Gross Capital Formation in India for
1948/9 to 1960/1. (ii) NCAER Saving in India, 1950/1
to 1961/2 (New Delhi: Publication Division, July,
1965). (iii) Deshpande et al "Estimates of Saving
and Investment in the Indian Economy, 1950/1 to 1962/
3 "Reserve Bank OF India Bulletin, (March, 1965).

TABLE 19.5

Estimates of Consumption function, 1948/9 to 1960/1
(Rs.'0 million)

RBI Data

1. (Private consumption = 865.0 + .856   (Disposable income at constant
   (at constant prices) (294.0)   (.027)   1959 prices)

   $\bar{R}^2$ = .988   VNR = 1.10

2. Indirect tax receipt = -884.87 + .139 GNP (net) at current prices
   at current prices   (96.03)   (.008)

   $\bar{R}^2$ = .961   VNR = 2.71

3. $\left\{ \dfrac{\text{Private Income at current price}}{\text{GNP (Net) at current prices}} \right\}$ x 100 = $\underset{(.132)}{100.6} + \underset{(.017)}{.007t}$

   $\bar{R}^2$ = .629   VNR = 1.097

4. Log private consumption = .798 + .907 Log   (private disposable income at
   (at constant prices)   =(.285) (.031)   constant 1959 prices)

   $\bar{R}^2$ = .986   VNR = 1.029

5. Log indirect taxes at = -13.4 + 2.147 Log $\left\{ \text{GNP (net) at current prices} \right\}$
   current prices   (1.42)   (.152)

   $\bar{R}^2$ = .943   VNR = 2.475

6. $\text{Log} \left\{ \dfrac{\text{Private Income}}{\text{G.N.P. (net) at}} \right\}$ = 4.609 + .004 Logt.
   current prices   (.001)   (.0006)

   $\bar{R}^2$ = .800   VNR = 2.145

NCAER Data

7. Private consumption = 653.8 +   .852   (Disposable income at constant
   at constant prices   (279.0)   (.026)   1959 prices)

   $\bar{R}^2$ = .989   VNR = 2.604

8. Log private consumption = .593 + .926   Log private disposable income at
   at constant 1959 prices (.276) (.030)   constant prices

   $\bar{R}^2$ = .989   VNR = 2.507

---

number of assumptions. In the above model it was
found extremely difficult to relate income to
expenditure directly for individual items because
the details of the expenditure items are available
on a cross-section basis (for individual items of
consumption), while the data on income is available
only in aggregation and on a time-series basis.
Besides, it appeared that, conceptually, any information on expenditure was a better proxy of permanent
income, and the expenditure habits of the people
were supposed to have a more stable relation with
permanent income than with income at a specific period.
Hence this two-stage approach was preferred.

In our approach, it is assumed that the difference
in consumption behavior amongst persons with different
incomes at a given moment of time are the same as
the differences in consumption behavior of the same
person if his income is changed from one level to
another. This assumption may prove to be slightly
unrealistic under certain circumstances. It is
generally assumed that family budget surveys reveal
a long-run stable relation between aggregate expenditure and expenditure on an individual item. Thus
cross-section elasticities for the purpose of predicting future demand assume away autonomous changes in
tastes over time, irrespective of changes in income
and in the quality of the product.

Moreover, a family budget survey in a given
year may contain many transitory components of income
and expenditure, and hence may not reveal the long-
run permanent relationship between them, insofar as
temporary components of income and expenditure are
unrelated to each other and to the permanent
components.

Lastly, the elasticity of demand with reference
to the value of expenditure on individual items of
consumption includes the effect of changes in quality
as well as in price. When one considers only the
quantity elasticity of demand, i.e., changes in the
quantity consumed in response to changes in total
expenditure or income, the changes in the quality
of the product cannot be incorporated in it. But

the problem comes when the value of an expenditure
item is taken into consideration.

As income goes up, the value of expenditure on
any individual item may go up, not only because the
quantity consumed may go up but also because the
price of the commodity (even under the same head) is
higher. This arises because of quality improvement,
i.e., charging higher prices for the same commodity
consumed by higher income brackets. For example,
the ratio of the value of expenditure on food to
total consumer expenditure on all goods and services
has remained fairly constant throughout in the United
Kingdom and the United States, even though every
budget study carried out since the days of Engels
shows income elasticity for food always less than
unity.[3] This is because the value of expenditure
on food does not have the same real content in terms
of quality over a period of time (Improvement in
quality is visualized.)

Indeed, an analysis of family budgets, which
gives a still picture of commodity technology as
well as of consumer preference at a given point of
time, is likely to be misleading when used for the
purposes of prediction, unless allowance is made
for changes in tastes and nature or quality of the
commodities in the shopping list.

Lastly, we have total per capita expenditure
as an explanatory variable in the place of total
per capita income. The use of total per capita
expenditure as an independent variable may tend to
introduce bias in the estimates of regression
coefficients.

Suppose the linear model underlying income/
consumption relationships is as follows:

$$Y_i = A_i + B_i I + U \qquad\qquad\qquad (1)$$

$$\sum_i Y_i = X = A_j + B_j I + U \qquad\qquad (2)$$

where Y_i is per capita expenditure on ith commodity,
I per capita income, and X per capita total expenditure

on all items. The expenditure on the ith commodity
as a function of per capita total expenditure can
be derived from the above model as follows:

$$Y_i = A_i + B_i \frac{(X - A_j - V)}{B_j} + U$$

$$= A_i + \frac{B_i}{B_j} X - \frac{A_j B_i}{B_j} - \frac{B_i}{B_j} V + U$$

$$= (A_i - \frac{A_j B_j}{B_j}) + \frac{B_i}{B_j} X + (U - \frac{B_i}{B_j} V)$$

$$= P + Q X + W \text{ where } P = (A - \frac{A_j B_j}{B_j})$$

$$Q = (\frac{B_i}{B_j}) \text{ and } w = (U - \frac{B_i V}{B_j}) \tag{3}$$

The new error term is a linear combination of the
error terms in the previous system of equations.
The new error term (w) contains V which is related
to variations in x. (vide Equation 2.) Thus,
additional relationships between the new error term
(W) and the explanatory variable is introduced in
equation (3). Accordingly, the estimate of the
coefficient B will be biased. Total per capita
expenditure is by definition equal to the sum of
per capita expenditure on various individual items;
if, during a survey period, expenditure on a given
item is particularly high, there is automatically
an increase in the total expenditure.

For example, if the purchase of rice or wheat
increases, both expenditure on food as well as total
expenditure increases. Thus there is a dependence
between random elements affecting food expenditure,
i.e., variable to be explained, and the explanatory
variable, i.e., total expenditure. The extent of
the bias is not merely a function of the relative
importance of the particular item in total expenditure.[4]

Empirical studies reveal that upward biases tend to occur in the case of durable articles and clothing, which are generally considered to be unstable and variable items of expenditure, whereas in the case of more stable items of expenditure, such as food and rent, the bias is usually downwards.[5] It should be recognized that the bias arises out of the assumptions made and relations postulated in the first set of equations, from which the expenditure equation is derived. The basic assumption underlying that model is that individual items of expenditure as well as total expenditure are both functions of income and are simultaneously determined as such.

One could, of course, think of an alternative model. One may assume that a household first decides on its total expenditure and then, in the second stage, distributes its total expenditure among various commodities included in the budget. Decision is thus taken in two stages, so that the relationship between errors and explanatory variables no longer exists in the equation for particular items of expenditure.

The basic data for this study is drawn from the National Survey reports, (conducted as a part of a regular multipurpose socio-economic sample survey) in the form of several rounds, each round relating to a specific period of time and some special subject of enquiry. But fortunately data on household expenditure has been collected in all rounds since 1950. However, the published volumes gave information only on total expenditure and expenditure on individual items. Attempts have been made to estimate two variable equations from this data. In this connection, the choice of the functional form has been made mainly in the light of goodness of fit and the practice followed in Indian planning. Thus, finally, the expenditure elasticities are estimated by Iyengar's method of Engel's elasticity, double log relations between the total expenditure and expenditure on individual items per capita for all income classes, and simple linear relationship (Stone's type), all for the year 1960/1.

Data are also available for earlier rounds, and
accordingly, the concentration coefficients and
elasticities are estimated for three earlier rounds
(March-August 1957, September 1957-May 1958, July
1959-June 1960), for both rural and urban population,
separately and altogether.

The number of subdivisions used in these
exercises, in terms of commodity consumed, differs
from round to round. To bring comparability with
the 22-sector classification used in the present
model, we have reclassified the consumption entries
of the National Sample Survey (NSS) data into five
broad groups: (1) Food grains, (2) food, beverages,
and tobacco, (3) "other" agriculture, (4) textiles,
and (5) Electricity, other types of fuel, and
miscellaneous expenditure.

Subsequently, further subdivisions within each
of the groups are made in the proportions in which
they are available in the 1959 consumption basket
given in the 1959 inter-industry table.

The expenditure elasticities and the concentration
ratios show a good degree of stability over all the
rounds with very minor differences, and with no
observable trend effect.[6]

This suggests that the 1960/1 estimated expenditure elasticities can be used with confidence in
the final programming model.

Table 19.6 gives the different fits between
aggregate consumption expenditure and consumption
expenditure on individual commodities, all on a per
capita basis, for rural and urban sectors combined
for 1960/1. Item 4 of this table gives the relation
between consumption of an individual item and of the
total in the light of Stone's linear expenditure
system.

TABLE 19.6

ESTIMATES OF ENGEL ELASTICITIES FOR COMMODITY GROUPS:
FOURTH ROUND 1960
(Rural and Urban Population)

	Constant Term	Elas-ticities	R-Bar Squared	Von Neumann Ratio
	A	B	$\bar{R}^{-2}$	
I FOOD GRAINS				
Iyengar's method		0.4543		
Log-Log Regression	1.2255	0.4822	0.9322	0.5380
(Standard Error)	(0.1586)	(0.0391)		
Linear Regression	14.9300	0.1451	0.8071	0.4617
(Standard Error)	(1.6735)	(0.0212)		
II FOOD-BEVERAGES-TOBACCO				
Iyengar's method		1.4156		
Log-Log Regression	-3.7222	1.4134	0.9984	0.9495
(Standard Error)	(0.0686)	(0.0169)		
Linear Regression	-3.5683	0.2042	0.9941	0.5019
(Standard Error)	(0.3746)	(0.0047)		
III OTHER AGRICULTURE				
Iyengar's method		1.4165		
Log-Log Regression	-3.0308	1.4147	0.9984	0.9554
(Standard Error)	(0.0686)	(0.0169)		
Linear Regression	-7.1795	0.4104	0.9941	0.5011
(Standard Error)	(0.7523)	(0.0095)		
IV TEXTILE				
Iyengar's method		1.9513		
Log-Log Regression	-7.2867	2.1171	0.9782	1.1425
(Standard Error)	(0.3863)	(0.0952)		
Linear Regression	-5.1722	0.1786	0.9704	0.8253
(Standard Error)	(0.7424)	(0.0094)		
V ELECTRICITY GENERATION				
Iyengar's method		0.8400		
Log-Log Regression	-1.8681	0.8393	0.9969	2.8148
(Standard Error)	(0.0571)	(0.0141)		
Linear Regression	0.9900	0.0617	0.9834	1.8683
(Standard Error)	(0.1911)	(0.0024)		

As only the combined estimates for rural and urban sectors are needed for the model, it was decided to omit any presentation of separate tables for rural and urban sectors.

In general, log-linear fits between aggregate consumption and consumption of individual items are slightly better than the linear ones. Hence, it was decided to choose the former estimates for this model.

As an alternative, the parameters derived from Iyengar's method of estimation were used as an experiment. Again, the estimated elasticities were found to be more or less the same.

The expenditure elasticities estimated in the earlier sections are used in the steady-state model for converting the scalar value of private consumption expenditure into its vector counterpart. This is done for 1975/6, (the terminal year of the plan horizon). The following relations are used for this purpose:

$$c_{it} = c_{io} + c_{io} \left(\frac{x_{it} - x_{io}}{x_{io}}\right) e_i$$

$$P.c_{it} = C_{it}$$

P = Projected population

c_{io} = Per capita aggregate consumption of item i in the base

x_{io} = Per capita aggregate consumption in the base

x_{it} = Targeted per capita aggregate consumption for the terminal year

e_i = Expenditure elasticity of the ith item

c_{it} = Total per capita consumption of ith element in period t

C_{it} = Total consumption of ith element in period t

The expenditure classes are divided into five subgroups in this "expenditure elasticity" model. This is necessary to bring comparability between inter-industry and the NSS expenditure classifications.

NOTES

1. N. S. Iyenger, "Some Estimates of Engel
Elasticities Based on National Sample Survey Data,"
Royal Statistical Society, 130, (1967).

2. See article by Dr. Khat Khate and K. L.
Deshpande in Reserve Bank of India, Bulletin (March,
1965), p. 314; and National Council of Applied
Economic Research, Saving in India, 1950-1 to 1961-2,
(New Delhi, July, 1965).

3. J. A. C Brown, "The Use of Income Elasticities
in Predicting Food Consumption," (Unpublished paper,
Cambridge Department of Applied Economics, 1959).

4. R. Summers, "A Note on Least Square Bias
in Household Expenditure Analysis," Econometrics,
Vol. 29, No. 3, (July, 1961).

5. N. Liviatan, "Errors in Variables and Engel
Curve Analysis," Econometrics, Vol. 29, No. 3, (July,
1961), pp. 336-61.

6. (C.A. Devos), "A Consumption Model for a
Growing Economy," (Unpublished M. A. dissertation,
Manchester University, England, 1967).

20

THE
MACRO-ECONOMIC
FRAMEWORK

The national income estimate at factor cost in the macro-model is attempted from three distinct approaches: the future growth rates in terms of broad national-income (i.e., value-added) sectors derived primarily on the basis of mechanical extrapolation of past growth rates; the estimate of national income for 1975/6 based on a "demand" or "requirement" approach calculated from some welfare norm--for example, the minimum requirement of the people (these estimates initially appear as a consumption expenditure per capita satisfying given consumption needs of the people: The breakdown between public and private consumption is made at a subsequent level of decision; and adoption of the estimates of national income given in the draft Fourth Plan. These draft plan estimates are a mix of technical information regarding capacity expansion, past performances, political aspirations, and broad value judgement of the planners.

The detailed working stages of the first line of approach are well illustrated in the Economic decision; sion's exercise on the Fourth Plan formulation. The second approach is highly subjective, as the very concept of minimum or decent standard of living is relative to the values of life. In this book, although this approach has been adopted, to make it less subjective the estimate is made very close to the living standard prescribed in the draft outline of the Fourth Plan.

TABLE 20.1

MACRO-ECONOMIC MODEL
(DRAFT FOURTH PLAN)

Item	(Rs. billion at 1960/1 market prices)		
	1960/1	1970/1	1975/6
National income	141.4	231.0	323.0
Net domestic product at factor cost	141.9	233.1	362.0
Add indirect taxes and miscellaneous receipts (net subsidies)	11.9	23.5	35.0
Net domestic product at market price	153.8	256.6	361.0
Add depreciation provisions	6.1	13.5	21.0
Gross domestic product at market price	159.9	270.1	382.0
Add excess of import of food and services over their exports	4.1	2.5	-4.8 (for repayment of loans)
Gross domestic expenditure	164.0	272.6	377.2
Gross capital formation	20.8	49.4	73.8
Public consumption	11.6	31.8	45.5*
Private consumption	131.6	191.4	257.9*
Population (millions)	439	560	630
Per capita private consumption	300	342	409

*The estimate of public consumption entering into the model is Rs.86.8 billion, and for private consumption is Rs.244 billion, both valued at factor cost and 1959 prices. The corresponding material components are Rs.34 billion and Rs.221.7 billions.

In this connection, it is important to note that
the consumption standards in the draft outline for
1970/1 and for 1975/6 are based primarily on the recommendations of a technical paper prepared by the
Perspective Planning Division of the Indian Planning
Commission under the heading "Minimum Standard of
Living in the Perspective Plan of India." Table 20.1
gives the macro-framework presented in the material
balance paper of the Indian Planning Commission for
the Fourth and Fifth Plans.

Given that in the present model, the estimates
of consumption, investment, and exports are at producer's prices, it follows that the estimates of
private consumption and public consumption for 1975/6
given in the above macro-model have to be revalued at
producer's prices by subtracting the indirect taxes
(net of subsidies) from the respective values, to
bring comparability with our estimates. Further, as
our steady-state and transient-state models treat the
material and labor component separately in two different submodels, we have to separate the estimates
of private and public consumption into two parts before
being fed into the principal models as exogenous
variables.

The steady-state model contains the following exogenous variables:

Item 1: Private consumption, as a scalar and a vector
Item 2: Post-terminal rates of growth of private consumption
Item 3: Public consumption, as a scalar and a vector
Item 4: Post-terminal rates of growth of public consumption
Item 5: Exports, as a scalar and a vector
Item 6: Post-terminal rates of growth of export

Item 1 is estimated as a scalar value from the macro-model and as a vector (together with item 2) from the consumption-income disaggregated submodel already discussed. In the macro-model, the per capita private consumption for 1975/6 is estimated as Rs. 441.5 per annum and total private consumption as Rs.280.0 billion at 1959 producer's prices.

Further, the estimate is made net of direct expenses on services by households and placed at Rs.351.9 per capita per annum, to make it comparable with the specification of the 1959 matrix.

The consumption vector for 1959 is at current prices at factor cost and is divided into 22 sectors. On the other hand, the expenditure elasticities estimated in the consumption-income submodel are divided only into five broad groups. Hence, for

projecting in the year 1975/6, it is necessary to
aggregate the 22 sectors into the above five groups.
Later on, before being fed into the steady-state model,
they are expanded again into 22 sectors, assuming
that the base-period (1959) product composition within each of the five groups remains unchanged over
this period. The services component of private consumption is maintained at the base-period level on
a per capita basis.

    Table 21.1 presents the consumption vector for
1975/6 and the post-terminal growth rates.

    The rate of growth of income in the post-terminal
period in the steady-state formulation is assumed
to be 7 percent per annum. This targeted income
growth rate is borrowed from the Fourth Plan draft
outline. Assuming a 2.5 percent rate of growth of
population in the post-plan period, this gives a 4.5
percent rate of growth of per capita income. Again,
the estimated expenditure elasticities of this model
give the percentage changes in expenditure on a single
item corresponding to a unit percentage change in
aggregate consumption. Assuming the average propensity
to consume to remain constant over the whole of the
post-plan period, it suggests that one should expect
a 4.5 percent compound rate of growth of consumption
per capita in the post-plan period. Subsequently,
by using the estimates of expenditure elasticities
derived in the consumption-income submodel, the
exponential rates of growth of each element of consumption in the post-1975/6 period are estimated in
a rough-and-ready manner.

    The public-consumption estimate (item 3) appears
initially as a scalar value at market prices and is
derived from the macro-model. Afterwards, it is
revalued at factor cost.* This revalued figure is
further converted into a vector on the basis of a
22-sector classification by using the base-period

----

    *Salary component is excluded.

commodity and service composition of public-consumption expenditure.

Item 4 is estimated by assuming an unchanged level of per capita public consumption in the post-terminal period.

As has already been explained, the estimates of exports are initially made in four major groups and are based on four regression equations, computed from time-series data and relating changes in the volume of exports (f.o.b.) at constant prices with changes in price relatives between domestic and world prices and income growths in the absorbing countries. The importing countries, in this context, are divided broadly into developed and developing. Details are given in the export model.

The following two major alternative exercises are attempted regarding the export projection in the present model: (i) A pessimistic one, assuming devaluation would have no effect on the volume of export;* and (ii) an optimistic one, assuming devaluation would have the full effect in reducing export prices.

Subsequently, these projected estimates are expanded into 22 sectors, assuming the product mix within each sector remains the same as in 1959.

To elaborate, the pessimistic estimates assume a rate of increase in the ratio of domestic prices to international competitive prices of 1 percent per annum beyond the sample period in the agricultural sector, 2.5 percent in the industrial sector mainly based on agrigulture, and 2 percent in the industrial sector based on mining. The estimates of these per-centages are not determined completely arbitrarily, but have been calculated by mechanical extrapolation from the past time-trend of the internal and external price movements of comparable goods, together with

---

*Say, by a corresponding increase in export duty.

the subjective assessments of the different ministries
and government organizations responsible for Indian
exports. For the exports of "metal-based" manufactured
goods, no price sensitivity is noticed, and they are
estimated primarily on the basis of growth of income
of the developing countries, including the Middle
East and South East Asia.

For the second alternative exercise, an attempt
is made to take account of the effect of rupee
devaluation in India in the year 1964/5, in a more
optimistic manner. It is assumed that

1. the price of domestic goods in the foreign
market will go down by the full extent of devaluation.

2. the full effect will be perceptible with a
two-year lag.

3. The rise in the import costs of domestic
industries will be completely compensated by corresponding import substitution.

To be more specific, the effect of rupee devaluation in India (in 1965) is assumed to lower relative
prices (domestic versus foreign) in the export market
by nearly 36.7 percent. Conceptually, it is too
optimistic to expect the full effect of devaluation
to work in the above fashion: hence this exercise
is branded optimistic.

The export estimates thus derived are in four
broad groupings and are all at f.o.b. 1958/9 prices.
As a result, "two-stage" price corrections are needed
to bring them on to an identical price footing to
that of the other economic variables in the present
model. Thus, all the estimates are converted first
into 1959 prices, and second to producer's cost, by
subtracting from the export estimates the distribut-
ing margin appropriate for the four relevant sectors
and the respective indirect taxation. Finally, these
estimated values of exports (classified into the
above four broad groups) are further expanded into
22 sectors, as has already been discussed.

The processing of data is divided into five major parts:

(i)   Computation of the base configuration

(ii) Estimation of the target variables relating to the terminal year of the plan

(iii) Computation of the exogenous variables for each year of the plan

(iv) Processing of the parameters of the model (discussed earlier)

(v) Laying out of the policy variables relating to the plan.

The first major task in the processing of data for the transient-state model is the computation of the base-period configuration (i.e., current flow transaction matrix for the year 1964/5) of the economy. To begin with, the 1964/5 current flow matrix is estimated (Table 21.2), and is based mainly on the 1959 matrix prepared by the ISG, as follows:

The input coefficients of the 1959 table are assumed to remain unchanged for 1964/5.

The production trends of the major commodity groups, derived from the Ministry of Agriculture and Commerce production series, are combined into the 22 corresponding aggregated sectors of the inter-industry classification by using the 1959 gross outputs as weights.

After subtracting the intermediate use of material inputs (AX, where A is the current flow coefficient matrix and X is the gross output vector), the total final demand, net of imports, is estimated for each of the 22 activity sectors.

The public consumption vector is estimated by analyzing the central and state government budgets for the year 1964/5.

TABLE 21.1

PRIVATE CONSUMPTION VECTOR FOR 1975/76

Sectors	1959 Consumption* (Rs. million)	1959 per capita consumption (Rs.)	NSS Expenditure Groups	Elasticities	Increment of consumption per capita (Rs. million)	1975/76 per capita consumption (Rs.)	1975/76 Consumption** (Rs. million)	Growth rates of per capita consumption (post-terminal)	Growth rates of each element of consumption (post-terminal)
1	0	0	V	0	0	0	0	0	0
2	386	0.9	III	1.414	5.2	1.4	882	.064	.089
3	822	1.9	V	0.839	6.5	2.6	1,638	.038	.063
4	745	1.7	III	1.414	9.9	2.7	1,701	.064	.089
5	13,432	31.4	II	1.413	182.3	49.6	31,248	.064	.089
6	7,113	16.6	IV	2.117	143.7	31.0	19,530	.095	.120
7	138	0.3	IV	2.117	2.5	0.6	378	.095	.120
8	687	1.6	III	1.414	9.2	2.5	1,575	.064	.089
9	33,368	77.4	I	.482	153.7	92.8	58,464	.022	.047
10	17	0	III	1.414	0	0	0	.060	0
11	2,734	6.4	III	1.414	37.0	10.1	6,363	.064	.089
12	478	1.1	III	1.414	6.4	1.7	1,071	.064	.089
13	25	0.1	V	0.839	0.3	0.1	63	.022	.047
14	23,767	55.5	III	1.414	321.3	87.6	55,188	.064	.089
15	0	0		0	0	0	0	.060	0
16	190	0.4	V	.839	1.3	0.5	315	.038	.063
17	337	0.8	V	.839	2.8	1.1	693	.038	.063
18	0	0	0	0	0	0	0	.030	0
19	0	0	0	0	0	0	0	0	0
20	0	0	0	0	0	0	0	0	0
21	0	0	0	0	0	0	0	0	0
22	461	1.1	V	.839	3.8	1.5	945	.038	.063
	21,082	49.2	V	.839	169.0	66.1	41,643	.038	.063
Total	105,782	247.0			1,054.9	351.9	221,697		

*1959 consumption deflated by the population of 1959 (428.3 million)

**1975/76 per capita consumption multiplied by the estimated population of 1975/76 (630.0 million)

302

TABLE 21.2

CURRENT FLOW TRANSACTION MATRIX, 1964/5
(At 1959 producers' prices: Rs. million)

Consuming Sector / Producing Sector	I	II	III	IV	Sub-Total	Private Consumption	Public Consumption	Gross Capital Formation	Imports of Capital and Consumption Goods	Exports	Gross Domestic Output
I Cash crop and cash-crop-based industries	5,604	484	346	1,049	7,843	9,007	625	679	400	2,200	19,594
II Food and food-based industries	881	36,079	455	2,373	39,789	76,243	2,990	1,973	2,632	2,706	121,069
III Mining-based industries	196	484	4,117	1,260	6,067	1,604	40	19,008	8,979	477	18,217
IV Trade, transport, chemicals, misc. industries	3,076	8,596	4,481	6,568	22,722	26,558	2,499	3,466	407	355	55,193
Sub Total	9,757	45,623	9,400	11,260	76,042	113,412	6,154	25,126	12,418	5,738	214,073
Noncompeting imports	118	20	692	386					1,216*		
Wages and non-wages incl. depreciation	9,719	75,426	8,125	43,547		17,100	10,910	5,340			
Depreciation		8,000									
Gross domestic output	19,594	121,069	18,217	55,193							

*Total noncompeting imports.

303

Exports are estimated from the annual abstract at f.o.b. prices for 1964/5 and are converted into ex-factory prices by using the trade and transport margins as available in the 1959 table. Similarly, imports are estimated c.i.f., and intermediate imports are subtracted from the total import vector, in order to have the estimates of the combined capital-goods and consumption-goods import vector.

The capital formation (gross) and the consumption estimates (on a commodity basis) are estimated on a residual flow basis,* and in those cases where the same commodity contributes both to consumption and to capital formation, the 1959 ratios are used to allocate their contribution to respective sectors.

The value-added component is estimated by again assuming that the wage and non-wage components (as percentages) of 1959 total gross output remain unchanged in the year 1964/5.

Finally, the sectors are aggregated into four broad groups according to the specification of the transient-state model, and, as a cross-check, these aggregates are matched with the CSO national-income aggregates for 1964/5.

The next task in connection with the base con-figuration is to estimate the amount of capital stock available at the beginning of the transient state. This is achieved in three main stages. The estimation of the capacity output in each individual sector is obtained basically from the estimation of idle capacities arrived at in Chapter 13 of this study. To be more precise, the above estimates are initially combined into the corresponding transient-state classifications and subsequently, in conjunction with the output estimates for 1964/5, are used for the computation of the planned-capacity figures for the base year. Idle capacity as a percentage of the

----

*Gross output + Import of capital goods or con-sumption goods - Intermediate demand - Exports.

total is estimated at 9.2 percent in sector I, 8.9
percent in sector II, 13.3 percent in sector III and
2.9 percent in sector IV, in the year 1961/2. It is
assumed that these proportions remain unchanged for
the year 1964/5.

The capital-flow coefficient matrix and the
stock-flow coefficient matrix are combined similarly
into the above four groups in order to arrive at
consolidated estimates for the fixed and working-
capital matrix for the transient stage.*

The commodity component of net investment is
estimated by subtracting the replacement needs of
that year (arrived at by multiplying the replacement
matrix with the corresponding capacity vector for
1964/5) from the gross investment estimates.

The target variables (i.e., capital stock requirements) relating to the terminal year of the plan are
calculated by multiplying the consolidated capital-
flow and stock-flow matrix (22 x 22) with the desired
output vector (22 x 1) derived as a solution value of
the steady-state model* (See Table 21.3), and subsequently combined into four sectors to conform to the
transient-state classification.

The public consumption estimates conceptually
include all expenditure (less transfer payments) on
the revenue budget of the government. The estimates

---

*The capital-flow coefficient matrix and the
inventory-flow coefficient matrix must be on the
average basis in this case. Unfortunately, however,
only marginal coefficients are computed for this model.
That, however, does not affect the result, because
in the system of equations which has gone into this
model, the capital coefficients appear only in marginal
sense. For example, the system of equation (VII)
page 224 given in the algebraic formulation of this
model, and describing the terminal conditions of
capital stock acting as a constraint, in the final
analysis, reduces to a marginal concept.

TABLE 21.3

DATA RELATING TO THE BASE AND TERMINAL YEARS OF THE TRANSIENT-STATE MODEL
(Rs. million: at 1959 prices)

Sectors*	Gross output 1964/5 (Q_O)	Planned capacity 1964/5 (C_O)	Total Capital Stock for 1964/5 ($\underline{K}\ C_O$)	Gross Investment 1964/5	Net Investment 1964/5	Planned Idle Capacity (Percent)	Gross Output 1975/76	Total Capital Stock 1975/6 (material component)
I	19,594	21,397	8,940	679	301	92	55,854	22,838
II	121,069	132,934	60,643	1,973	1,750	89	297,511	139,836
III	18,217	21,022	117,928	19,008	12,394	133	64,855	287,116
IV	55,193	56,849	81,759	3,466	2,681	29	135,662	195,060

*Including public administration, banking, insurance, and construction activities.

inter-industry table. For later years it is assumed
that per capita needs for public goods would increase
by 3 percent per annum, a rate of growth derived
roughly on a mechanical extrapolation basis (Table
21.4).

Export projections are made in four broad groups:
(a) Cash crop and industries based on cash crops, (b)
food crops and industries based on food crops, (c)
industries based on mining and minerals, and (d)
mining industries, assuming a 3.5 percent growth rate
of real income in the developed countries and 4.5
percent in the developing countries, and assuming
that the benefits of devaluation in terms of a reduction in price differentials will be realized with a
two-year lag.

The export estimates thus derived are at f.o.b.
prices. They are converted into ex-factory prices
by assuming a given trade and transport margin for
each sector separately, derived from 1959 relations.
They are 14 percent in sector I, 13.9 percent in
sector II, and 9.3 percent in sector III, and 40
percent in sector IV.

Foreign aid is defined in the present model as
the total amount of import surplus in a particular
period on visible exports (f.o.b.). Hence, it refers
to a net concept, the whole of which can be used for
financing the excess of imports over exports.

To elaborate, two alternative aid estimates are
formulated (in Table 21.4), the second of which
(Alternatives V, VI, and VII of Table 9.1) is a true
reproduction of the aid estimates made in the Perspective Planning Division's document, Draft Fourth
Plan - Material and Financial Balances, (1964-5,
1970-1 and 1975-6). This document gives a figure of
Rs.14,500 million as payments for total servicing
charges on past aid and Rs.37,000 million as the
total level of gross external assistance projected
over the years 1966/7 to 1970/1. For 1965/6 no
estimate is available in this document. Hence, in
this particular alternative formulation, a figure
of net aid similar to that received in 1964/5 is

TABLE 21.4

LAYOUT OF PUBLIC EXPENDITURE
OVER THE TRANSIENT-STATE MODEL
(Rs. million, at 1959 prices)

Sectors	1964/5	1965/6	1966/7	1967/8	1968/9	1969/70
I	625	656	689	724	760	798
II	2,990	3,140	3,296	3,461	3,634	3,816
III	40	42	44	46	49	51
IV	2,499	2,624	2,755	2,893	3,038	3,189
V		10,200	10,500	11,900	12,500	13,200

Sectors	1970/1	1971/2	1972/3	1973/4	1974/5
I	838	879	923	970	1,018
II	4,007	4,207	4,418	4,638	4,870
III	54	56	59	62	65
IV	3,349	3,516	3,692	3,877	4,071
V	13,700	14,600	15,200	15,900	16,700

assumed. For the period 1970/1 to 1974/5 the estimates
of the total amount of aid are given in the above
document, but the phasing of the servicing costs is
not available in detail and is therefore estimated
arbitrarily. The aid inflow in all these periods
includes private capital.

Finally, the post-devaluation amount of net aid
is estimated by assuming that the amount of aid
increases by the full extent of the rupee devaluation
and is further adjusted by a subsequent devaluation
in the pound sterling.

In the first alternative (alternative I - III
of Table 21.5) it is assumed that the net aid available in 1965/6 amounts to zero. This is because we
suspect that in that year the whole amount of aid was
used up in defense expenditure, and this has not been
allowed for in the present model's estimates of public
consumption for 1965/6. For the other years, the aid
phasing is conducted on the basis of the information
available at the time.

As an experiment, in the third alternative exercise (alternative IV of Table 21.5, the total amount
of aid, net of all servicing expenses, over the ten
years of our plan, is assumed to be Rs.87,200 million
(with the same aid phasing as in alternative I) at
the post-devaluation rate.

In the last alternative, the model has been
asked to prescribe an optimum intertemporal phasing
of aid, the total amount being given over the ten-
year period (as in alternative V). Of course the
unreality of this exercise is well admitted. In real
life, the problem of aid allocation is much more
complex. Mostly the intertemporal phasing of aid or
its sectoral allocation is decided by the donor
countries and hence it is exogenous to the model.
But such an exercise may act as a guide to future
negotiation.

The two important policy conditions grafted into
this model are that the consumption of any item per
capita must not fall in absolute amounts in any

TABLE 21.5

PHASING OF FOREIGN AID IN THE TRANSIENT-STATE MODEL
(Rs. million)

Years	Aid under alt. I, II, III				Aid under alt. V, VI, and VIII			
	Gross Aid	Servicing Charges	Net Aid	Net at devaluation aid	Gross Aid	Servicing Charges	Net Aid	Postdevaluation aid
1965/6	1,210	1,210	0	0	4,580	1,210	3,370	4,720
1966/7	6,750	2,646	4,104	5,755	7,250	1,800	5,450	7,630
1967/8	8,450	3,312	5,138	7,193	9,000	2,350	6,650	9,310
1968/9	8,300	3,254	5,046	7,064	8,900	2,850	6,050	8,470
1969/70	7,500	2,940	4,560	6,384	8,150	3,500	4,650	6,510
1970/71	6,000	2,352	3,648	5,107	6,700	4,000	2,700	3,780
1971/2	5,140	1,700	3,440	4,816	6,000	3,400	2,600	3,640
1972/3	4,280	1,700	2,580	3,612	5,900	3,900	2,000	2,800
1973/4	3,420	1,700	1,720	2,408	5,600	3,800	1,200	1,680
1974/5	2,560	1,700	860	1,204	5,350	4,850	500	700

Source: Computed from Planning Commission, Perspective Planning Division, Draft Fourth Plan: Material and Financial Balances: 1964/5, 1970/1 and 1975/6, (September, 1966).

TABLE 21.6

EXPORT PROJECTIONS FOR THE TRANSIENT-STATE MODEL
(Rs. million: at 1959-60 prices)

Sectors	1965/6	1966/7	1967/8	1968/9	1969/70
I	2,276	3,865	3,935	4,006	4,082
II	2,860	4,369	4,530	4,698	4,872
III	1,041	1,063	1,094	1,212	1,340
IV	1,160	1,759	1,818	1,982	2,151

Sectors	1970/1	1971/2	1972/3	1973/4	1974/5
I	4,194	4,240	4,317	4,399	4,484
II	5,058	5,242	5,435	5,636	5,845
III	1,482	1,642	1,822	2,023	2,249
IV	2,330	2,602	2,985	3,274	3,452

particular year of the plan period of the model, and
that the country must be self-sufficient in her needs
for foreign exchange by 1975/76.

The demand coefficients of the manpower model
have been computed in three succesive stages: the
calculation of manpower requirement coefficients for
the different sectors of the economy, the construction
of the occupation-employment matrix, and the estimation
of parameters for engineers and scientists, expressed
as a function of the professional labor force, and of
agricultural and veterinary graduates as a function
of gross agricultural output.

For the first stage of this model, the economy
is divided into 19 sectors in the steady-state model,
and 7 sectors in the transient-state model (see Tables
22.1 and 22.2). In the former, the coefficients of
employment per unit of output in organized manufacturing are derived for 1960. The necessary data are
obtained from the ASI report and computed as coefficients in Table 22.3. As a result, these estimates
can be regarded as unbiased in so far as the year 1960
can be regarded as representive of the entire period.*
This means that there is no technical change and no
labor-capital substitution over the projected period.

---

*Conceptually, the parameters should be built
by regression analysis over time-series data to exclude random movements.

For the small-scale industries (including the household
sector), parameters are derived separately, and are
combined with the organized sector to derive aggregate
employment coefficients and transport correspond to
sector 22 of the inter-industry classification, combined with necessary weights. Construction and service sectors correspond to our model classification.

An attempt is also made to convert the parameters
of professional and technical people obtained in the
occupation-employment matrix of the nonagricultural
sector into engineers and scientists, by assuming that,
of the total professional labor force, 8.1 percent
constitute engineers and 2.5 percent constitute scientists. (They were calculated as follows:

a) Total incremental professional and technical
hands, required over the plan (1968/9 to 1973/4) =
1.0 million.

b) Total increase in engineers required over
the same period. = 81,000

c) Total increase in scientists required over
the same period. = 25,000)

Estimation in the agriculture sector (8,9,10,11,
12 and 14 of the 22 sector inter-industry matrix) is
a difficult problem because of lack of data. Conceptually, we are to estimate the marginal coefficients
of agricultural and veterinary graduates for all
sectors of agriculture. However data is limited to
students passing from agricultural and veterinary
colleges each year, so we must be satisfied with a
single norm for agriculture as a whole.

From the information supplied by the council of
Agricultural Research the number of students who have
enrolled and passed over 9 years (between 1954/5 and
1962/3) were estimated, (Table 22.5). The weights
are derived from Table 11.3. An alternative source
(the population census of India) gives the estimated
numbers of workers distributed between the different
sectors of the economy for each census year. But
these figures contain persons unemployed and

TABLE 22.1

SECTOR CLASSIFICATION OF THE TRANSIENT-STATE MODEL

Principal Model (1)	Export Model (2)	Import Model (3)	Manpower Model (4)	Public Exp. Model (5)	Income and Exp. Model (6)
1. Cash crop and cash-crop-based industries (3,4,6,7,8,10)	1 to 4 sectors	1 to 4 sectors	A. Employment 1 to 4 sectors B. Occupation 1) Agn. mining and manufacturing ii) Services iii) Construction iv) Education	1 to 6 sectors	A. Saving Income (2 sectors) B. Expn. pattern (6 sectors) C. Tax sector 1. Direct Taxes 2. Indirect Taxes
2. Food crop and food-crop-based industries (2,5,9,11,12,13,14)					
3. Mining and metal-based industries (1,15,16,17,18,19,20,21)					
4. Trade, transport, chemicals, power, and misc. industries (22)					
5.* Banking, insurance and other services, incl. education					
6.* Construction					

*Treated exogenously of the principal model but dependent on its solution values.

315

TABLE 22.2

SECTOR CLASSIFICATION OF THE STEADY-STATE MODEL

Principal Model 1	Export Model 2	Import Model 3	Manpower Model 4	Public Exp. Model 5	Macro-Economic Model 6	Income and Exp. Model 7	Tax Model
1. Cement	1 to 22 sectors	1 to 22 sectors	A. Employment Sector	1 to 24 (as in col.1)	Two Sectors	A. Saving Income (2 sectors)	1. Direct Taxation
2. Glass, wood, nonmetallic			1. Cement				2. Indirect Taxes.
3. Rubber and leather			2. Glass and wood			B. Expn. pattern (24 sectors)	
4. Paper and paper products			3. Rubber and leather		1. Consumption goods		
5. Food, beverages, and tobacco			4. Paper and paper products				
6. Textiles			5. Food, beverages and tobacco				
7. Jute and Coir			6. Textiles		2. Investment goods		
8. Cotton			7. Jute and coir				
9. Food grains			8. Fertilizer				
10. Jute			9. Transportation equipment				
11. Oil seeds			10. Electrical equipment				
12. Plantations			11. Aluminum, etc.				
13. Fertilizers			12. Iron and steel				
14. Other agriculture			13. Nonelectrical equipment				
15. Iron ore			14. Chemicals, power, etc.				
16. Transportation equipment and allied			15. Agriculture				
17. Electrical equipment			16. Mining				
18. Aluminum and nonporous metals			17. Services excluding education				
19. Other mining			18. Construction				
20. Iron and steel			19. Education				
21. Nonelectrical equipment and ferrous, nonporous prod.			B. Occupation Sector				
22. Chemicals, power, transport, etc.			1. Manufacturing				
23.* Banking, insurance, and other services, including education			2. Mining				
24.* Construction			3. Agriculture				
			4. Trade and commerce				
			5. Construction				
			6. Services excluding education				
			7. Education				

*Treated exogenously of the principal model but dependent on its solution values.

TABLE 22.3

STRUCTURAL COEFFICIENTS OF EMPLOYMENT
AND EARNINGS RATES (MANUFACTURING) 1960.

Sectors 22-Sector inter-industry matrix classification	per man rupee earnings per annum	Employment norms: No. of employee per Rs.100 per annum	per nonworkers eupee earnings per annum	Employment norms: No. of nonworkers per Rs.100
1	1977.50	0.0052	2966.49	0.0011
2	1073.89	0.0198	2224.85	0.0017
3	2326.02	0.0052	5234.26	0.0007
4	1893.46	0.0103	3215.72	0.0018
5	1094.87	0.0055	2030.45	0.0008
6	1701.77	0.0127	3023.91	0.0009
7	1320.51	0.0140	2522.18	0.0010
13	2075.91	0.0071	2630.54	0.0020
16	1955.88	0.0112	3301.00	0.0014
17	2077.68	0.0071	3476.33	0.0013
18	2556.95	0.0038	4476.71	0.0007
20	2501.34	0.0061	3669.60	0.0010
22	1834.58	0.0107	3472.43	0.0013
22	2430.13	0.0045	4087.69	0.0009
TOTAL	1718.71	0.0091	3111.60	0.0010

underemployed. Their relation to output cannot,
therefore, be regarded as a technical norm. Attempts
may be made to adjust these figures for the number
of unemployed. The estimates of unemployment can be
obtained from two sources: National Sample Survey
reports and the population census. But the definitions of employed are extremely liberal in both these
reports. In the former "employed" is defined as
anyone employed even for one day (for any number of
hours) of the week of calling; in the latter, anyone
employed for even one day of the two weeks prior to
the period of enumeration. If we take these definitions, then the percentage unemployment in India
would be as low as 2 percent to 3 percent in 1959,
in the first case, and .6 percent in 1961, in the
second case. These estimates are widely different
and evidently suggest a large underemployed labor
force within the employed population.

What is needed for the computation of employment
norms for planned projection is a ratio of optimally
employed labor force to output. For the present model,
a suitable definition of an optimum labor force is
one in which any individual labor will be employed,
in the organized sector of the economy, for the
average of working days (5.5 days) of any normal year
(figures will be adjusted for seasonal industries).
Hence our preference is for the average number of
laborers employed per day to total gross output in
individual sectors given in the ASI reports, as the
employment parameter. An estimation of these parameters for nearly 350 industries was made separately
and the results combined with 22 sectors and 6 sectors,
according to the model's specifications. When our
presently computed parameters were used to estimate
the total labor force optimally used in 1961 and when
these findings were compared with the estimates given
in the 1961 census, underemployment in the region of
20 percent was observed in the nonagricultural sector
of the economy.

For the construction and services sectors, it
is necessary to assume that the earnings rates per
labor per year in these sectors will correspond to
the nonworker and worker earnings rates respectively

in the manufacturing sector. This is admittedly very
heroic, but no other source of information exists.
For the education sector, the employment figures are
borrowed from the Ministry of Labor.[1]

For the agricultural sector, it is extremely
difficult to build employment norms from the existing
information. The estimates of working population from
the population census contain a very high degree of
underemployment. Hence, no attempt is made to estimate the employment coefficient in this sector. As
will be explained shortly, the demand for skilled
labor in this sector is derived directly.

In the transient state model, the following sector
classifications are adopted:

Sector I. Cash-crop and cash-crop-based industries, comprising sectors 3, 4, 6, 7, 8, and 10 of
the original 22-sector inter-industry matrix

Sector II. Food-crop and food-crop-based industries, comprising sectors 2, 5, 9, 11, 12, 13, and
14 of the same matrix.

Sector III. Metal and metal-based industries,
comprising sectors 1, 15, 16, 17, 18, 19, 20, and 21
of the same matrix.

Sector IV. Power, chemicals, transport, and
services, corresponding to sector 22 of the original
matrix.

Sector V. Banking, insurance, etc., as in the
steady-state model.

Sector VI. Construction, similar to the steady-
state model.

Sector VII. Educational institutions.

The employment norms of the detailed 22-sector
classification of the economy are combined with relevant weights to arrive at the corresponding sector
norms of sectors I to IV.

At this stage an attempt is made to estimate
parameters for the occupation-employment matrix.
These parameters are based on the 1961 population
census and corrected for technological changes likely
to occur between 1968/9 and 1978/9. The projected
occupational pattern of nonagricultural employment
(1968/9 to 1978/9) is given in Table 22.4. The mining
and manufacturing sectors of this matrix correspond
to sectors 1 to 7 and 13 to 21 (excluding 14) of our
22-sector inter-industry matrix. Electricity, gas,
trade, and commerce, correspondingly, value-added
(net) figures for agriculture over the same period
are available in the national-income-and-expenditure
statistics published by the CSO. Accordingly, gross
output for agriculture has been estimated for all
these years by using the gross/net ratio from the
1959 inter-industry matrix. Skilled manpower is one
of the inputs in Indian agriculture, but with the
cyclical nature of rainfall in India, there is an
unstable relation between increased skilled manpower
and incremental agricultural output from year to
year. But assuming the cyclical and random effects
on output changes will cancel when several years are
aggregated, the ratio of incremental skilled manpower
over incremental output over the eight years may be
taken to represent a stable technical relationship.
This is estimated in this paper as:

Years	Incremental Skilled Manpower	Incremental Net Output	Incremental Gross Output	2÷4 per Rs.100
1	2	3	4	5
1954/55 to 1961/2	17,401	Rs.25.4 billion	Rs.40.3 billion	.000043

Source: For basic data see Indian Agriculture
in Brief, (Delhi: Government of India Press, 1967).

TABLE 22.4

PROJECTED OCCUPATIONAL PATTERN OF NONAGRICULTURAL EMPLOYMENT
(1968/9 to 1978/9)
(Percent)

	Mining	Manu-facturing	Construction	Electricity, gas etc.	Trade and commerce	Transport and communications	Services*
Professional, technical	3.0	2.5	3.0	9.0	0.5	1.5	8.0
Administration and managerial	1.0	1.5	5.0	1.0	1.5	1.5	8.0
Clerical	4.5	2.5	4.0	16.0	90.0	10.0	7.0
Farmers	-	-	-	-	-	-	0.5
Miners	46.0	-	-	-	-	-	-
Workers in transport and communications	1.5	0.5	2.0	2.5	0.5	50.5	0.5
Craftsmen	9.5	90.0	60.0	32.0	2.0	10.0	1.0
Service workers	1.0	0.5	0.1	0.5	0.5	1.0	24.5
Unskilled	33.5	2.5	25.9	39.0	5.0	25.5	50.5
TOTAL	100.0	100.0	100.0	100.0	100.0	100.0	100.0

*The distribution for services has been worked out after excluding teachers, for whom calculations have been made independently.

TABLE 22.5

ADMISSION AND OUTPUT OF AGRICULTURAL COLLEGES
(B.Sc. COMMERCE)

YEARS	NO. OF AGRICULTURAL COLLEGES	NO. OF STUDENTS ADMITTED	NO. OF STUDENTS PASSED
1954/5	24	1454	886
1955/6	30	1989	806
1956/7	32	2344	994
1957/8	31	2789	1387
1958/9	32	3077	1700
1959/60	40	4633	2090
1960/1	53	5634	2612
1961/2	55	6392	2912
1962/3	62	7483	n.a.

ADMISSION AND OUTPUT OF VETERINARY COLLEGES

1954/5	10	910	268
1955/6	14	1269	322
1956/7	14	1204	509
1957/8	14	1170	591
1958/9	16	1293	801
1959/60	16	1281	831
1960/1	17	1301	858
1961/2	18	1381	988
1962/3	18	1219	n.a.

TABLE 22.6

ESTIMATED OUTTURN OF ENGINEERS DURING THE FOURTH PLAN*

Year	Engineers (Degree Holders)	Engineering Diploma Holders	Total
1969/70	18,700	27,300	46,000
1970/1	19,600	28,300	47,900
1971/2	21,000	28,900	49,900
1972/3	21,050	29,100	50,150
1973/4	21,050	29,100	50,150
	101,400	142,700	244,100

*Excluding practical engineers--i.e., those trained on the job without having undergone any formal training in engineering.

Source: India, Ministry of Labor and Employment, India's Manpower Requirement-Some Preliminary Estimates (1968/9 to 1978/9), (New Delhi: Government of India Press, January, 1969).

TABLE 22.7

ENGINEERS AND SCIENTISTS: COEFFICIENTS OF THE TRANSIENT-STATE MODEL
(MANUFACTURING SECTOR)

Sector classifications, (serial no. corresponding to 22-sector matrix classification).	Sector heads.	Combined engineering norm per Rs.100 output**	Combined scientist norm per Rs.100 output**
I Cash crops and industries based on cash crops (79 percent non-agr.)	3 4 6 7 8* 10*	.000020	.0000079
II Food crops and industries based on food crops (18.5 percent non-agr.)	2 5 9* 11* 12* 13 14*	.000021	.0000066
III Mining and metal-based industries	1 15 16 17 18 19 20 21	.000027	.0000086
IV Power, transport, trade, chemicals, and mixed industries	22	.000041	.0000130

*As they belong to agriculture, they are excluded from each group (having zero scientists and engineers) by the gross output of 1975/6 as weights.

**Combined on the basis of 1975/6 gross outputs as weights.

TABLE 22.8

MANPOWER COEFFICIENTS OF THE STEADY-STATE MODEL (MANUFACTURING SECTOR)

Industry classifications (Serial no. corresponding to 22-sector classification)		No. of employees Rs. 100 gross output. Large scale	No. of employees per Rs. 100 of gross output Combined*	Percent professional of total labor force	Percent engineers of total professional force	Percent scientists of total profession force
1		2	3			
1. Cement	(1)	.0052	.0052	2.5	8.2	2.5
2. Glass, wood and non-metallic products	(2)	.0198	.0202	"	"	"
3. Rubber and leather	(3)	.0052	.0069	"	"	"
4. Paper and paper products	(4)	.0103	.0104	"	"	"
5. Food, beverages and tobacco	(5)	.0055	.0079	"	"	"
6. Textiles	(6)	.0127	.0150	"	"	"
7. Jute and coir	(7)	.0140	.0154	"	"	"
8. Fertilizer	(13)	.0071	.0071	"	"	"
9. Iron ore	(15)	.0410	.0410	3.0	"	"
10. Transport Equipment	(16)	.0112	.0118	2.5	"	"
11. Electrical equip.	(17)	.0071	.0071	.	"	"
12. Aluminum and nonferrous products	(18)	.0038	.0038	"	"	"
13. Other Mining	(19)	.0410	.0410	3.0	"	"
14. Iron and steel	(20)	.0061	.0061	2.5	"	"
15. Nonelectrical equipment	(21)	.0107	.0140	"	"	"
16. Chemical, power, transport, trade and other industries	(22)	.0100	.0240	"	"	"

*"Combined" of large-and small-scale sectors on the basis of 1959 gross outputs as weights.

325

Finally, a 2 percent allowance for depreciation or replacement of the total skilled labor force of any year is provided for in all sectors of the economy.

In estimating the future supply of manpower, it was decided to confine our attention solely to engineers and scientists. The supply of unskilled manpower is guided by the rate of growth of the working population. But due to the existence of a large unemployed and underemployed labor force, its supply for our computational purposes can be assumed to be infinitely elastic over the Fourth Plan period. Hence, it is felt that in our programming scheme we can afford to ignore the equation referring to the supply constraint of unskilled manpower.

For engineers and scientists no such priori information regarding their constraining effects on the growth of the economy is available. Hence, it is necessary to formulate all the supply constraints of these resources. The supply of engineers and scientists depends on the level of enrollments, dropouts, degree of success in examinations, and the gestation period of training and education. As the intention is to calculate the supply of these resources over a five-year period, then with a gestation lag of four or five years they are mostly predetermined over the plan period under consideration. Hence the supply figures given by the Directorate General of Employment and Training of the Government of India are adopted.

NOTE

1. Ministry of Labor, India's Manpower Requirements: Some Preliminary Estimates, 1968/9 to 1978/9, (Delhi: Government of India Press, 1969)

PART

IV

MODEL
SOLUTION

THE COMPUTATIONAL SEQUENCE

The model is computed in three stages: a fore-cast, to formulate the base-period structure of the economy; a mathematical model of the Stone-Brown type with infinite time horizon, to formulate the conditions of the terminal state of the economy in the plan; and a programming technique to bring out the element of choice between alternative growth patterns in the transient state of the economy. The first stage has already been described in detail. The second stage is defined as the steady state of our model, with its major economic variables borrowed from the Draft Fourth Plan. Two broad alternatives are attempted, based mainly on different export as-sumptions, owing to the uncertain effect of rupee devaluation in India at that time. The first alter-native is defined as pessimistic and the second as optimistic.

The basic assumptions of the first alternative are that exports are exogenous to the model and de-valuation has no effect on the volume of exports and imports, that current inputs and replacement invest-ments are related to gross output in fixed proportions, that marginal fixed capital and inventory holdings are related to marginal gross output, that intermediate imports are proportional to sectoral outputs, while

capital-goods imports are related linearly to net
fixed-capital formation and time, and no consumption
goods are imported, and the whole of the import surplus is balanced by foreign aid (i.e., foreign aid
is endogenous).

In the second alternative, it is assumed that
devaluation has its full effect in the reduction of
prices of export goods and that net foreign aid will
amount to zero in this period; the other assumptions
of the first alternative are retained.

The following computational sequence is adopted
in both the alternatives:

Round 1.

Stage 1. Estimation of the gross-output vector,
assuming no imports and satisfying the terminal consumption and export conditions (already set exogenously).

Stage 2. Estimation of the needs for intermediate imports vis-à-vis stage 1 output.

Stage 3. Estimate of the needs for capital
goods imports vis-à-vis stage 1 net fixed-capital
formation.

Stage 4. The vector conversion of the scalar
capital-goods imports.

Stage 5. The surplus of export earnings over
intermediate and capital-goods imports which is
available for consumption-goods imports, and their
vector conversion.

Round II.

Stage 1. The estimation of gross output, assuming the imports estimated in Round I, stages 2 +
4 + 5 to take place, and satisfying the terminal
consumption provisions and exports of Round 1 stage 1.

Subsequently, stages 2 to 5 are repeated as

before. Thus, all the stages of earlier rounds are
repeated from round to round until the gross output
attained in round (n + 1) will almost equal that of
round (n) (a maximum difference of 1 percent is permitted in any single element of the gross-output
vector between the (n + 1)th and (n)th round).
In the present exercise, the convergence in the above
sense is reached monotonically in the optimistic
case and with fluctuations in the pessimistic case.

For estimating the net fixed-capital formation
and the working-capital needs of the terminal year,
the rates of growth of each industry sector in the
post-terminal year are computed as follows:

$$\sum_{i=1}^{n} \left[\left\{ (1 - (A+R) - r_{i}(pr) \ (K+S) \right\}^{-1} c_{i}(pr) \right] = \left| Qc1 \right| = \begin{bmatrix} Q_{11}^{c1} + Q_{12}^{c1} = + Q_{1i}^{c1} \dots + Q_{in}^{c1} \\ \dotfill \\ Q_{\ell 1}^{c1} + Q_{\ell 2}^{c1} \dots + Q_{\ell i}^{c1} + Q_{\ell n}^{c1} \\ \cdots \\ Q_{n1}^{c1} + Q_{n2}^{c1} + Q_{ni}^{c1} + Q_{nn}^{c1} \end{bmatrix}$$

similarly

$$\sum_{i=1}^{n} \left[\left\{ (1 - (A+R) - r_{i}(Pu)(K+S) \right\}^{-1} c_{i}(pu) \right] = \left| Q_{c2} \right| = \begin{bmatrix} Q_{11}^{c2} + Q_{12}^{c2} + Q_{1i}^{c2} + Q_{in}^{c2} \\ \cdots \\ Q_{\ell 1}^{c2} + Q_{\ell 2}^{c2} + Q_{\ell i}^{c2} + Q_{\ell n}^{c2} \\ \cdots \\ Q_{n1}^{c2} + Q_{n2}^{c2} + Q_{ni}^{c2} + Q_{nn}^{c2} \end{bmatrix}$$

and

$$\sum_{i=1}^{n} \left[\left\{ (1 - (A+R) - r_{i}(e)(K+S) \right\}^{-1} Ej \right] = \left| Q_{e3} \right| = \begin{bmatrix} Q_{11}^{e3} + Q_{12}^{e3} + Q_{1i}^{e3} + Q_{in}^{e3} \\ \cdots \\ Q_{\ell 1}^{e3} + Q_{\ell 2}^{e3} + Q_{\ell i}^{e3} + Q_{\ell n}^{e3} \\ \cdots \\ Q_{n1}^{e3} + Q_{n2}^{e3} + Q_{ni}^{e3} + Q_{nn}^{e3} \end{bmatrix}$$

and

$$\sum_{i=1}^{n} \left[\left\{ (1 - (A+R) - ri(m)(K+S) \right\}^{-1} \left| Im(Cap)_{i} + Im(Con)_{i} \right| \right] = \left| Qm4 \right|$$

$$= \begin{bmatrix} Q_{11}^{m4} + Q_{12}^{m4} + Q_{1i}^{m4} + Q_{in}^{m4} \\ \cdots \\ Q_{\ell 1}^{m4} + Q_{\ell 2}^{m4} + Q_{\ell i}^{m4} + Q_{\ell n}^{m4} \\ \cdots \\ Q_{n1}^{m4} + Q_{n2}^{m4} + Q_{ni}^{m4} + Q_{nn}^{m4} \end{bmatrix}$$

Footnote: Vector $\left| Q_{1i} \right| = \left\{ 1 - (A + R) - r_i \; (pr) \; (K+S) \right\}^{-1}_{c_i} \; (pr)$ when

$c_i = (\; o, \; o, \; o, \; o, \; \dots \; \text{ith element} > o, \; o, \; o, \; o, \; \dots \text{nth element})$

Hence if Q_i^R represents the post-terminal rate of growth of the ith sector, then

$$Q_i^R = \frac{\sum_{i=1}^{n} (Q_{li}^{c1}) \; ri \; (pr) + \sum_{i=1}^{n} (Q_{li}^{c2}) \; r_i \; (pu) + \sum_{i=1}^{n} (Q_{li}^{e3}) \; r_i \; (e) - \sum_{i=1}^{n} (Q_{li}^{m4}) \; r_i \; (m)}{\sum_{i=1}^{n} (Q_{li}^{c1}) + \sum_{i=1}^{n} (Q_{li}^{c2}) + \sum_{i=1}^{n} (Q_{li}^{e3}) - \sum_{i=1}^{n} (Q_{li}^{m4})}$$

quently, on the basis of the estimated values of gross output, consumption, and investment, we compute the manpower requirements (in the manpower submodel) and the tax requirements (in the tax-subsidy submodel). The flow sequence of computation is shown on page 333.

In the third stage, the choice between the alternative patterns of development of the economy, that will transform it from an initial to a final configuration, is computed. This stage is named the transient state of the model. There are infinite alternative patterns of development, all lying within the feasibility range, which can lead to the same goal, and the final choice is made in the light of any given objective. There are three major types of constraints in this present model: technology constraints, foreign-aid contraints and behavior contraints. The first and third type are assumed to be given exogenously, and the second becomes the policy constraint. Hence, the alternative optimal development patterns are explored almost exclusively in the light of alternative aid assumptions. The transient-state formulation is solved by linear programming techniques. Some variables for different periods are treated as different variables. All the parameters and variables are fed into the model in the form of a set of equations. The objective function is placed as a linear function of the utility of consumption.

The solution has been reached in a single stage by an ABL program which was run in the Chilton Atlas

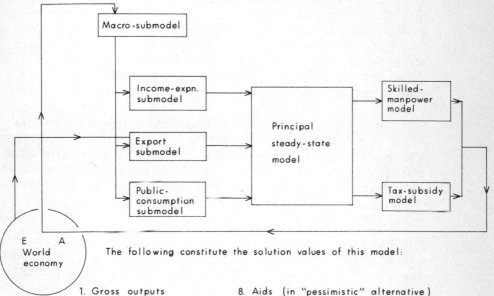

The following constitute the solution values of this model:

1. Gross outputs
2. Gross national income
3. Net national income
4. Replacement investment
5. Working capital
6. Fixed capital
7. Imports

8. Aids (in "pessimistic" alternative)
9. Income generation in construction
10. Income generation in services
11. Income generation in public administration
12. Demand for (a) engineers, (b) scientists, and (c) agricultural products
13. Direct tax needed
14. Savings propensity needed

laboratory in Harwell, England. However, to assess
the sensitivity of a prescribed plan program to
changes in discount rates, it was necessary to pro-
ceed by two stages: through the optimum allocation
pattern for any arbitrarily chosen value of the rate
of time discount (r) and the minimum and maximum
limiting value of r when the above optimal base will
not be destroyed (that is, when any of the nonbase
evaluator zj- cj becomes favorable to be included in
the base.) The two-stage solution is necessitated
because the price coefficient of the objective function of our present model is a nonlinear function of
the rate of time discount. The relation presumed is

$$c_t = \frac{c_o}{(1+r)} t-1,$$ when c_t is the price coefficient in

tth period of the objective function, t is the time
suffix, r is the rate of time discount, and co is
the price coefficient at the base year of the plan.
The flow sequence of transient-state computation
adopted is shown on page 335.

The Findings. The solution of the first (pessimistic)
alternative of the steady-state model is obtained on
the sixth iteration, and of the second (optimistic)
alternative on the fifth iteration. Tables 23.1 and
23.2 show the path of convergence. The convergence
(defined as the point when all the sectoral outputs in
the nth and n-1 th iterations become identical:
a 1 percent difference is permitted) is reached by
a cyclical movement in the first alternative, but
monotonically in the second. Tables 23.1 and give
the solution values of the two alternative exercises
respectively. The first column gives the intermediate
consumption vector (ID), the second column the replacement-investment vector (RI), the third one the
fixed-investment vector (FI), the fourth one the
inventory-investment vector, and the fifth one combines both the capital- and consumption-goods-imported
vector. The last two columns present the post-terminal rates of growth of output of individual sectors
and the absolute gross-output vector for all the 22
sectors in the year 1975/6.

    The aggregate national income (net domestic pro-
duct) for 1975/6 in the first alternative has been

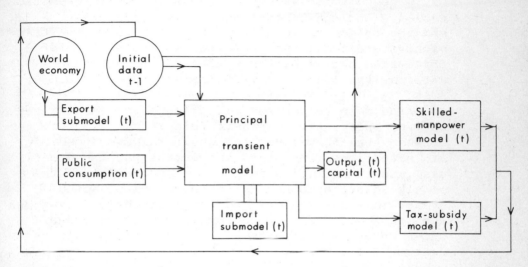

The following constitute the solution values of this model:

1. Gross output
2. Private consumption
3. Replacement investment
4. Fixed capital
5. Working capital
6. GNP
7. Imports
8. Income generated in construction
9. Income generated in services

10. Income generated in public administration
11. Demand for (a) engineers, (b) scientists, and (c) agricultural graduates
12. Direct tax needed
13. Savings propensity needed
14. Ideal aid phasing
15. Shadow price of trade balances
16. Sensitivity of aid of social time discounting

computed at Rs.348.1 billion and in the second alternative at Rs.381.8 billion. (The manpower implications and other details are discussed later and
given in Table 23.5.)

The solution values of gross output, consumption,
capital- and consumption-goods imports, foreign aid,
and the shadow price of foreign exchange in the transient-state model are presented in Table 23.1 for
three alternative patterns of aid phasing, under
alternatives I, V, and VIII (as set out in Table 9.1).

The main reason for selecting these three alternatives and presenting their full results is that
between them they cover the whole range of possible
aid situations; one gives the latest-published official assessment (alternative V), another gives the
likely adjustments needed in the light of actual
events (alternative I), and the third helps to assess
the state of conditions which is likely to prevail
under an optimum intertemporal aid pattern (alternative VIII).

In solving the present allocation problem, alternative I needed 329 iterations, alternative V 330
iterations, and alternative VIII 413 iterations, in
a two-phase simplex iterative method.

Due to the enormous size of the program, we
faced the difficult problem of rounding errors. In
fact, in almost all the cases, the machine reached
phase 1 of the computation with a value of the imag-
inary objective at a "non-zero" (though very near to
zero) level. From a study of the magnitude of the
rounding errors, it is my belief that the results of
all our alternative runs should be read as approximate, correct only to the units of Rs.10 millions,
although originally they were fed into the model in
the units of millions.

Tables 23.7, 23.8, and 23.9 give the results of
the above three alternatives in macro terms (in
national-income accounts), and these tables also
include the results of the fiscal submodel and the
consumption/income submodel. The reasons for

TABLE 23.1

COMPUTATIONAL PATH OF CONVERGENCE OF STEADY-STATE
MODEL (ALTERNATIVE I)
(Rs. million)

Sectors	GO I	GO II	GO III	GO IV	GO V	GO VI (Final)
1.	4,177	4,112	4,118	4,113	4,116	4,115
2.	11,587	11,393	11,411	11,398	11,404	11,400
3.	3,935	3,884	3,888	3,885	3,886	3,885
4.	6,473	6,393	6,399	6,394	6,398	6,396
5.	41,107	41,081	41,083	41,082	41,083	41,082
6.	29,083	29,070	29,071	29,070	29,070	29,070
7.	3,134	4,105	3,107	3,105	3,107	3,106
8.	9,884	9,875	9,878	9,878	9,878	9,878
9.	113,516	113,444	113,440	113,435	113,434	113,434
10.	1,127	1,117	1,117	1,117	1,117	1,117
11.	10,683	10,681	10,681	10,681	10,681	10,681
12.	4,978	4,953	4,955	4,954	4,954	4,954
13.	1,408	1,405	1,405	1,405	1,405	1,405
14.	112,177	111,813	111,845	111,821	111,833	111,821
15.	462	445	447	446	446	446
16.	4,950	3,749	3,848	3,774	3,813	3,795
17.	6,294	5,335	5,413	5,355	5,385	5,375
18.	2,143	1,975	1,990	1,979	1,984	1,980
19.	3,581	3,459	3,469	3,461	3,467	3,463
20.	19,523	18,748	18,819	18,766	18,793	18,780
21.	30,057	26,613	26,938	26,696	26,820	26,758
22.	137,049	134,937	135,126	134,985	135,058	135,022

Note: GO = Gross Output
       I, II, etc. = Number of interation.

TABLE 23.2

COMPUTATIONAL PATH OF CONVERGENCE OF STEADY-STATE
MODEL (ALTERNATIVE II)
(Rs. million)

Sectors	GO I	GO II	GO III	GO IV	GO V (final)
1.	4,260	4,154	4,143	4,143	4,143
2.	11,810	11,512	11,486	11,485	11,485
3.	4,184	4,109	4,102	4,102	4,102
4.	6,536	6,159	6,072	6,066	6,066
5.	42,246	42,180	42,168	42,167	42,167
6.	31,218	31,095	31,054	31,051	31,051
7.	3,187	3,141	3,135	3,135	3,135
8.	10,425	10,385	10,376	10,373	10,373
9.	114,018	113,740	113,639	113,682	113,682
10.	1,145	1,129	1,127	1,127	1,127
11.	10,765	10,760	10,759	10,759	10,759
12.	5,707	5,677	5,677	5,678	5,678
13.	1,426	1,415	1,413	1,413	1,413
14.	113,828	112,587	112,343	112,327	112,327
15.	470	448	448	448	448
16.	5,099	3,776	3,813	3,821	3,821
17.	6,438	5,365	5,387	5,392	5,392
18.	2,189	1,985	1,985	1,986	1,986
19.	3,656	3,489	3,491	3,491	3,491
20.	19,880	18,892	18,869	18,871	18,871
21.	30,741	26,652	26,685	26,703	26,703
22.	140,561	136,441	135,708	135,662	135,662

Note: GO = Gross Output.
        I, II, etc. = Number of interation.

TABLE 23.3

SOLUTION VALUES OF THE STEADY-STATE MODEL (ALTERNATIVE I)
(Rs. million)

Sectors	Investment Demand	Replacement Investment	Fixed Investment	Inventory Holding	Import of Capital Goods	Growth of Output (%p.a.)	Gross Output
1.	106	2,228	31	31		7.7	4,115
2.	2,089	3,591	4,545	284		7.8	11,400
3.	1,635			76		6.0	3,885
4.	2,521			207		6.1	6,395
5.	7,725			613		8.5	41,082
6.	5,295			464		10.4	29,071
7.	1,801			166		7.0	3,106
8.	7,391			725		9.8	9,878
9.	33,029			1,202		5.2	113,436
10.	1,080			37		7.0	1,117
11.	3,936			382		8.8	10,681
12.	1,936			107		5.1	4,954
13.	1,319			23		6.8	1,405
14.	46,315	2,956	5107	673		7.9	111,821
15.	394			18		8.0	446
16.	543		3778	41	927	8.5	3,795
17.	881	2,170	2073	57	701	7.8	5,375
18.	1,817			86		8.0	1,980
19.	2,676			440		7.5	3,463
20.	5,541	5,332	5522	508		8.3	18,780
21.	7,549	15,014	4877	506	2,273	8.2	26,758
22.	59,417		11527	2,314		6.6	135,022

TABLE 23.4

SOLUTION VALUES OF THE STEADY-STATE MODEL (ALTERNATIVE II)
(Rs. million)

Sectors	Investment Demand	Replacement Investment	Fixed Investment	Inventory Holding	Import of Capital Goods	Growth (percent)	Output
1.	107	2,241	1,769	26		7.8	4,143
2.	2,109	3,710	4,594	181		7.9	11,485
3.	1,664			77		5.9	4,102
4.	2,489			208	298*	6.2	6,066
5.	7,845			618		8.4	42,167
6.	5,629			474	116*	9.4	31,051
7.	1,825			171		7.0	3,135
8.	7,834			734		9.4	10,373
9.	33,273			1,204		5.2	113,682
10.	1,090			37		7.1	1,127
11.	4,013			383		8.8	10,759
12.	2,191			116		4.8	5,678
13.	1,328			22		6.7	1,413
14.	46,671	2,972	5,135	668	689*	7.9	112,327
15.	396			18		8.1	448
16.	546		3,802	50	987	8.8	3,821
17.	882	2,185	2,083	92	745	8.0	5,392
18.	1,821			88		8.1	1,986
19.	2,695			449		7.5	3,491
20.	5,549	5,367	5,607	471		8.3	18,871
21.	7,603	15,158	4,931	547	2446+ 175*	8.2	26,703
22.	60,071		11,697	2,300	1,817*	6.7	135,662
Total	197,631	31,633	39,636	8,934	4178+3,095*		563,962

*Denotes consumption-goods imports

TABLE 23.5

THE SUPPLY-DEMAND BALANCE OF ENGINEERS AND
SCIENTISTS. OVER THE FOURTH Plan

YEAR	DEMAND FORECAST
A. Engineers	
1968/9	284,000
1973/4	366,968
Net increase between 1973/4 and 1968/9	82,968
Replacement need	32,548
TOTAL DEMAND	115,516
TOTAL SUPPLY*	244,000
B. Scientists	
1968/9	103,000
1973/4	132,322
Net increase between 1973/4 and 1968/9	29,322
Replacement needs	11,766
TOTAL DEMAND	41,088
TOTAL SUPPLY*	94,752

*The supply figures are taken from Directorate
General of Employment and Training, India's Manpower
Requirements 1968/9 to 1978/9, (January, 1969). But
it is not clear whether these estimates are actual
or forecast. In the second case, they have to be
scaled down because of poor performance of the Indian
economy in this period. The supply over the period
1968/9 to 1973/4 is guided by the activities in these
sectors, already taken place in the years 1964/5 to
1969/70 in the form of enrollments of students in
the first-year class.

TABLE 23.6

ANNUAL PHASING OF THE ESTIMATES OF GROSS OUTPUT,
PRIVATE CONSUMPTION, IMPORTS, FOREIGN AID AND
SHADOW PRICE OF FOREIGN EXCHANGE, 1965/6 to 1974/5
(Endoverous variables of the transient-state model)
(Rs. million)

ALTERNATIVE I

Variables		1965/6	1966/7	1967/8	1968/9	1969/70	1970/1	1971/2	1972/3	1973/4	1974/5
	1	2	3	4	5	6	7	8	9	10	11
Gross Output											
Sector 1	Q_1	19,594	19,594	22,363	23,690	25,381	27,017	27,947	29,554	33,091	37,850
Sector 2	Q_2	132,416	138,031	143,715	150,442	158,408	167,919	173,080	183,019	213,350	271,182
Sector 3	Q_3	34,146	34,146	35,507	40,233	45,362	52,805	53,125	53,097	53,066	53,064
Sector 4	Q_4	57,095	58,113	62,707	69,545	78,966	91,196	114,150	132,696	142,976	142,940
Sector 5	Q_5	9,549	13,675	16,732	20,114	24,229	32,097	30,242	27,508	27,840	20,341
Sector 6	Q_6	29,038	30,110	31,109	32,141	33,302	34,499	35,825	37,093	38,298	39,542
Private Consumption											
Sector 1	e_1	9,225	9,456	9,692	9,934	10,183	10,437	10,698	10,969	12,891	13,213
Sector 2	e_2	78,149	80,103	82,105	84,158	86,262	88,418	90,629	92,895	108,302	160,134
Sector 3	e_3	1,644	1,685	1,727	1,770	1,815	1,860	1,907	1,954	2,003	2,053
Sector 4	e_4	27,331	28,014	28,715	29,433	30,168	30,923	53,163	68,405	74,502	80,435
Sector 5	e_6	17,600	18,100	18,500	18,900	19,400	11,900	20,500	21,000	21,400	21,800
Capital Goods											
Imports	m_3	0	2,419	3,965	5,555	8,801	11,884	9,837	8,209	6,414	890
Consumption-goods imports											
Sector 1	M_1	572	1,500	1,523	1,359	940	469	726	856	1,004	1,582
Sector 2	M_2	943	2,299	2,332	2,693	1,481	793	1,168	1,357	1,575	2,418
Sector 3	M_3	254	699	710	631	431	205	328	390	461	738
Sector 4	M_4	2,779	8,120	8,253	7,309	4,899	2,186	3,665	4,412	5,268	8,591
Aid (Net)		0	5,757	7,193	7,064	6,384	5,107	4,816	3,612	2,408	1,204
Aid (Gross)		1,694	9,459	11,830	11,620	10,500	8,400	7,196	5,992	4,788	3,584
Shadow price of trade balance		210.5	41	26.8	18.1	12.6	8.9	3.4	3.2	4.7	0.3

Variables		1965/6	1966/7	1967/8	1968/9	1969/70	1970/1	1971/2	1972/3	1973/4	1974/5
1		2	3	4	5	6	7	8	9	10	11
Gross output											
Sector 1	Q_1	19,594	19,594	22,531	24,152	26,300	28,936	34,183	52,662	53,739	54,540
Sector 2	Q_2	138,360	138,823	145,262	153,382	164,616	186,045	258,860	287,109	292,866	297,549
Sector 3	Q_3	32,820	32,947	37,407	42,189	46,129	49,990	53,990	57,357	57,326	57,292
Sector 4	Q_4	55,196	58,962	64,519	72,989	84,466	97,207	97,593	102,239	115,874	126,614
Sector 5	Q_5	10,792	15,350	18,768	22,834	27,322	30,316	27,969	28,005	25,741	25,210
Sector 6	Q_6	29,038	30,110	30,709	32,141	33,302	33,499	35,825	37,093	38,298	39,542
Private Consumption											
Sector 1	e_1	9,225	9,456	9,692	9,934	10,183	10,437	10,698	28,517	29,230	29,960
Sector 2	e_2	78,149	80,109	82,105	84,158	86,262	88,418	149,034	171,429	175,715	180,108
Sector 3	e_3	1,644	1,685	1,727	1,770	1,815	1,860	1,907	1,954	2,003	2,053
Sector 4	e_4	27,331	28,014	28,715	29,432	30,168	30,928	31,700	35,269	49,624	61,962
Sector 6	e_6	17,600	18,100	18,500	18,900	19,400	19,900	20,500	21,000	21,400	21,800
Capital-goods imports	m_3	819	3,555	5,193	7,178	10,627	10,355	7,091	5,978	3,833	1,751
Consumption-goods imports											
Sector 1	M_1	1,147	1,597	1,615	1,322	738	498	916	1,025	1,221	1,420
Sector 2	M_2	1,783	2,441	2,467	2,039	1,184	835	1,446	1,604	1,891	2,181
Sector 3	M_3	530	745	754	614	335	220	419	471	565	660
Sector 4	M_4	6,090	8,683	8,785	7,098	3,730	2,356	4,759	5,385	6,513	7,656
Aid (Net)		4,720	7,630	9,310	8,470	6,570	3,780	3,640	2,800	1,680	700
Aid (Gross)		6,414	10,150	12,600	12,460	11,410	9,380	8,400	8,260	7,000	7,490
Shadow price of trade balance		10	5.1	3.5	2.5	1.8	1.3	0.9	0.6	0.5	0.5

(continued)

TABLE 23.6 (Continued)

ALTERNATIVE VIII

Variables		1965/6	1966/7	1967/8	1968/9	1969/70	1970/1	1971/2	1972/3	1973/4	1974/5
1		2	3	4	5	6	7	8	9	10	11
Gross Output											
Sector 1	Q_1	19,594	29,657	29,657	29,643	29,650	34,067	53,551	53,526	54,574	54,541
Sector 2	Q_2	135,375	145,710	162,077	175,584	242,509	281,028	287,078	287,052	294,598	294,564
Sector 3	Q_3	36,380	37,378	44,461	44,450	46,823	52,552	54,672	57,938	57,907	57,872
Sector 4	Q_4	55,193	69,575	73,027	91,197	91,181	91,161	93,227	103,663	116,886	128,792
Sector 5	Q_5	23,809	16,757	28,495	26,522	23,124	20,650	23,888	28,149	25,595	23,917
Sector 6	Q_6	29,038	30,110	31,109	32,141	33,302	34,499	35,825	37,093	38,293	39,542
Private Consumption											
Sector 1	e_1	9,225	9,456	9,692	9,934	10,183	10,437	27,784	28,479	29,191	29,920
Sector 2	e_2	78,149	80,103	82,105	84,158	137,856	161,764	165,808	169,958	174,202	178,557
Sector 3	e_3	1,644	1,685	1,727	1,770	1,815	1,860	1,907	1,954	2,003	2,058
Sector 4	e_4	27,331	28,014	28,715	29,432	30,168	30,922	31,695	32,488	49,566	64,806
Sector 5	e_5	17,600	18,100	18,500	18,900	19,400	19,900	20,500	21,000	21,400	21,800
Capital goods imports	m_3	10,011	3,892	10,910	8,771	6,294	2,222	3,722	6,016	3,670	874
Consumption goods imports:											
Sector 1	M_1	3,730	694	2,114	89	250	603	1,044	403	1,009	1,431
Sector 2	M_2	5,557	1,122	3,196	238	473	1,210	1,632	698	1,581	2,198
Sector 3	M_3	1,765	313	993	24	101	270	480	174	464	665
Sector 4	M_4	10,958	3,486	11,656	220	928	2,955	5,500	1,808	5,293	7,722
Aid (Net)		29,770	0	19,470	0	0	0	0	0	0	0
Aid (Gross)		31,464	2,520	22,760	3,990	4,900	5,600	4,760	54,560	5,320	6,790
Shadow price of trade balance		0.04	0.01	0.03	4	0	0.17	0.13	0	0.36	0.69

formulating the results in macro-economic terms are
mainly two: First, as the official plan runs mostly
in terms of macro-dimensions, any comparison of the
model estimates with the official estimates would be
impossible unless they were aggregated under similar
broad groupings; and second, any fiscal implication
of the above plan allocations (and their fiscal
feasibility) could only be brought out in aggregate
terms, both because many of the fiscal tools operated
in India are more aggregative than the details of
plan allocations, and because much information on fiscal
and behavioral indicators, such as tax rates and
savings rates, are available only in aggregate terms.

These tables lay out the following indentities:

(i) Gross domestic product = Consumption (private and public) + Gross Investment (fixed, working-
capital, and replacement investment) - net aid.

(ii) Net domestic product = Gross domestic product - Replacement investment.

(iii) Capital stock in any period = Capital
stock of the earlier periods + net investment of the
earlier period.

(iv) Idle capital capacity in any period =
unused capital stock in any period = "slack" variable
of the equation $kq_t \leq kq_{t-1} + I_{t-1}$

In our present formulation, the material-balance
equation is presented as an inequality, and as a
result the machine has given some solutions with positive non-zero values of some of these slack variables.
They represent the excess of material output that
cannot be used for consumption or investment or export
under the model - constraint. Hence, it is assumed
that this amount will not be produced, although the
corresponding capital capacity will be generated.
These outputs multiplied by the capital flow matrix
will thus add to the existing idle capacity of that
period. Row 12 of Tables 23.7, 23.8, and 23.9 present the idle capacity in the economy over the plan
as defined above.

TABLE 23.7

MOVEMENTS OF THE MAJOR ECONOMIC VARIABLES: ALTERNATIVE I
(Rs. billion)

	Variables	1965/6	1966/7	1967/8	1968/9	1969/70	1970/1	1971/2	1972/3	1973/4	1974/5	1975/6
1.	Gross Output	295.2	312.8	335.6	364.3	399.5	450.4	476.7	501.5	547.6	593.3	
2.	Gross Domestic Product (GDP)	183.8	199.3	214.0	230.7	251.5	279.4	301.7	321.8	352.3	386.0	433.6
3.	Net Domestic Product (NDP)	159.8	174.7	188.1	202.6	220.8	245.3	264.8	282.2	308.9	337.6	381.8
4.	Extension Investment (incl. Working Capital)	8.0	24.3	34.3	44.8	57.6	75.9	68.7	65.4	65.8	33.4	51.0
5.	Replacement Investment	24.0	24.6	25.9	28.1	30.7	34.1	36.9	39.6	43.4	48.4	51.8
6.	Total Consumption	151.8	156.2	160.4	164.9	169.6	174.3	200.9	220.4	245.5	305.4	330.8
7.	Exports	7.3	11.1	11.4	11.9	12.4	13.1	13.7	14.6	15.3	16.0	16.9
8.	Total Imports	7.3	16.9	18.6	19.0	18.8	18.2	18.5	18.2	17.7	17.2	16.9
9.	Consumption Imports	4.5	12.6	12.8	12.0	7.8	3.7	5.9	7.0	8.3	13.3	3.1
10.	Aid	0	5.8	7.2	7.1	6.4	5.1	4.8	3.6	2.4	1.2	0
11.	Total Capital Stock	303.9	311.9	336.2	370.5	415.3	472.9	548.8	617.5	682.9	748.7	782.1
12.	Idle Capacity as p.c. of Capital Stock	16.8	9.7	1.4	1.3	1.2	1.0	0.9	0.8	0.7	0.6	0
13.	Domestic Saving (Desirable)	32.0	43.1	53.5	65.1	79.3	104.9	100.8	101.4	106.8	80.6	102.8
14.	Domestic Saving (Projected)	31.5	35.3	39.0	43.1	48.2	55.1	60.6	65.6	73.1	81.4	93.2
15.	Inflationary Gap	0.5	7.8	14.5	22.0	31.1	49.8	40.2	35.8	33.7	-0.8	9.6
16.	Inflationary Gap as p.c. of GDP	.3	3.9	6.8	9.5	12.4	17.8	13.3	11.1	9.6	-0.2	2.2
17.	Direct Taxes	13.5	24.3	33.9	44.3	58.3	78.4	68.3	64.3	63.1	23.5	67.7
18.	Direct Taxes as p.c. of Household Income	8.4	13.9	18.0	21.9	26.4	32.0	25.8	22.8	20.4	7.0	17.7
19.	Rate of Growth of GDP	7.1	8.4	7.4	7.8	9.0	11.1	8.0	6.7	9.5	9.6	7.2
20.	Gross Investment as p.c. of GDP	17.4	24.5	28.3	31.6	35.1	39.3	35.0	33.0	31.0	21.2	23.7
21.	Capital/Gross Output Ratios	1.03	1.00	1.00	1.02	1.04	1.05	1.15	1.23	1.25	1.26	

TABLE 23.8

MOVEMENTS OF THE MAJOR ECONOMIC VARIABLES: ALTERNATIVE V
(Rs. billion)

Variables		1965-6	1966-7	1967-8	1968-9	1969-70	1970-1	1971-2	1972-3	1973-4	1974-5
Gross Output	1.	300.9	317.2	345.4	379.6	420.4	469.5	547.5	603.7	619.9	636.0
Gross Domestic Product (GDP)	2.	183.3	204.8	219.3	239.1	263.5	294.2	343.3	376.7	390.6	405.0
Net Domestic Product (NDP)	3.	159.2	180.3	192.8	210.1	231.6	258.4	300.0	329.4	341.4	354.3
Extension Investment (incl. Working Capital)	4.	12.1	31.8	41.6	53.6	68.6	87.8	66.2	48.8	38.6	31.3
Replacement Investment	5.	24.1	24.5	26.5	29.0	31.9	35.8	42.9	47.3	49.2	50.7
Total Consumption	6.	151.8	156.4	160.4	164.9	169.6	174.3	237.8	283.4	304.4	323.7
Exports	7.	7.3	11.1	11.4	11.9	12.4	13.1	13.7	14.6	15.3	16.1
Total Imports	8.	12.0	18.7	20.7	20.4	19.0	16.9	17.3	17.4	17.0	16.8
Consumption Imports	9.	9.5	13.5	13.6	11.1	6.0	3.9	7.5	8.5	10.2	11.9
Aid	10.	4.7	7.6	9.3	8.5	5.6	3.8	3.6	2.8	1.7	0.7
Total Capital Stock	11.	303.9	316.0	347.0	389.4	443.0	511.6	549.4	665.6	714.4	753.0
Idle Capacity as p.c. of Capital Stock	12.	14.3	1.7	1.6	1.4	1.2	1.1	0.9	0.8	0.8	0.7
Domestic Saving (Desirable)	13.	31.5	48.7	58.8	74.1	93.9	119.8	105.5	93.3	86.1	81.3
Domestic Saving (Projected)	14.	31.4	36.7	40.3	45.2	51.2	58.8	70.9	79.1	82.6	86.1
Inflationary Gap	15.	0.1	12.0	18.5	28.9	42.7	61.0	34.6	14.2	3.5	-4.8
Inflationary Gap as p.c. of GDP	16.	.05	5.9	8.4	12.1	16.2	20.7	10.1	3.8	.09	-1.2
Direct Taxes	17.	-2.9	29.9	38.6	51.8	69.1	91.5	60.4	37.9	26.8	18.8
Direct Taxes as p.c. of Household Income	18.	8.1	16.6	20.0	24.7	29.8	35.4	20.1	11.5	7.9	5.3
Rate of Growth of GDP	19.	7.1	11.2	7.1	9.0	10.2	11.7	16.7	9.7	3.7	3.7
Gross Investment as p.c. of GDP	20.	16.6	27.5	31.1	34.5	38.1	42.0	31.7	25.5	22.5	20.2
Capital/Gross Output Ratios	21.	-.01	1.00	1.00	1.03	1.05	1.09	1.09	1.10	1.15	1.18

347

TABLE 23.9

MOVEMENT OF THE MAJOR ECONOMIC VARIABLES: ALTERNATIVE VIII
(Rs. billion)

Variables		1965/66	1966/67	1967/68	1968/69	1969/70	1970/71	1971/72	1972/73	1973/74	1974/75
Gross Output	1.	332.1	352.6	408.3	436.7	499.0	542.9	581.6	606.9	623.6	632.7
Gross Domestic Product (GDP)	2.	204.3	219.6	241.2	271.6	312.1	326.1	353.3	376.0	388.7	409.9
Net Domestic Product (NDP)	3.	179.8	192.2	210.8	238.2	272.7	282.1	307.3	328.4	339.1	359.1
Extension Investment (incl. Working Capital)	4.	57.8	36.0	69.8	73.3	51.6	34.4	35.6	49.4	36.3	34.3
Replacement Investment	5.	24.5	27.4	30.4	33.4	39.4	44.0	46.0	47.6	49.6	50.8
Total Consumption	6.	151.8	156.2	160.4	164.9	221.2	247.7	271.7	279.1	302.8	324.8
Exports	7.	7.3	11.1	11.4	12.0	12.4	13.1	13.7	14.6	15.3	16.0
Total Imports	8.	37.1	11.2	30.9	12.0	12.4	13.1	13.7	14.6	15.3	16.0
Consumption Imports	9.	22.0	5.6	18.0	0.5	1.8	5.3	8.7	3.1	8.3	12.0
Aid	10.	29.8	0.1	19.5	0	0	0	0	0	0	0
Total Capital Stock	11.	303.9	361.7	397.7	467.5	540.8	592.4	626.8	662.4	711.8	748.1
Idle Capacity as p.c. of Capital Stock	12.	1.3	5.3	11.3	3.1	2.6	10.5	6.2	1.8	2.5	0.5
Domestic Saving (Desirable)	13.	52.5	63.3	80.8	106.7	91.0	78.3	81.6	97.0	85.9	79.1
Domestic Saving (Projected)	14.	36.6	40.3	45.7	53.2	63.2	66.6	73.4	79.0	82.1	85.9
Inflationary Gap	15.	15.9	23.0	35.1	53.5	27.8	11.7	8.2	18.0	3.8	-6.8
Inflationary Gap as p.c. of GDP	16.	7.8	10.5	14.6	19.7	8.9	3.6	2.3	4.8	0.1	-1.7
Direct Taxes	17.	33.5	41.8	56.6	79.9	49.9	29.5	28.1	41.9	26.5	16.2
Direct Taxes as p.c. of Household Income	18.	18.6	21.7	26.9	33.5	18.3	10.4	9.1	12.8	7.8	
Rate of Growth of GDP	19.	7.1	7.4	9.8	12.6	14.9	4.5	8.3	6.4	3.4	3.9
Gross Investment as p.c. of GDP	20.	40.3	28.9	41.5	39.2	29.2	24.0	23.0	25.8	22.1	20.8
Capital/Gross Output Ratios	21.	0.92	1.25	1.32	1.28	1.22	1.18	1.19	1.21	1.19	1.18

In discussing the results derived from other
alternatives of the transient-state formulations,
only relevant features such as the sensitivity of
plan allocations to changes in discount rates and aid
and/or the presence of "bang-bang" effect in some of
the formulations of the model, are dealt with in this
book.

THE MANPOWER SUBMODEL

Manpower requirements for engineers, scientists,
and agricultural graduates are estimated for the
year 1975/6 and also for 1973/4, from the model contained in this chapter. The year 1975/6 is chosen
because it is the terminal year of the planning
model. Further, as the estimates of supply of skilled
manpower are only available for the year 1973/4 from
reliable official sources, an attempt is made to
estimate their demand for the same year. This will
help in assessing the constraining effect of these
resources in the growth pattern prescribed in our
model.

Table 23.11 presents the demand forecast of
skilled manpower for the year 1975/6. The stages of
computation are: (1) estimates of total employees,
(2) estimates of professional hands, and (3) estimates of engineers and scientists.

The estimates of total employees for construction
and services are computed by deflating their net
output (i.e., value added) by Rs.3,111.6 and Rs.
1,718.7 only. The percentage of professionals in
the total employed labor force and in construction
and services is 3.0 and 8.0 respectively. This is
derived from the occupation employment matrix (Table
22.4). For the education sector, all employees are
identified as professionals (i.e., as teachers).
The requirements of this sector have been estimated
by the Indian Government at 4 million for 1975/6.
In converting their estimates into engineering and
scientists components, the percentage of engineers
to professionals is reduced from 8.1 to 4.0. Table
23.5 gives the demand forecast for 1975/6. For

agriculture, the number of agricultural and veterinary
graduates needed is derived directly from the planned
gross output of Rs.253,948 million for 1975/6.

For the year 1973/4, the coefficients for engineers and scientists for the detailed manufacturing
sectors are aggregated into four sectors, and the
demand forecast of these four sectors, together with
agriculture, construction, services and public administration, and education are presented in Table 23.10.
As is obvious from Table 23.5, neither the supply of
engineers nor the supply of scientists will act as
constraints in the proposed development plan given
in this book. Conceptually, the constraining effect
of the supply of any resource should be assessed not
only sectorally but also intertemporally. But
unfortunately no data are available on the supply
pattern of engineers and scientists phased annually
over the Fourth Plan period (1969/70 to 1973/4).
Hence, it was necessary to confine ourselves in the
supply-demand analysis to the year 1973/4.

                        THE FISCAL SUBMODEL

The estimate of tax realization in this model
is not a forecast but is demand-oriented. The main
purpose here is to estimate the amount of purchasing
power that is to be siphoned off from the private-
expenditure stream in order to maintain price stability. Thus, the role of taxation in this scheme
is essentially confined to price stabilization, and
since the desired allocation of resources in these
models is conducted at constant prices, maintenance
of price stability is of the highest priority in the
execution of the plans.

Taxation is broadly divided into direct and
indirect. Assuming a part of the incidence of indirect taxes is passed over to consumers through price
changes, it is difficult to deal with the problem of
the shifting of incidence of taxation in our present
simplified model. So we assume that the rate of indirect taxation advalorem will not change over the
plan period. This will leave us with direct taxation

TABLE 23.10

DEMAND FOR SKILLED MANPOWER 1973/4

	Engineers*	Scientists*	Agricultural* and Veterinary Graduates
I. Cash-crop-based industries	8,490	3,353	
II. Food-crop-based industries	11,377	3,576	
III. Mining and mining-based industries	15,594	4,930	
IV. Power, transport, trade, chemicals, and misc. industries	47,507	15,063	
V. Agriculture (a part of sector I and II			107,109
VI. Construction	20,000	6,200	
VII. Services, including public administration	144,000	44,200	
VIII. Education	120,000	75,000	
	366,968	132,322	

*As the norm derived for engineers and scientists is aggregate for the whole economy, the sectoral estimates are of doubtful validity and less reliable than the totals.

351

TABLE 23.11

SKILLED MANPOWER REQUIREMENTS FOR 1975/6.
(Thousands)

Industries. Sector No. of inter-industry classifications	Total Employees	Total Professionals	Total Engineers	Total Scientists
1	215	5.4	)	)
2	2,320	58.0	)	)
3	283	7.1	)	)
4	631	15.8	)	)
5	3,331	83.3	)	)
6	4,657	116.4	)	)
7	483	12.1	)	)
13	100	2.5	)	)
15	184	4.6	) 459.8	) 192.5
16	451	11.3	)	)
17	383	9.6	)	)
18	75	1.9	)	)
19	1,431	35.8	)	)
20	1,151	28.8	)	)
21	3,747	93.7	)	)
22	32,558	651.1	)	)
Construction	7,800	234.0	)	)
Services	29,100	2,328.0	)	)
Education	4,000	4,000.0	)	)
Agriculture	152,319			) 109.0*

*Directly calculated from gross output in agriculture. (They comprise agriculture and veterinary graduates.)

as the only tool for combating inflation. (Later
on, the directional changes in the rates of indirect
taxes are estimated under restricted assumptions in
order to tackle sectoral imbalance.)

Given the income/consumption relation as:
Private consumption at constant prices = 865.0 + .856
(private income at constant prices net of direct
taxes measured in Rs. ten million), the inflationary
gaps in the plan can be calculated, assuming certain
tax rates, or alternatively, tax rates can be calculated assuming a zero inflationary gap.

Direct taxes in India take the form of corpora-
tion tax, other income taxes, and land revenue, but
this disaggregation is not considered in this model,
and the effects of direct taxes on the ability and the
desire to work and invest are overlooked.

As to the possible imbalance in the investment
sector between the desired level and the actual level
of investment, given the level and pattern of income
and taxes, it is presumed that the government, with
its large public sector and nationalized banking
system, will be capable of carrying out whatever
financial manipulation is needed to bring about a
balance. (More than 70 percent of investment is in
the public sector.)

In this highly simplified fiscal framework, the
surplus or deficit budget of the government will act
as residual and neutral to the price structure. In
real life, a part of the burden of the anti-inflation-
ary drive will be shared by indirect taxation and a
part by voluntary saving of the community, by improving its propensity to save. Tables 23.7, 23.8, and
23.9 give the absolute figures and percentage share
of taxes for different years of the plan.

The findings are analyzed under five heads:

a) A study of the salient features of the model's layout of both the macro-and sectoral variables.

b) A probe into its feasibility considerations.

c) An analysis of the implications of the model's findings under alternative aid assumptions.

d) A search for the principal constraining sectors of the economy in the growth process.

e) An exploration of the technical limitations of a typical linear-programming planning model.

Conceptually, the solutions given under (a) should lie within the feasibility area, and therefore no separate check to feasibility is warranted. But a separate treatment under (b) is needed because the savings/consumption submodel and the tax/subsidy submodel (two major tests of feasibility) have not been incorporated into the two principal models giving the aforesaid solutions.

Tables 23.7, 23.8, and 23.9 present the movements of the major macro-variables over ten years of the plan (1965/6 to 1975/6) for the three principal

355

alternative formulations, shown as alternative I, V,
and VIII (Table 9.1 in the model. Table 23.6
similarly gives the sectoral movements of outputs,
consumption, imports, exports, etc., over the same
ten-year horizon.

These macro-variables are computed by aggregating
the estimates of the six sectors of the transient-
state model, four derived from the principal models
and the other two (e.g., construction and services,
including public administration) from two separate
submodels. The rate of growth of gross domestic
product over this transient phase (between 1964/5
and 1975/6) of the model is recorded as 8.8 percent
per annum, and the rate of growth of consumption is
7.6 percent per annum. This suggests an increase
in the average savings rate over the period.

The difference between the alternative formulations of the model is exhibited in terms of the
optimum time path (i.e., intertemporal movements)
that the output, consumption, investment, and
capital stock have taken to reach a desired targeted
situation from a given initial position. The time
paths are different because the availibilities of
foreign resources in the different exercises are
different. As the tables show, the larger and more
favorable the supply of foreign resources, the
quicker the growth of capital stock, and the greater
the supply of consumption goods to the community
over the plan period.

The capital stock in all three cases starts at
Rs.303.9 billion and ends at Rs.781.1 billion in
1975/6. Idle capacity as a percentage of total
capacity declines in all the cases over the plan
period. When an economy moves from one consumption-
income configuration to another, the adjustment
process is time-consuming. This is because of the
long gestation of production in some cases, the
lack of perfect substitutability between different
production inputs and the less-than-infinitely
elastic supply of foreign resources as substitutes
for domestic ones. This results in the appearance
of idle capacity in specific sectors in the early
years of the plan.

Also, it is evident from our findings that the capital/output ratio increased over this period in all the alternative exercises. This is mainly due to the faster growth of the capital-intensive sector relative to the others. For example, the sectors of transport, power, etc., which have the highest capital/output ratio, have a much higher-than-average growth. The capital/net income (net domestic product) ratio increased over this period from 1.9 to 2.2 in alternative I, from 1.9 to 2.1 in alternative V, and from 1.7 to 2.1 in alternative VIII. These ratios seem to be slightly lower than those found in contemporary studies. Of course, one major explanation is that our concept of capital/optimum capacity relations differs from the conventional capital (used and unused)/output relations.

The rates of growth of income (GDP) fluctuate widely between 7 percent and 11 percent in alternative I, 3.7 percent and 16 percent in alternative V, and 3.4 percent and 14.9 percent in alternative VIII. They exhibit in all cases a sort of normal distribution, with the peak rate being reached near the middle of the plan. In alternatives V and VIII, the rates of growth slow down very near the tail-end of the plan. This is an extremely common feature in these types of planning models, and goes by the name of "flip-flop" behavior.

The consumption movements in the alternative formulations trail the minimum floor path in the initial years of the plan. During this phase the real income of the community per capita is maintained at the base level. Also, the following percentage changes would take place over the plan period in the composition of the consumption basket offered to consumers in the plan. (The implications of these changes will be discussed later on.) Gross investment as a percentage of gross domestic output in the first two alternatives reaches its peak near the middle of the plan period. In both these cases, it reaches its maximum (approx. 40 percent of GDP) in the year 1970/1. In contrast, in the last alternative we find a negatively skewed distribution, starting from a figure of as high as 40 percent in the first year of the plan.

TABLE 24.1

MOVEMENTS IN THE COMPOSITION OF CONSUMPTION

ITEMS	1959	1965/6	1974/5 Alt.I	1974/5 Alt.II	1974/5 Alt.III	1975/6
1. Cash crop and based industries	7.9	6.9	4.8	10.1	10.1	10.1
2. Food crop and based industries	62.0	58.5	57.6	60.9	60.1	62.8
3. Metal-based Industries	0.9	1.2	0.7	0.7	0.7	0.8
4. Power, transport, trade, etc.	17.6	20.5	28.9	20.9	21.8	17.00
5. Services	11.6	13.2	7.8	7.4	7.3	9.1

To obtain a general long-term perspective of the
projected macro-variables of the present model as
given in alternative I, vis-a-vis past trends in the
economy, Graph 24.1 traces the movements of the relevant economic variables between 1950/1 and 1975/6.
In Schedule 2 of this graph, representing total gross
investment, a break appears between 1960/1 and 1963/4
because of lack of data. Investment data between
1950/1 and 1960/1 are drawn from the CSO estimates.[1]
The figures for 1964/5 to 1975/6 are estimated by the
model.

One of the main purposes in formulating the above
programming model is to map out and recommend a pattern
of integrated movements of the key economic variables
(which are otherwise guided by multiple, and not
necessarily integrated, decision units), in order to
maximize certain social objectives.

The important question that normally arises under
the circumstances is whether these recommended layouts
are feasible for implementation in the society concerned. Feasibilities in this case are tested prin-
cipally from three major angles--technical (relating
to technology and knowledge on the one hand, and
resource availability on the other), behavioral, and
political and administrative.

Both our steady-state and transient-state models
satisfy all the technical conditions by using the
base-period (adjusted for technical changes) current
and capital flow matrices for developing their production relations and observing the capacity constraints (at every time period) that arise from the
problems of resource availability. The constraining
effect of land, however, is not explored. The constraining effect of labor, both in its aggregate and
sectoral aspects, is taken care of in the manpower
submodel (page 349). The results show that over the
Fourth Plan period (1969/70 to 1973/4) the supply of
engineers is 111 percent and scientists is 130 percent
of requirements. Hence feasibility in this field is
safely assured. The behavioral feasibility of this
model is mainly tested in the savings/income submodel.
The principal models have behavior considerations only

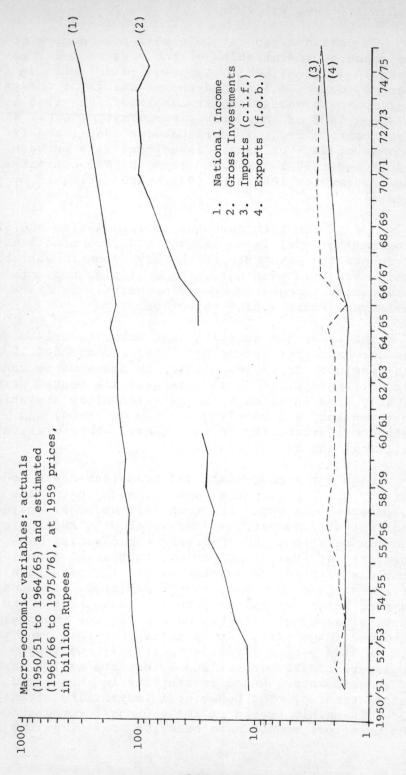

GRAPH 24.1

Macro-economic variables: actuals
(1950/51 to 1964/65) and estimated
(1965/66 to 1975/76), at 1959 prices,
in billion Rupees

1. National Income
2. Gross Investments
3. Imports (c.i.f.)
4. Exports (f.o.b.)

Source: Present model.

360

TABLE 24.2

MOVEMENTS OF CAPITAL STOCK AND IDLE CAPACITY IN THE INDIAN ECONOMY
(Rs./million)

Alt. I	1965/6	1966/7	1967/8	1968/9	1969/70	1970/1	1971/2	1972/3	1973/4	1974/5	1975/6
Total capital stock	3,039	3,119	3,362	3,705	4,153	4,729	5,488	6,175	6,829	7,487	7,821
Idle capacity as percent of capital stock	16.8	9.7	1.4	1.3	1.2	1.0	0.9	0.8	0.7	0.6	0
Alt. V											
Total capital stock	3,039	3,160	3,478	3,894	4,430	5,116	5,994	6,656	7,144	7,530	7,843
Idle capacity	14.3	1.7	1.6	1.4	1.2	1.1	0.9	0.8	0.8	0.7	0
Alt. VIII											
Total capital stock	3,039	3,617	3,977	4,675	5,408	5,924	6,268	6,624	7,118	7,481	7,843
Idle capacity	1.3	5.3	11.3	3.1	2.6	10.5	6.2	1.8	2.5	0.5	0

Note: Idle capacity is defined as icle capital stock.

in the treatment of export forecasting. In general,
these models meticulously cover technical considerations and prescribe a technically consistent pattern
of economic development and resource allocation. But
if the society has a free market where economic
decision units such as households or institutions can
exercise a free choice, then there is no automatic
guarantee that resource allocation under market
influences will match that of the planned one. If
not, then the price structure of the market will
change, the plan allocation will not be realized, and
feasibility will be destroyed. In the savings/income
submodel, attempts are made to locate and measure the
pressure points both in the aggregate and in the
sectors by identifying demand/supply disequilibrium.
The pressure may develop in either the consumption or
the investment markets. In the investment market,
70 percent of the activities are in the public sector
and the rest also under strict government control.
In the consumption market, the pressure is measured
as the gap between the demand for, and supply of,
consumer goods. This can also be represented as the
gap between the demand for, and supply of, domestic
saving. This behavioral aspect is neglected in most
Indian planning models. This pressure may also work
differently within each individual sector.

The desirable level of domestic saving is defined
as total gross capital formation minus import surplus.
The supply of domestic saving is estimated on the
assumption of a linear relationship between gross
domestic output and gross domestic saving at constant
prices. This relation is estimated from time-series
data spreading over ten years, ending in 1961 and
obtained from a study by the NCAER. Of the different
alternatives attempted, the linear one gives the best
fit.

Gross domestic saving at constant price = -13.9 +
.247 domestic product at constant prices. [Measured
(.026)
in Rs. 10 million].
          R^2 = .897, D-W statistics. = 2.72.

Tables 23.7, 23.8, and 23.9 give the value of

the gaps, in absolute terms and as percentages of GDP
for all plan years for alternatives I, V, and VIII.
The gap (inflationary pressure) becomes as high as
17.8 percent in alternative I in the year 1970/1,
20.7 percent in alternative V in the same year, and
27.8 percent in alternative VIII in the year 1969/70.
In absolute terms, they become as high as Rs.60
billion (approximately) in these years. These findings
convince one of the inflationary potential of the
prescribed plans. In fact, only a doubling of the
average propensity to save could remove these gaps,
but this is very ambitious, especially in a free
society where the chance of a voluntary change to
this degree in the propensity to save is very remote.
Recourse to compulsory saving is normally undertaken,
through rationing or price control, or increased
taxation. The feasibility of a given fiscal measure
will be discussed in the tax/subsidy submodel. Even
when inflationary pressure in the economy as a whole
is removed, sectoral imbalance may still exist. In
Table 24.4 the demand for, and the supply of, goods
and services in the consumer market, are formulated.
Supply here refers to planned supply, while demand is
estimated from the respective expenditure elasticities
derived from the NSS surveys. The demand/supply ratios
in each sector of this table will measure the sectoral
price rise, with market forces given free play. The
patterns of price rise, as defined above, are seen
to be almost similar in alternatives V and VIII.
Sector I has the highest price rise of 28 percent to
30 percent, and sector IV has the greatest fall of
20 percent to 23 percent, in the year 1974/5. Any
judgements as to whether a given plan allocation would
be feasible or not under the corresponding sectoral
imbalances will depend on the acceptance by the
community of the efforts required to remove these
imbalances. This will again mean a study of the
political and administrative feasibility of the plan.

      The last group of behavioral constraints springs
from import propensities. Import propensities for
capital and intermediate goods are essentially technological, and are thus fully respected in the computed solution of this model. On the other hand,
the behavioral aspect of import propensities of

consumer goods is not guaranteed in the model solutions. In our attempt to build an econometric behavior relation between gross domestic product and
consumption-goods imports, we met with no success.
Hence a macro-relation is computed between aggregate
imports and the level of GDP in any period. This
is based on a time-series data covering the period
1950/65, as follows:

Imports at constant price = -.668 + .0766 GDP. at
constant price.   (2.207)   (.0184)

$$R^{-2} = .598. \quad D/W = 2.174.$$

Using this functional form, the demand for, and
supply of, total imports over ten years of the plan
is computed in table 24.4. This means that, if left
to market forces, inflation in the import sector will
rise to nearly 23 percent aggregating the plan period
as a whole. In all probability, it will be still
higher in reality, since there are some individual
years within the plan period where the gap is much
higher, and since we know that the sum total effect
of each year's gap will normally exceed the aggregate
gap. The feasibility of removing these gaps from
the plan will again depend on the fiscal and administrative performance of the plan.

As has been discussed, the feasibility of a
plan is to be assessed mainly in terms of the workability of removing the "gaps" (i.e., demand/supply
imbalances) in the domestic and foreign-trade sectors.
These gaps can be removed by direct participation by
the state in the physical allocation of resources,
price control and rationing, tax-subsidy methods, and
general guidance and persuasion. The investment
sector in India is almost exclusively treated by
the first two methods: 70 percent is in the public
sector and the rest under strong licensing controls.
The feasibility of any action in this field is to be
judged in terms of its political acceptability.
The consumer-goods market, on the other hand, is
almost wholly laissez-faire. Further, this sector
is largely regulated by the third method (price control and rationing). An attempt will be made to

TABLE 24.3

DEMAND – SUPPLY IMBALANCES (SECTORAL), 1974/5

(Rs. million)

Sectors	Alternative I			Alternative V			Alternative VIII		
	Demand	Supply	Implied price changes (percent)	Demand	Supply	Implied price changes (percent)	Demand	Supply	Implied price changes (percent)
I	35,091	13,213	165.5	38,575	29,960	28.8	38,827	29,920	29.8
II	171,665	160,134	7.2	183,267	180,108	1.8	184,130	178,557	3.1
III	2,211	2,053	7.6	2,356	2,053	14.8	2,363	2,058	14.8
IV	47,048	80,435	-41.5	50,091	61,962	-19.2	50,331	64,806	-22.3

TABLE 24.4

DEMAND FOR AND SUPPLY OF IMPORTED GOODS
(Rs. billion)

Years	Demand	Supply	Balance
1965/6	13.3	12.0	+1.3
1966/7	15.0	18.7	-3.7
1967/8	16.1	20.7	-4.6
1968/9	17.6	20.4	-2.8
1969/70	19.5	19.0	+0.5
1970/1	21.8	16.9	+4.9
1971/2	25.6	17.3	+8.3
1972/3	28.2	17.0	+11.2
1973/4	29.2	16.8	+12.4
1974/5	30.3	16.9	+13.4
TOTAL	216.6	175.9	+40.9

measure the extent of direct and indirect taxes needed
to remove gaps in this sector under the tax-subsidy
submodel. Assuming the demand for consumption in
any period is a function of the economy's disposable
private income, (i.e., private income net of direct
taxes), the rates of direct taxes needed (expressed
as percentage of private income), for removing these
gaps reach their maximum at 32.0 percent in alternative
I, 35.4 percent in alternative VIII (both in 1970/1),
and 33.5 percent in alternative VIII in 1968/9 (see
Tables 23.7, 23.8, and 23.9). These contrast sharply
with a figure of 4 percent or less of direct taxation
to private income during the whole of the last decade.
From this one gets the feeling that only a very
efficient administrative machinery and a strong and
popular government will be able to attain this high
rate of achievement. But if we take the plan period
as a whole, it means an additional rate of taxation
of only 10-15 percent. This sounds much less ambitious, but aggregating many of the plan efforts will
underestimate the ambitiousness of a plan. Even
when the overall imbalance is eliminated by the
necessary rate of direct taxation, the sectoral imbalance may develop in a free market depending on
consumer choices. Sectoral resource allocation in
the plan is determined in the context of an unchanged
(base-period) price structure. This price structure,
in its role as a guide to resource allocation, should
be maintained in the plan. What is presumed in this
simplified planning model is that the rate and structure of indirect taxation should be so manipulated
as to siphon off the sectoral-demand gaps by raising
the demand prices, but at the same time maintaining
the existing supply/price structure. This is possible
if the whole gap between demand and supply in each
sector can be removed by indirect taxation. Assuming
the elasticity of demand as zero, the increment in
the indirect tax receipt will be equal to the absolute
level of these gaps.* In general, owing to these

---

*If elasticity is more than zero, then the amount
of indirect taxation must be more than the gap, and
the supplier will be compensated by a corresponding
subsidy.

gaps, a price rise is expected in sectors I and III
and a fall in sector IV. Hence the rate of indirect
taxation should be revised upwards in the first two
sectors and reduced in the last sector (in fact, a
subsidy might be needed). In reality, this is the
existing trend of indirect taxation in India. The
detailed pattern of changes can only be worked out
in a more sophisticated model where the elasticities
of demand and supply of goods and services would be
available separately. Similarly, in the import market, a rise in custom duties or import control will
be needed to combat excess demand. The overall effect
on the budget in any year is the sum total of the
tax receipts (under the new rates) less the public
expenditure of that year: In our present case heavy
budget surpluses are implied.

The practicability of the necessary changes in
the tax structure evidently depends on the existing
administrative machinery and the political and social
norms that the country professes. Our general impression is that the efforts needed to make the above plan
successful are indeed very ambitious.

AID IMPLICATIONS

The level and pattern of foreign aid is essentially the outcome of international negotiations.
It is thus justifiably treated exogenously in this
model. At the same time, attempts to forecast the
level of foreign aid ten years hence (as in this
model) must be regarded as heroic. To avoid the
problem, the popular practice is to work planning
models with alternative aid assumptions. As Tables
24.5 and 24.6 show, the higher the level of aid, the
less the strain on the domestic economy in achieving
certain goals, and the higher the value of its social
maximand.

The productivity of foreign aid should be defined
in a way that enables one to increase the increment
in the total value product (GDP) per unit change in
foreign aid. In a dynamic planning model, aid is
spread over time. Hence redefined, it should measure

the increment of GNP at the end of the plan period,
compared to the base, for a unit change in aid, the
phasing of aid remaining unchanged.[2] In our present
model, however, it is difficult to compute productivity in the above sense. This is because our
terminal-period GNP is constrained to a fixed targeted
value and our objective function is the maximization
of consumption and not income. Hence increasing aid
supply results in greater consumption and hence higher
income within the plan period (investment needs
remaining unchanged by the terms of reference given
to the model), although the terminal-year income
remains unchanged. Therefore, an indirect method is
adopted for calculating the productivity of foreign
aid in the context of the present model formulation.

    Productivity is defined as the sum of the GNP in
each year over the plan period per unit change in
foreign aid (phasing remaining unchanged), divided by
the number of years in the plan. This is calculated
by comparing alternative V with alternative I as
3.5.* The savings constraint in the present model
is policy-oriented and not behavioral, and being much
less stringent it only guarantees against a fall in
per capita consumption over the plan period, compared
to the base. However the model solution permits an
improvement in the per capita consumption of the
people, which suggests that the plan period as a
whole has no effective savings constraint. The above
figure can therefore be interpreted as the productivity
of foreign aid under a trade constraint. When an
economy acts under a savings constraint, foreign aid
supplements doemstic investible resources. Therefore,
its capital productivity (i.e., capital coefficients)
will be similar to those derived from the capital
flow matrix of the country, which is estimated by
the ratio of incremental output to the total extension
investment (with one and a half year's gestation lag)
over the plan period in our model. But productivity
as defined above will depend very much on the phasing
of aid. Assuming phasing as in alternative I or V,

─────────────

*Unfortunately, their phasing is exactly the same.

the productivity of aid in this case is estimated at
0.2.   This compares favorably with Chenery's findings
of 2.6 and .3 in the case of Greece, for the trade
constraint and savings constraint respectively.[3]
The above results show that under the model's assumptions and prescribed pattern of growth, the economy
will suffer from a trade gap.

We come next to the economic interpretations
of the shadow prices of duality values for the trade
balances appearing in the model solution.   They must
not be identified with the conventional productivity
concept of foreign aid or foreign exchange.   They
represent the additions to the discounted consumption
stock over the whole plan period.   The declining
trend in duality values over time suggests that if
one takes the plan utility or welfare into consideration (measured as the sum total of the discounted
value of consumption), the utility from unit foreign-
exchange earning is higher in the initial years of
the plan.   The logical corollary of this is that
the ideal phasing of aid should be positively skewed.
This hypothesis is corroborated by the findings of
our third alternative exercise (VIII in Table 23.9).

Lastly, the divergences in the marginal contribution to the discounted sum of consumption (i.e.,
duality values of trade balances) for each period
are seen to go down as the phasing of aid approaches
the optimum.   This substantiates the theory of
equimarginal returns between alternative uses, for
output maximization.

As is evident from our findings and from other
contemporary sources, the productivity of foreign
aid is very high in plan formulation in developing
economies.   Evidently, therefore, any error in forecasting the aid supply is quite likely to disrupt
the entire structure of the plan.

In order to avoid a recasting of the strategy
and allocation of resources in a plan, the formulation
of the upper and lower limits of foreign aid could
be conducted for each year separately.

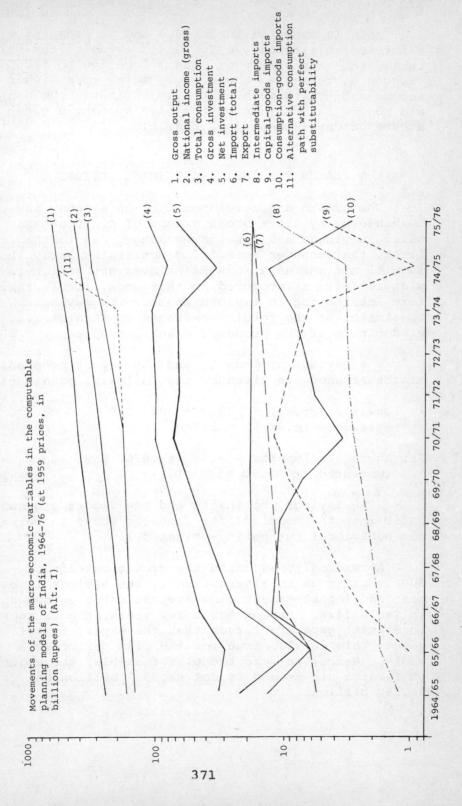

GRAPH 24.2

Movements of the macro-economic variables in the computable
planning models of India, 1964-76 (at 1959 prices, in
billion Rupees) (Alt. I)

1. Gross output
2. National income (gross)
3. Total consumption
4. Gross investment
5. Net investment
6. Import (total)
7. Export
8. Intermediate imports
9. Capital-goods imports
10. Consumption-goods imports
11. Alternative consumption
    path with perfect
    substitutability

371

This is shown in Table 24.5 and is computed with
reference to alternative V. As is evident from this
table, the sensitivity of plan allocation to aid
changes decreases as the economy moves to a higher
income-and-growth path. It also estimates the minimum
aid needed in any year of the plan to make a given
scheme of development just feasible.

A SEARCH FOR THE CONSTRAINING SECTORS

The growth and development of an economy may
be hindered by three broad groups of constraints:
skill, savings, and foreign exchange. As to the
first, the manpower submodel demonstrates amply that
it will not act as a constraint over any medium-term
plan in India as proposed in this book. It is therefore interesting to explore whether the savings
constraint or the foreign-exchange constraint will
predominate if the proposed plan is adopted.

The savings propensity and the import propensity
of the economy are given by the following equations:

1.   Savings (gross) = -13.9 + .247 GNP
      [Measured in Rs.10 million]

2.   Aggregate imports = -.668 + .0767 GNP
      [Measured in Rs.10 million]

(The savings propensity and the import propensity
built into the model differ from the above in being
not behavioral but policy-oriented.)

Accordingly, assuming the growth pattern of
GDP is given as in alternative V, the savings-invest-
ment and import-export gaps are estimated as shown
in Table 24.6. Except for a few years, the savings-
investment gaps are larger than the export-import
gaps. This is also true for the plan period as a
whole. Hence, to make the plan feasible, the amount
of foreign aid needed is not Rs.89.7 billion but
Rs.260 billion.

TABLE 24.5

THE SENSITIVITY OF THE REQUIREMENT VECTOR (FOREIGN EXCHANGE)
AND THE ESTIMATES OF MINIMUM AID UNDER ALTERNATIVE V

(Rs. million)

Entries	1965/6	1966/7	1967/8	1968/9	1969/70	1970/1	1971/2	1972/3	1973/4	1974/5
a) Export earnings	9,283	11,056	11,377	11,897	12,445	13,064	13,726	14,559	15,331	16,030
b) Aid (net)	4,720	7,630	9,310	8,470	6,510	3,780	3,640	2,800	1,680	700
c) Total availability of foreign exchange (a) + (b)	12,003	18,686	20,687	20,367	18,955	16,844	17,366	17,359	17,011	16,730
d) Lower range (−)	390	473	1,974	6,761	7,773	4,375	7,824	6,218	7,930	12,343
e) Upper range (+)	98	191	282	3,992	558	2,089	756	2,611	2,657	6,319
f) Minimum aid needed for the existing optimum plan program in any year	4,300	7,157	7,336	1,709	0	0	0	0	0	0

The logic of this approach deserves attention:
Conceptually, it is irrational to assume, especially
in a planned economy, that all past behavior, such
as propensity to consume and propensity to import,
will be preserved as sanctified during the planned
period, irrespective of whether they contain wastage
or irrationality; and empirical estimation of these
parameters will raise an identification problem unless
they are computed from a period when both the gaps
were exactly equal. The possibility of the latter
conditions being fulfilled in India over the sample
period is very remote. Under the circumstances, the
propensity to import is likely to be overestimated
and that to consume underestimated. It is extravagant
to say, for example, that India needs Rs.260 billion
to achieve the prescribed rate of growth in the plan.
Due to the international scarcity of aid, only the
barest minimum of imports--those justified on technological and humanitarian grounds--should be allocated
to a country.

This is what is attempted in our planning model,
where the need for aid is reduced to Rs.43 billion,
with the possibility of even further economy (see
Table 24.5).

TECHNICAL LIMITATIONS

From the technical viewpoint, the present type
of programming models are said to contain two major
limitations: high sensitivity of the plan outlays
to the discount rates used, and "flip-flop" behavior
in the movement of some of the major macro-variables
like consumption and output. In layterms, this means
that consumption shows a tendency to concentrate at
the tail-end of the plan period, and the rate of
growth of output falls sharply near the end of the
plan.

In this study, the first objection does not
appear significant. In alternative V, for example,
it is found that resource allocation shows complete
insensitivity to a change in the discount rate over
as wide a region as 3.2 percent to 13.1 percent per

TABLE 24.6

"GAPS" IN THE PROPOSED PLANNING MODEL (Alt. I)

Year	Gross Savings	Gross Invest- ment	Saving Minus Inv.	Imports	Exports	Imports Minus Exports	Nature of Constraint
1965/6	36.2	31.4	4.8	13.3	7.3	6.0	Trade gap
1966/7	56.3	36.7	19.6	15.0	11.1	3.9	Savings gap
1967/8	68.1	40.3	27.8	16.1	11.4	4.7	"
1968/9	82.6	45.2	37.4	17.6	11.9	5.7	"
1969/70	100.5	51.2	49.3	19.5	12.4	7.1	"
1970/1	123.6	58.8	64.8	21.8	13.1	8.7	"
1971/2	109.1	70.9	38.2	25.6	13.7	11.9	"
1972/3	96.1	79.1	17.0	8.2	14.6	13.6	"
1973/4	87.8	82.6	5.2	29.2	15.3	13.9	Trade gap
1974/5	82.0	86.1	4.1	30.3	16.1	14.2	"
TOTAL	842.3	582.3	260.0	216.6	126.9	89.7	Savings gap

TABLE 24.7

INTERTEMPORAL, INTERSECTORAL RESOURCE
ALLOCATION UNDER ALTERNATIVE
RATES OF TIME DISCOUNT
(Rs. million)

ALTERNATIVE V

Period 1965/6	10%	20%	30%
Gross output Q_1	19594	19594	19594
Q_2	138360	138360	138360
Q_3	32820	32824	32824
Q_4	55196	55196	55196
Q e_1 Private consumption	9225	9880	9880
e_2	78149	78149	78537
e_3	1644	1644	1644
e_4	27331	27331	27331
Capital-goods^m imports	819	825	799
Consumption imports M	9550	9544	9567
Period 1966/7			
Gross output Q_1	19593	19593	19593
Q_2	138823	138771	139317
Q_3	32947	32847	32827
Q_4	58962	59010	55821
Private consumption e_1	9456	10127	10127
e_2	80103	80103	80500
e_3	1685	1685	1685
e_4	28014	28014	28014
Capital-goods imports m_3	3555	3538	3492
Consumption imports M	13466	13487	13536

TABLE 24.7 (Continued)

Period 1967/8	10%	20%	30$
Gross output Q_1	22531	23443	22463
Q_2	145262	145163	145763
Q_3	37407	37237	37207
Q_4	64519	64376	64302
Private consumption			
e_1	9692	10380	10380
e_2	82105	82105	82513
e_3	1727	1727	1727
e_4	28715	28715	28715
Capital-goods imports m_3	5193	5081	5111
Consumption imports M	13621	13740	13714
Period 1968/9			
Gross output Q_1	24152	25024	23988
Q_2	153382	153215	153974
Q_3	42189	41944	41855
Q_4	72989	72700	72658
Private consumption			
e_1	9334	10640	10640
e_2	84158	84158	84575
e_3	1776	1770	1770
e_4	29432	29432	29432
Capital-goods imports m	7178	7196	7061
Consumption imports M	11073	11245	11208
Period 1969/70			
Gross output Q_1	26300	27009	25829
Q_2	164616	164400	165782
Q_3	46129	45834	45590
Q_4	84466	83966	83891
Private consumption			
e_1	10183	10906	10906
e_2	86262	86262	86690
e_3	1815	1815	1815
e_4	30168	30168	30168
Capital-goods imports m	10627	10403	10322
Consumption imports M	5987	6226	6316

377

TABLE 24.7 (Continued)

Period 1970/1	10%	20%	30%
Gross output Q_1	28936	29043	27456
Q_2	106045	185968	190680
Q_3	49990	49774	29668
Q_4	97207	96399	95338
Private consumption			
e_1	10437	11179	11179
e_2	88418	88418	92479
e_3	1860	1860	1860
e_4	30923	30923	30923
Capital-goods imports			
m	10355	10070	9670
Consumption imports			
M	3909	4209	4620

Period 1971/2			
Gross output Q_1	34183	32078	29302
Q_2	258860	259821	262682
Q_3	53990	54238	54442
Q_4	97593	96375	95814
Private consumption			
e_1	10698	11458	11458
e_2	149034	149829	152468
e_3	1907	1907	1907
e_4	31700	31696	31696
Capital-goods imports			
m	7091	7221	7242
Consumption imports			
M	7540	7410	7389

Period 1972/3			
Gross output Q_1	52662	42320	35126
Q_2	287109	287005	286932
Q_3	57357	57377	57358
Q_4	102239	103303	104037
Private consumption			
e_1	28517	18167	11458
e_2	171429	171429	171428
e_3	1954	1954	1954
e_4	35269	35391	35467
Capital goods imports			
m	5978	6639	7100
Consumption imports			
M	8485	7817	7351

TABLE 24.7 (Continued)

Period 1973/4	10%	20%	30%
Gross output Q_1	53739	53739	53739
Q_2	292866	292866	292866
Q_3	57326	57326	57326
Q_4	115874	115874	115870
Private consumption e_1	29230	29230	29230
e_2	175715	175715	175714
e_3	2003	2003	2003
e_4	49624	49624	49624
Capital-goods imports m	3833	3834	3835
Consumption imports M	10190	10190	10189
Period 1974/5			
Gross output Q_1	54540	54541	54541
Q_2	297549	297549	297549
Q_3	57292	57292	57292
Q_4	126614	126614	126612
Private consumption e_1	29960	29961	29960
e_2	180108	180108	180107
e_3	2053	2053	2053
e_4	61962	61963	61958
Capital goods imports m	1751	1750	1752
Consumption imports M	11917	11917	11917

Note: Numbers 1 to 4 refer to sectors

379

annum. This range covers the normal variations of
the discount rate used in most plan evaluations.
Alternatively, we use 10 percent, 20 percent, and
30 percent discount rates. The findings are tabulated
in Table 24.7. In no case does the allocation pattern,
(even at a disaggregated level) change more than
2 to 3 percent. These findings may, of course, be
peculiar to India, and should not be generalized
without further evidence. One of the reasons for
low sensitivity in the present case may be almost
deterministic pattern of the economy's growth pattern,
with very low income and insufficient choice.

The second objection is removed by using time-
discount rates in the objective function and by
introducing a monotonicity assumption in the movement
of output. In formulations which do not contain
these two assumptions, the "flip-flop" behavior
becomes marked: consumption moves along the minimum
level (constrained as lower bound in the model) and
jumps to a very high figure in the last year of the
plan.

                            NOTES

    1. Central Statistical Organisation, National
Income Statistics, Estimates of Gross Capital Forma-
tion in India for 1948-9 to 1960-1, (New Delhi:
Government of India Press, 1961).

    2. H. B. Chenery and A. M. Strout "Foreign
Assistance and Economic Development", The American
Economic Review, (September, 1966).

    3. I. Adelman and H. Chenery, "Foreign Aid and
Economic Development," Review of Economics and
Statistics, 48 (February, 1966), pp. 1-19.

APPENDIX:
A FEASIBILITY
AND CONSISTENCY
CHECK TO
THE FOURTH PLAN

This appendix demonstrates the operationalization of a computable planning model of the type contained in this book. Due to the changing conditions of a dynamic society, the periodic revision of the plan layouts at very short notice is an essential requisite. Revisions of this kind, however, are difficult for two major reasons: the inflow of detailed disaggregated data, needed for this type of comprehensive model, comes with a considerable time lag, and although the inflow of macro or aggregated information comes more promptly, it lacks comparability over time. Given these data limitations, it would be extremely unrealistic to work exclusively with either backdated comprehensive data or recent but macro or global data. In the present model, a compromise is therefore attempted in order to combine the best of both worlds, "comprehensiveness" and "up-to-datedness."

For this purpose, the base period is made synonymous with the year that possesses the necessary detailed information. This may even be a few years in the past. Later, all the information, micro and macro, available over the intervening period (i.e., up to the time of writing), is injected into the model frame in the form of constraints. The model is then run with the new set of constraints. The plan layout of the model from the base to the present period in this case represents the estimates of "actuals" over this period. Provided all information is injected, it will exactly represent the facts; otherwise, the model will present a picture whose proximity to the actual situation will depend upon the availability of information. In the process of revision, new or changed values of exogenous or policy variables could also be accommodated. However, due to its exploratory nature, this part of the study is separated from the main body.

Our original model covers a period of eleven years: 1965/6 to 1975/6, and it relies on the detailed data available up to 1964/5 and on the policy assumptions formulated in the Draft Fourth Plan. Further information is now available concerning several major macro-variables, such as national income, consumption, investment, exports/aid, etc., up to and including

1967/8, provisional national-income estimates (revised series) for the year 1968/9, and a new set of exogenous and policy variables embodied in the final Fourth Plan document.

This additional information can be incorporated in our model. Thus, in the present exercise, the period between 1965/6 and 1968/9 represents the "actuals," and the plan horizon is reduced to seven years from 1969/70 to 1975/6. The final, official Fourth Plan covers the period 1969/70 to 1973/4. Hence, this exercise will also be used to work out the Fourth Plan layouts and to check broadly their consistency and feasibility.

Initial Period Adjustments

The effective base of the model has been shifted from 1964/5 to 1968/9, and all available information between 1964/5 and 1968/9 has been introduced into the model as constraints. Data for 1967/8 contains detailed macro-economic information, whereas we are limited to national-income data for the other years, including 1968/9. This information is supplied mainly by the Fourth Plan document. But before it could be fed into our model, a threefold correction was needed, regarding--prices (from a 1967/8 base to a 1960/1 base), the method of evaluation (from market prices to factor cost), and coverage (converting from new to old series).

Table A.1 gives the information for the year 1967/8. As has already been mentioned, we are limited to the net national-product figure for 1968/9 at 1967/8 prices. Converted to 1960/1 prices, and on the basis of the old series, it stood at Rs.185.2 billion.*

───────────────

*The national-income series was revised by the Central Statistical Organization of India, on the basis of changed coverage and concepts in 1967. The earlier national-income figures were revised accordingly. As our model was formulated on the basis of prerevised series, we decided to convert the present

TABLE A.1

NATIONAL AGGREGATES 1967/8
(At factor cost Rs. billion)

	at 1967/8 prices revised series	at 1960/1 prices revised series	at 1960/1 prices old series
Net domestic product	281.9	168.8	179.3
Private consumption	234.2	140.1	148.8
Public consumption	25.5	17.3	18.5
Net investment	30.0	14.5	15.3
Aid	7.8	3.1	3.3

Policy Adjustments

First, we have the adjustments in the consumption targets of the plan. In the Fourth Plan document, per capita private consumption for the year 1973/4 has been given as Rs.559 at 1967/8 market prices. This implies total private consumption of Rs.334.4 billion at 1967/8 market prices; converted to a factor-cost base and at 1960/1 prices, it comes to Rs.181 billion. It stands at Rs.195 billion when converted to the old series.

The Terminal Stock Adjustments

In the official plan report, total private and public consumption are assumed to grow at 22.5 percent and 25 percent over the five years of the Fourth Plan (1969-1974). In our present exercise, it is assumed that this growth rate will prevail over a slightly longer period, i.e., between 1969/70 and 1975/6. The plan also assumes that a consumption growth rate of 6 percent per annum will be guaranteed after 1975/6, i.e., for the post-terminal period of the plan.[1]

This brings private and public consumption at 1960/1 factor cost to Rs.212.7 billion and Rs.28.9 billion respectively, giving a total of Rs.241.6 billion in the year 1975/6. The comparable estimate of total consumption in our original model was Rs.330.8 billion. Then, using the formula KX=K (1-A-rK)-1 (Cg+Cp+E-M), already discussed in the steady-state formulation, and adjusting for the use of idle capacity in the economy, the terminal-period capital-stock requirement has been estimated accordingly for the year 1975/6.

Aid Assumptions

The net aid estimates taken for the years 1965/6 to 1976/8 are those given in the Economic Survey, 1968/9, in million-dollar equivalents: $841, $614

Fourth Plan information based on this revised series, to its old base.

and $667 millions in the years 1965/6, 1966/7 and
1967/8. These figures are then converted to rupee
equivalents, assuming a pre-devaluation exchange rate
before 1967/8 and a post-devaluation rate for 1967/8:
Rs.4.5, 4.6, 3.3 and 5.0 billion for the years 1965/6,
1966/7, 1967/8 and 1968/9 respectively.

For the period 1969-74, no annual estimates of
expected aid are available, but the estimates of
total aid (including PL 480) over this period have
been placed in the plan document at Rs.25.4 billion
(including Rs.3.8 billion from PL 480 aid). In this
exercise, the annual phasing of this level of aid
has been assumed to be in the same pattern as the
one recommended by Perspective Plan Division in connection with the Fourth Plan. We have treated foreign
aid as excluding PL 480 aid over the period 1965-9,
but have included it beyond this period, since no
definite annual estimates of PL 480 aid were available.

Thus, the aid figures were finally revised as
follows:

(Rs billion)

Year	65/6	66/7	67/8	68/9	69/70*	70/1*	71/2*	72/3*	73/4*	74/5*
Net Aid excluding PL 480	4.5	4.6	3.3	5.0	9.0	5.2	4.7	3.5	3.0	0.7
PL 480 Aid	2.7	3.6	3.1							

*Estimates

Monotonic Assumptions

As the period 1965-9 experienced an absolute
fall in per capita consumption, it was decided to drop
the usual monotonic assumption of per capita consumption over this period in our model. In its place, a
guarantee of a minimum consumption standard was
inserted.

THE MOVEMENTS OF THE MACRO-ECONOMIC VARIABLES OVER THE FOURTH PLAN
(Rs. billion at 1960/1 prices: National Income Old Series)

Variables	Fourth Plan Period					1974/5
	1969/70	1970/1	1971/2	1972/3	1973/4	
Gross national product	234.5	242.7	260.8	262.8	270.4	280.4
Net national product	204.6	211.9	229.8	230.6	237.3	246.4
Private consumption	174.7	179.1	184.3	189.2	195.5	200.8
Public consumption	21.8	22.9	24.0	25.2	26.5	27.7
Total investment	47.0	45.9	57.2	51.8	51.8	52.6
			253.7			
Total net investment	17.1	15.1	25.7	17.6	18.7	18.6
			94.2			
Aid (net)	9.0	5.2	4.7	3.5	3.0	0.7
Inflationary gap as percent of GNP	-2.6	-2.2	0.8	-1.0	-1.5	-1.2
Rate of growth of GNP	9.5	3.6	7.5	0.5	3.7	5.0
Average rate of growth of income per annum			4.9			
Direct taxes as per-cent of household income	5.2	6.0	10.7	7.7	8.2	--

TABLE A.3

NATIONAL AGGREGATES 1967/8
(1960/1 factor cost, old series Rs. billion)

	Model Solution	Actuals
Net national income	178.8	179.3
Private consumption	150.5	148.8
Public consumption	19.7	18.5
Net investment	11.8	15.3
Aid	3.3	3.3
(Net national income, 1968/9	187.6	185.2

The movement of the major macro-variables in our model over the period 1969-75 is presented in Table A.2.

The macro allocations for the year 1967/8 and the national-income estimates for the year 1968/9, derived from the model, match very well with the actuals obtained from the Economic Survey, 1968/9, and the final Draft Fourth Plan document (1969) of the Indian Planning Commission. They are given in Table A.3.

NOTE

1.   Fourth Five Year Plan: Draft, (Delhi: Government of India Press, 1970).

BIBLIOGRAPHY

BOOKS

Adler, J. H. Capital Movements and Economic Development. London: Macmillan, 1967.

Baran, A., Scitovsky, T., and Shaw, E. S. The Allocation of Resources. Stanford, Calif.: Stanford University Press, 1959.

Battacharyya, K. N. A Generalist Approach. London: Asia Publishing House, 1963.

Becherman, W., et al. The British Economy in 1975. Cambridge, England: Cambridge University Press, 1965.

Belshaw, H. Population Growth and Level of Consumption with Special Reference to Asia. London: George Allen and Unwin, 1954.

Bipin, Behari. Imports in Developing Economy. Bombay, India: Vora and Co., 1965.

Bhagwati, Jagdish N., and Desai, P. India Planning for Industrialization, London: Oxford University Press, 1970.

Brahmand, Prasad. Planned Capital Formation in India. Bombay, India: Vora and Co., 1965.

Carter, A. P., and Brody, A. Application of Input-Output Analysis. Amsterdam, Holland: North Holland Publishing Company, 1970.

Chakrabarty, S. Contribution to Economic Analysis: The Logic of Investment Planning. Amsterdam, Holland: North Holland Publishing Company, 1959.

Dorfman, R., Samuelson, P., and Solow, R. Linear

Programming and Economic Analysis. New York:
    McGraw-Hill, 1958.

Eckaus, R. S. "Planning in India." National Economic
    Planning. Edited by Max F. Millikan. New York:
    National Bureau of Economic Research, 1967.

Eltis, W. A. Economic Growth: Analysis and Policy.
    London: Hutchinson University Library, 1966.

Ghosh, A. Experiments with Input-Output Models: An
    Application to the Economy of the United Kingdom
    1948-55. Cambridge, England: Cambridge Univer-
    sity Press, 1964.

_____. Efficiency in Location and Inter-regional
    Flows: The Indian Cement Industry During the
    Five-Year Plans, 1950-59. Amsterdam, Holland:
    North Holland Publishing Company, 1965.

Hadley, H. Linear Programming. Reading, Mass.:
    Addison Wesley Publishing Company, 1965.

Hagen, Everett E. Planning Economic Development.
    Homewood, Ill.: Richard D. Irwin, 1963.

Hanson, A. H. The Process of Planning: A Study of
    India's Five-Year Plans, 1950-64. London:
    Oxford University Press, 1966.

Healey, J. M. The Development of Social Overheads in
    India. Oxford, England: Basil Blackwell, 1965.

Hicks, J. Capital and Growth. Oxford, England: The
    Clarendon Press, 1965.

Hirschman, A. O. The Strategy of Economic Delelopment.
    New Haven, Conn., and London: Yale University
    Press, 1964.

Islam, Nurul. Studies in Consumers' Demand. Vols.
    I and II. Bureau of Economic Research, Dacca
    University. Oxford University Press, Pakistan
    branch, 1965-6.

Quyum, A. Theory and Policy of Accounting Prices.
     "Economic Analysis" series. Amsterdam: North
     Holland Publishing Company, 1960.

Reddaway, W. B. Some Observations on the Capital Out-
     put Ratio (with special reference to India's
     Third Plan). "Reprint Series" 168. University
     of Cambridge, Department of Applied Economics,
     1960.

_____. Importance of Time Lag for Economic Planning.
     "Reprint Series" 161. University of Cambridge,
     Department of Applied Economics, 1960.

_____. The Development of the Indian Economy.
     London: George Allen and Unwin, 1965.

Rosen, G. Industrial Change in India. London: Asia
     Publishing House, 1958.

Rosenstein-Rodan, P. N. Capital Formation and Economic
     Development. London: George Allen and Unwin,
     1964.

_____. Pricing and Fiscal Policies. London:
     George Allen and Unwin, 1964.

Rostow, W. W. The Stages of Economic Growth. Cam-
     bridge, Cambridge University Press, 1967.

Sandee, S. A Demonstration Planning Model of India.
     "Indian Statistical Institute Series" No. 7.
     Calcutta: Asia Publishing House, Statistical
     Publishing Society, 1960.

Sahani, B. S. Saving and Economic Development.
     Calcutta: Scientific Book Agency, 1967.

Sen, S. R. The Strategy for Agricultural Development.
     Second Edition. London: Asia Publishing House,
     1966.

Stone, R., ed. A Programme for Growth. Series 1 to 6.
     Cambridge, England: Published for the Department

of Applied Economics, University of Cambridge,
by Chapman and Hall, 1963.

Stone, R. and Brown, J. A. C. Output Investment for
Exponential Growth in Consumption.   "Reprint
Series," 192. University of Cambridge, Depart-
ment of Applied Economics, 1963.

Streetan, Paul, et al. The Crisis of Indian Planning.
Oxford, England: Oxford University Press, 1968.

Tilanus, C. B. Input Output Experiments: The Nether-
lands 1948-1961. Economic Series, Vol. 5.
Rotterdam: Rotterdam University Press, 1966.

Tims, W. Analytical Technique for Development Planning:
A Case Study of Pakistan's Third Five-Year Plan,
(1965-70). Karachi: Pakistan Institute of
Development Economics, 1968.

Tinbergen, J. Development Planning. London: World
University Library, 1967.

_____. Design of Development. Baltimore, Maryland:
The John Hopkins Press, 1958.

_____. Central Planning. New Haven, Conn., and
London: Yale University Press, 1964.

                         ARTICLES

Carter, A. P. "Studies in the Structure of the
American Economy, 1947 to 1958 and 1962," Review
of Economics and Statistics, (May, 1967).

Chakrabarty, S., and Leferber, L. "An Optimising
Planning Model," The Economic Weekly, Annual
Number (February, 1965).

Desai Padma. "The Development of the Indian Economy:
An Exercise," Oxford Economic Papers, (N.S),
Vol. 15 (1963).

Deshpande, K. L., and Khatkhate, D. R. "Estimates of

Saving and Investment in the Indian Economy, 1950/1 to 1962/3," Reserve Bank of India Bulletin (March, 1965).

Dutta Chowdhury Uma. "Income Consumption and Saving in Urban and Rural India," Review of Incomes and Wealth, Income and Wealth Series 14, No.1 (March, 1968).

Gupta, S. "Input Output Trends in British Manufacturing," Royal Statistical Society, 1963.

Iyenger, S. "Some Estimates of Engel Elasticities, Based on National Sample Survey Data," Royal Statistical Society, 130, (1967).

Komiya, R. "A Note on Professor Mahalanobis's Model of Indian Planning," Review of Economics and Statistics, Vol. 41 (1964).

Mahalanobis, P. C. "The Statistical Basis of the Plan Frame," Sankhya, Vol. 16, Part 182 (December, 1955).

_____. "Use of Capital Output Ratios in Planning in Developing Countries," Sankhya, Series B (December, 1967).

Manne, A. S., and Rudra, A. "A Consistency Model of India's Fourth Plan," Sankhya, Series B, Vol. 27, Parts 1 and 2 (September, 1965).

Mathur, P. N. "Output and Investment for Exponential Growth in Consumption - An Alternative Formulation," Review of Economic Studies, Vol. 31 (1964).

Simpson, D., and Tsukui, J. "The Fundamental Structure of Input Output Tables: An International Comparison," Review of Economics and Statistics (1965).

Walters, A. A. "Incremental Capital Output Ratios," Economic Journal (December, 1966).

MIMEOGRAPHED PAPERS

Bruno, M., Fraenkel, M., and Dougherty, C. "Dynamic
    Input-Output, Trade and Development," Paper
    presented to the Fourth International Input-
    Output Conference in Geneva, 1968. Bank of
    Israel and Hebrew University of Jerusalem, 1967.

Day, R. H., and Heiden, E. H. "Recursive Programming
    Models for Policy Formulation," Social System
    Research Institute, Wisconsin University, Sep-
    tember, 1966.

Devos, C. A. "A Consumption Model for a Growing
    Economy," unpublished M. A. dissertation, Uni-
    versity of Manchester, England, 1968.

Lung, T. N. "The Techniques of Economic Planning in
    India," unpublished M.Com. thesis, University
    of Melbourne, Australia, 1963.

Manne, Alan. "A Consistency Model of India's Fourth
    Plan." Studies on the Structure of the Indian
    Economy, Report No. 1, MIT. Center for for
    International Studies, Cambridge, Mass., July,
    1964.

Manne, Alan, and Weisskopf, Thomas E. . "A Dynamic
    Multisectoral Model for India, 1967-75." Mem-
    orandum No. 57, December, 1967, for presentation
    to the Fourth International Input-Output Con-
    ference at Geneva, January, 1968.

Pitamber, Pant. "Certain Dimensional Hypotheses
    Concerning the Third Plan." India: Planning
    Commission, Perspective Planning Division,
    November, 1954.

OFFICIAL REPORTS

India, Bureau of Minerals. Indian Minerals Year Book.

India, Central Statistical Organisation, Annual Survey

of Industries, 1959, 1961, 1962. Calcutta:
Department of Statistics, Industrial Statistical
Wing.

India, Central Statistical Organisation. "Estimates
of Gross Capital Formation in India for 1948/9
to 1960/1." Delhi, 1961. Mimeographed.

India, Chief Inspector of Mines. Monthly Coal Bulletin. Delhi: Government of India Press.

India, Directorate General of Supplies and Disposals.
Report.

India, Ministry of Agricluture. Farm Management
Studies.

India, Ministry of Food and Agriculture. Area, Production, Yield of Principal Crops in India 1949-
50 and 1965-6. Department of Commerical Intel-
ligence and Statistics.

India, Ministry of International Trade. Monthly
Statistics of the Foreign Trade of India.

India, Ministry of Railways. Annual Report of the
Railway Board. Vol. II (Statistics). Government
of India Press, 1956.

India, Central Statistical Office. National Income
and Expenditure. White Paper. Delhi.

India, Planning Commission. Annual Plans. New Delhi.

_____. Draft Fourth Plan: Material and Financial
Balances, 1964/5, 1970/1, and 1975/6. Perspective
Planning Division, September, 1966.

_____. First, Second, and Third Five-Year Plans.
New Delhi: Government of India Press, 1953;
1956; 1963 and 1967.

_____. Fourth Five-Year Plan: A Draft Outline.
Government of India Press, 1966.

_____. The Macro-Economic Hypothesis for the Fourth
Plan. Economic Division, April 17, 1964. Mineo-
graphed.

_____. Notes on Perspective of Development in India
1960/1 to 1975/6. Perspective Planning Division,
April, 1964. Mimeographed.

_____. Problems in the Third Plan: A Critical
Miscellany. The Publication Division, Ministry
of Information and Broadcasting, 1961.

_____. The Trird Plan Mid-Term Appraisal. November,
1963.

United Nations, Economic Commission for Asia and the
    Far East. Programming Techniques for Economic
    Development with Special Reference to Asia and
    the Far East. Developing Programming Techniques
    Series No. 1. Report by a group of experts,
    Bangkok, 1960.

Dr. S. Gupta, Lecturer in Economics at the University of Manchester, is on the United Nations panel of experts as planning and model analyst and has been appointed to the staff of the International Bank for Reconstruction and Development, Washington, D.C. He has had wide experience in economic planning, both academic and practical, serving as Deputy Director in the Indian Planning Commission for six years and as India's official delegate at U.N. planning conferences. Dr. Gupta was on the team of I.P.C. experts who drew up the country's first official input/output tables. At the University of Manchester Development Centre, he has guided research projects on development problems in South-East Asia, Africa, and Latin America.

He has published articles in learned economic and statistical journals, and co-authored Workshop Wage Determination (Pergamon Press, U.K., 1969). He holds an M.A. in Economics from the University of Calcutta and an M.Sc. and a Ph.D. in Economics from the University of London, and was Hallsworth Fellow in Economics at the University of Manchester.